The HUMAN SIDE of INTRANETS
Content, Style & Politics

Jerry W. Koehler
Thom Dupper
Marvin D. Scaff
Fred Reitberger
Patti Paxon

St. Lucie Press
Boca Raton, Florida

Library of Congress Cataloging-in-Publication Data

Koehler, Jerry W.
    The human side of intranets: content, style and politics/ Jerry W. Koehler...[et al.}
        p. cm.
    Includes bibliographical references and index.
    ISBN 1-57444-175-2
    1. Computers—intranet. 2. Internet
I. Title. II. Dupper, Thom. III. Scaff, Marvin D. IV. Reitberger, Fred. V. Paxon, Patti.
VM104.F6DL63 1997
574.5′.2325—dc20
for Library of Congress   97-41082
                                                                                                                                                              CIP

This book contains information obtained from authentic and highly regarded sources. Reprinted material is quoted with permission, and sources are indicated. A wide variety of references are listed. Reasonable efforts have been made to publish reliable data and information, but the author and the publisher cannot assume responsibility for the validity of all materials or for the consequences of their use.

Neither this book nor any part may be reproduced or transmitted in any form or by any means, electronic or mechanical, including photocopying, microfilming, and recording, or by any information storage or retrieval system, without prior permission in writing from the publisher.

The consent of CRC Press LLC does not extend to copying for general distribution, for promotion, for creating new works, or for resale. Specific permission must be obtained in writing from CRC Press LLC for such copying.

Direct all inquiries to CRC Press LLC, 2000 Corporate Blvd., N.W., Boca Raton, Florida 33431.

Trademark Notice: Product or corporate names may be trademarks or registered trademarks, and are used only for identification and explanation, without intent to infringe.

© 1998 by CRC Press LLC
St. Lucie Press is an imprint of CRC Press LLC

No claim to original U.S. Government works
International Standard Book Number 1-57444-175-2
Library of Congress Card Number 97-41082
Printed in the United States of America   1 2 3 4 5 6 7 8 9 0
Printed on acid-free paper

Preface

As we approach the millennium, technology seems to have taken on a larger, seemingly more ominous role in our lives. Computers are ubiquitous. Three- and four-letter acronyms fill the pages of our popular press. Most of us are on the Internet or wondering what the whole Internet thing is about.

Meanwhile, we all go about our daily lives and careers. We move in and out of relationships in our personal and professional lives. We communicate with other people every day. We give and receive information. We ask questions. We get answers.

Amid all the technology, we operate as human beings. Our lives may be more hectic than that of our parents, but our relationships may feel remarkably the same as theirs. Our work days seem to blur by at top speed, yet we still have time for some chit chat with our co-workers. Our desks may have computer monitors on them, but mine, at least, is partially covered with good-old sticky notes.

And that's a telling picture. Humans find creative ways to incorporate the most advanced technologies into everyday life. The story of the twentieth century is the story of humans embracing one technological revolution after another — and finding ways to preserve their humanity in the process.

The history of intranet technology is only a few years wide. There are no absolute success stories yet. There is precious little empirical evidence about intranets today. This is a technology in its early embryonic stage. We are witnessing the birth of a force with such potential it will most likely dwarf every technology that preceded it. Like most births, the newborn only provides the slightest hint of what maturity will bring.

Throughout all of technological history, from the printing press to television, from the wagon train to the bullet train, humans survive and adapt. Throughout this technology parade, the actual technology was neither the protagonist nor the antagonist — neither the answer nor the question. The real issue is how humans have reacted to technologies and incorporated them into the human condition.

Humans are generally flexible. Organizations often are not. One of the most painful lessons of corporate history is that organizations cling tenaciously to the status quo. For ages, the province of management was thought; the province of labor was labor. For ages, management conducted itself as benign dictator and hoarder of all knowledge. Like young children, employees were shielded from knowing too much — partly because management believed that employees could not handle the truth, and partly because all organizational power comes from knowledge.

This book takes a snapshot of the intranet phenomenon as it exists today, and makes some observations about how people are reacting to it. There is very little empirical data about intranets in this book. intranets have not been around long enough to have generated much in the way of empirical data.

This book is about change. It's about the evolution of traditional communication roles and relationships in the electronic age. It's about the impact of opening up organizational communication and what that means — and will mean — to organizations and to the humans that make them up.

Most of all, this book is about change agents. Everyone who gets involved in intranets — designers, writers, editors, Webmasters, technicians, administrators, managers, etc. — is an agent of change within their organization. Every corporate intranet user changes the organization every time they participate in an online forum.

This book is a roadmap of sorts. It is intended as a clear and comprehensive guide that can be used to guide an organization and its individuals through the complex and challenging process of creating a new organizational communication medium. In that regard, it begins with an analysis of strategic and management issues and then works through the actual process of rolling out an intranet.

We wrote the book specifically for the "deer in the headlights" professional who becomes involved in an intranet project — whether that involvement is voluntary or is the result of being pulled into it kicking and screaming. We have each experienced that feeling of absolute panic and sheer terror as we are presented with something new, something outside our own narrow history and experience.

Intranets are, indeed, new. They are a powerful new communication medium that begs for professional attention from communicators, marketers, human resource professionals, accountants, planners, and every other element within today's organization. They should not be relegated to the technical support department simply because computers are involved. They require full organizational backing and support. They demand the full attention of a full time staff. They need constant and continuing updates, additions and changes to become an integral part of the organization's daily life.

We hope this book will assist you in your journey through the intranet.

Dedication

We thank all the people who helped us make this book possible, particularly Dennis Buda, president of St. Lucie Press and Drew Gierman, our editor. Also we owe a special debt of gratitude to Angela Lahti, Debra Dupper and Elaine Reitberger. We also thank our coworkers who provided good examples for the book and who stuck with us throughout the publishing process. It has been a great trip.

The Authors

Dr. Jerry W. Koehler (jkoehler@bsn01.usf.edu) is a Professor of Management in the College of Business at the University of South Florida. His area of expertise is in Communication, Organization Design, Organization Development, Leadership and Total Quality Management. He has served as an advisor to numerous leading national and international organizations.

After graduating from the Pennsylvania State University in 1968 with his Doctorate in Communication, Dr. Koehler became Special Assistant to the Chief Executive Officer at Teacher's Management and Investment Company, Newport Beach, California. Later he joined American Express Investment Management Company and he became world-wide leader in sales.

In 1973, he became the Director, University of California, Irvine Executive Program and Lecturer in the Graduate School of Management.

At UCI, he completed his first book, *The Corporation Game: How to Win the War with the Organization and Make Them Love It* (Macmillan Publishing Company). BooksWest recognized him, along with Will Durant, Joseph Wambaugh and Ray Bradbury as Authors of the Year in 1975. *Business Week* referred to his book as a "well-written, down-to-earth description of how to succeed in a business by really trying." Also at UCI, he co-authored *Organizational Communication: Behavioral Perspectives*, (Holt, Rinehart, and Winston), now in its second edition.

Since 1976, Dr. Koehler has been associated with the University of South Florida where he has served as Assistant to the President, Chairman of the Department of Management, and Dean of Extended Studies. At USF, he has co-authored *Public Communication: Behavioral Perspectives*, (Macmillan Publishing Company), *Public Communication in Business and the Professions*, (West Publishing Company), and *Sell'Em*, (Contemporary Books), which was translated into Spanish. He has co-authored *Total Quality Management*, and produced a video on TQM (Total Quality Media), and has recently co-authored *Quality Government: Designing Developing, and Implementing TQM*, (St. Lucie Press, 1996); *Con-*

tinual Improvement Tools for Government, (St. Lucie Press, 1996); *Teams in Government*, (St. Lucie Press, 1996); *Transformational Leadership in Government*, (St. Lucie Press, 1997). Jerry has also authored numerous papers and articles, appeared on talk shows, lectured extensively throughout the world, and is a past Chairman of Leadership Tampa, a program sponsored by the Tampa Chamber of Commerce.

During the 1989 to 1990 academic year, while on sabbatical leave from USF, he served as a Total Quality Management consultant to Honeywell Space Systems Group, and the following year as advisor to the Frederick Commission and as a full-time TQM consultant to the Department of Revenue and the Department of Labor, State of Florida. For the next three years, he served as Deputy Secretary for Florida's Department of Labor and Employment Security. In 1995 he returned to his faculty position at USF and continues to serve as TQM Consultant to the Office of the Governor, State of Florida.

Thom Dupper (thom@sitedynamics.com) has spent more than 30 years in communication design and production. He was a pioneer in bringing multimedia into corporate communication (Honeywell 1987) and in embracing Web publishing (*St. Petersburg Times* — www.sptimes.com — the fourth newspaper on the Web, 1992). He left the Times to head up the best practices consulting group of Kinetoscope Inc, a leading online consulting and applications development company in Largo, Florida. Thom is now the Chief Strategic Officer of Site Dynamics, a spin-off of Kinetoscope and FKQ Advertising in Clearwater, Florida. In his new role, Thom is responsible for setting the strategic direction for the startup interactive communication company. Throughout his varied career, Thom has always embraced communication in all its forms. "I believe that communication is the cornerstone of every great relationship — whether personal or professional. As you examine highly successful businesses you find that communication is visible, ubiquitous and integral to every function within the organization. It's the great discriminator."

After graduating from Florida State University with a B.A. degree in mass communication (1969) Thom spent three years in the Army producing and directing training films at The U.S. Army Signal Center and School in Ft. Monmouth, New Jersey. Thom returned to Florida after the military and attended the University of South Florida (1976) graduating with an M.A. degree in organizational communication. It was at USF that Thom met Jerry Koehler and they formed a lifelong personal and professional relationship. They have collaborated on several classes, seminars and articles over the past two decades.

Thom took his communication passion to Honeywell's Space Systems Group in Clearwater where he spent nearly 14 years creating marketing and internal communication. In 1987 he introduced Honeywell's first interactive multimedia kiosk. He left Honeywell in 1991 to become a principal in Image Technologies, a multimedia development company recently acquired by World Color Press. As Image's first Executive VP, Thom helped build the company from a startup to a recognized leader in the field with such clients as Disney, Blockbuster Video and Ford Motor Co.

The Authors

Thom heard the call of online communication and joined the *St. Petersburg Times*, in 1992 to develop the newspaper's online presence. Thom served as the first Interactive Media Project Manager and with his staff created the *Times'* Web site (www.sptimes.com) now averaging over 1 million hits per month.

He left the Times to co-found Kinetoscope in 1996. Kinetoscope has worked with such companies as Ernst & Young LLP, Kaydon Corporation, Florida Trend Magazine, Florida Power Corporation and Continental Cablevision/U.S. West to help define and produce compelling online presences — both internal and external. Thom brought a depth of communication experience and expertise to the company. While at Kinetoscope, Thom worked with clients to help them define their online projects. His initial consulting enables clients to set realistic objectives, define audiences, construct messages and measure results from their online projects — on the Web and within the organization.

Thom taught business communication at the University of South Florida for six years. He served on the faculty of the Exhibitor Show in Las Vegas and Chicago for four years. Thom recently presented at the Internet Commerce Expo in Atlanta and Los Angeles and was chosen to judge the "Internet Open", a software competition sponsored by the show. He has published articles in professional periodicals on communication, management and human issues in technology. He is a frequent speaker at local communication, public relations and marketing associations.

Thom and his wife Debra live in Seminole, Florida where they have raised five daughters — Andrea, Michelle, Allison, Erica and Kimberly — a dog, a cat, a bird and some fish. Thom enjoys restoring classic American muscle cars, listening to almost all kinds of music, singing in his church choir and supporting his children in their athletic and academic pursuits.

Marvin D. Scaff (marvin@kinetoscopr.com) is the President and CEO of Kinetoscope, an Internet technology and software development company. Marvin began developing software professionally at the age of fourteen, writing an Apple II program for a local automobile auction in his hometown of Ashland, Kentucky.

Marvin brings 16 years of professional software development and 8 years of commercial product management to Kinetoscope. Prior to founding the company he served as the Director of Engineering for Hands-On Technology, a publisher of business multimedia applications based in Burlingame, California. Before joining HOT, Marvin was the Director of Development for Image Technologies, a multimedia development company in St. Petersburg, Florida. Prior to Image Technologies, Marvin designed the rule-based expert systems used in solving system configuration problems for Help! and Help! Network products from Teknosys. He is a regular columnist for *InterActivity* magazine as well as a frequent contributor to other major industry publications. He is also a speaker at key industry events.

One of his key strengths is his ability to translate complex technical issues for non-technical audiences. He is equally at home in a group of general managers discussing sales forecasts as he is in a group of high-level programmers. Marvin has successfully bridged the high technology world with his keen entrepreneurial insights. He truly understands technology, but more importantly, he understands the role of technology in our daily lives. He combines the pragmatism of the programmer with the vision of a futurist.

Fred Reitberger has been involved with high technology and marketing communication for over twenty years. He has worked for small businesses, Fortune 500 companies, and the government. He has consulted for utilities, Fortune 100 companies, and neighbors. He lives with his wife and two sons in Tampa, Florida.

His interest in technology started at his father's television repair shop in Ohio. Fred learned the importance of customer service and product knowledge as he helped his father during his summer high school breaks.

After graduating from high school, Fred attended Kent State University, where he met Elaine, his wife of 25 years. At Kent State he studied Television and Radio Broadcasting and graduated with a degree in Telecommunications. It was both the technology and its use for communication that excited him. Fred had the fortune to travel while in collage. He spent a semester studying and teaching at the University of Pahlavi in Shiraz, Iran.

Taking what he learned from his father's business, Fred opened his own television retail store in Ohio after graduating from Kent State. For five years he sold televisions, repaired them, learned how to market and sell them, as well as how to manage employees. Looking back, Fred says that was the best work experience he ever had. Recognizing that the area was headed for a economic downturn, Fred sold the business, and joined the Air Force.

As an Air Force Officer stationed in Tampa, Fred became part of the team that monitored high-tech radar equipment, watching for missile attacks against the United States. It was during this time that he discovered computers, purchasing one of the newly released Apple II personal computers. Using it he created reports, programmed training courses, did financial analysis on Visicalc, and tried to balance his checkbook on it—he was successful at everything except his checkbook! He established the first user group for the Apple II while in Tampa.. As president of the user group, he grew it from the original twenty members to over three hundred in just two years. It was then as he wrote for the many group newsletters that he realized writing is not easy.

After completing his enlistment with the Air Force, Fred and his family, now two boys, moved to Massachusetts to become part of a startup business. The new business focused on supporting the new desktop personal computers. With contracts from companies like Apple Computer and Digital Equipment the new company was off to a good start. As the Director of Information management Fred hired a staff, developed support procedures and even developed workgroup software before the industry developed the concept of workgroup software. In the beginning, Fred was deeply involved with the marketing and sales of new services but very quickly transitioned to delivery of the sold services.

Fred was recruited by a large Massachusetts utility company to redesign their entire communication and computer network. The utility was moving into new corporate headquarters and was taking the opportunity to replace every network wire, circuit and telephone system it had. He designed and implemented a wide-area voice and data network that was redundant and totally digital—one of the first in the nation. He also served as vice-president of the user group of Network Technologies equipment.

After a particularly harsh winter, Fred decided to return to Tampa. An old friend from the Apple II user group days introduced him to Apple Computer and the move was made. For the next four years, Fred worked and consulted with many of the major companies in Florida. He developed shop-floor management systems and software for Honeywell, databases for Rockwell and Rocketdyne at Kennedy Space Center in support of the Space Shuttle Program, customer-service applications and telecommunications integration for CSX Technologies, and became the regional expert on multimedia technologies. For both large and small companies, he presented new technologies, assisted in the development of new applications, and watched as each business organizationally adopted or rejected new ideas and methods.

With the downsizing of Apple, Fred joined the *St. Petersburg Times*. The *Times*, the nations 24th largest newspaper, had just decided to develop a new media department and start publishing in the electronic arena. While the early online adopters partnered with Prodigy, America OnLine, and CompuServe, Fred recognized the potential of the Internet and the World Wide Web. At his recommendation, *the Times* became the fourth newspaper to publish on the Web. It was an unqualified success winning many awards and recognitions.

Recently, Fred has turned his experience and talents to both this book and the creation of a new company, Site Dynamics.

Patti Paxson is a freelance public relations and advertising writer and creative director based in Tampa, Florida. She works for a wide range of regional and national clients and in nearly every medium of communication: print; television, video and film productions, radio, interactive audiovisual media, the internet, and live multimedia presentations and speeches, the latter of which includes writing presentations for First Lady Hillary Clinton, His Eminence Archbishop Spyridon of the Greek Orthodox Archdiocese of America, and various celebrity presenters at the Congressional Gold Medal Celebration Dinner honoring recipients Rev. and Mrs. Billy Graham in Washington, D.C. Additionally, Patti specializes in public relations and marketing communication strategic planning and management, creating and implementing identity/image campaigns, and media relations.

Before starting her freelance writing/creative direction business, Patti worked as a creative director for the Florida headquarters of the American Cancer Society, public relations manager for an advertising and public relations agency, staff writer and editor for an American Automobile Association (AAA) magazine, and a reporter for two daily newspapers. Patti has a Master of Science degree in Journalism and Mass Communications from Kansas State University, where she earned the Shiekh Ahmed Zaki Yamani (OPEC Oil Minister) Scholarship. After obtaining her Bachelor of Arts degree in Anthropology at the State University of New York at Buffalo and before beginning her writing career, Patti worked as an Arabic linguist for the U.S. government for more than four years. Her government work was distinguished by several awards and recognitions. In addition to Arabic, Patti has studied Italian, Greek and Latin, and has extensive international travel and multi-cultural experience.

Patti has been hired to teach business and public relations writing for national and international organizations, as well as the University of South Florida.

In her spare time, Patti actively volunteers for several charitable organizations.

Contents

1 Introduction   1
    Where Are We Today?   1
    Challenges and Issues   2
    Moving Toward Empowerment   2
    The Promise of Technology   2
    The Purpose of This Book   3
    Content, Style and Politics   4
        Content   4
        Style   5
        Politics   5
    The Human Side   6
    Book Organization   7

2 Intranet Benefits   9
    Intranet Springboards   9
        Grass Roots   10
        Guerrilla Operations   10
        Directives from the Chief   10
    Intranet Prerequisites   12
        Local Area Network (LAN)/Wide Area Network (WAN)   12
        Technology and Tools   12
        Collaborative Culture   12
        Budgetary Buy-In   13
    Online Advantages   13
    Faster, Cheaper, and Easier   13
        It Makes Everyone a Publisher   15
        Instant Updating   17
        Instant Global Distribution   17

Who's Doing What? Case Studies   18
Are You Ready for Real-time Interaction?   23
Content Providers   25
    Human Resources   25
    Communications   26
    Sales Automation   28
    Customer and Vendor Relations/Support   29
    Quality   29
    Training and Development   29

3 Electronic Empowerment   31

What Happens to Traditional Communications Functions   32
    The Way it Was   32
    The Gatekeeper   32
    The Trap   33
    Create a Plan   34
    The Filter   35
    The Grapevine   36
Who Wins, Who Loses?   36
How Much Information Is Too Much?   38
Should Everyone Know Everything?   39
Hanging On To Information Power   40
The New Communications Model   40
    Nonlinear Construction   40
    Real-Time Information   40
    Interactivity   41
The New Communications Roles   41
    Webmaster   41
    Content Provider   42

4 Managing Your Intranet   43

Managing Communication and Change   44
    Massaging Data   44
The Clash with Traditional Systems   45
Taking the Organization's Temperature   45
Managing an Effective Intranet Project   47
    Building Initial Support   47
    Developing an Action Plan   48
    Setting Realistic Expectations   48

Keeping a User Focus   49
Understanding the Technology   49
Encouraging Interaction   51
Managing Site Growth   51
Sustaining Momentum   52
Keeping a Fresh Face   52

5 Intranet Technology   53
Transmission Control Protocol/Intranet Protocol (TCP/IP)   53
Domains and URLs   53
Standards and Contents   54
Intranet Overview   54
   cgi   55
   SSI   55
   Image Mapping   55
   Page Security   56
   Remote Management and Monitoring   56
   Server Guidelines   57
   LAN/WAN   57
   Browser Standards   58
How an Intranet Works   60
   Universal Resource Locator (URL)   60
   Hypertext Transfer Protocol (HTTP)   62
   Hypertext Markup Language (HTML)   62
Connectionless Environment   63
   Firewall Issues   64
Putting It All Together   64

6 Intranet Strategies   65
Establishing Realistic Goals   65
Politics   67
What Will Your Intranet Add to What Exists Now?   67
How Will the Site Grow?   69
Typical Site Rollout Plan   69
   Step One — *Blue Sky It!*   69
   Step Two — *Deadline It*   69
   Step Three — *Phase It*   70
   Step Four — *Check It*   70

Determining Audiences   71
    Who Are Primary Users and What Do They Want?   71
    Secondary Users   73
    What Do They Want?   73
Surveying Communications Resources   76
What Is at Stake?   77
"Four Unnatural Acts"   78
Who Stands to Lose?   80
Reworking Strategic Communications Policies and Practices   81
Project Parameters   82

7 Planning Your Intranet   85
Inside or Outside — The Eternal Question   85
Allocation of Resources   85
    Hardware   85
    People   86
    Security Issues   86
    Remote Access   87
Obtaining User Involvement   87
    Surveys   87
    Focus Groups   88
    Ad Hoc Committee   88
    Soft Launch   89
Surveying Available Resources   90
    IT/IS Resources   90
    Content Resources   91
    Design and Production Resources   92
Understanding Nonlinear Information   93
    Growing the Content Tree   93
Designing An Internal Linking Scheme   95
Selecting Appropriate Content   95
    What Exists Now and In What Format?   96
    What Is Appropriate for Online Use?   96
    How To Repurpose Existing Materials and Information   97
    Surveying Your Current Enterprise for Inclusion   97
Building In Interactivity   97
    The Two-Way Street   97
Encouraging Feedback   98
    E-mail within the Site   98

       Forums   98
       Surveys   99
       Games   100
  Enlisting Management Support   101
       Strategic Planning Group   101
       Steering Committee   101
       Justifying the Resources   101
       Overcoming Objections   101
  Defining Responsibilities   102
       Content Generation and Maintenance   102
       Page Construction and Maintenance   102
       Technical Support   103
  Protecting Your Intranet from Copyright and Libel Violations   103
       Sidebar/Boxed Information   104
       Copyright Information Websites   105

8 Designing Your Intranet   107

"Look-and-Feel" Issues   108
Establishing a Unique Look for your Intranet   109
The Process   110
The Three-Phase Approach to Site Style   119
       Beginners Group   120
       Intermediate Group   120
       Advanced Group   121
The Limitations of Hypertext Markup Language (HTML)   121
       Style   121
       Print vs. Online   122
       Networks   122
       Download Time   122
       Graphics File Sizes   123
       Site Attitude   124
       Content Drives Style   126
Writing for Online Delivery   126
       Information Date Stamping   126
       Online Linking   127
       Keep It Short and Simple   127
       The One-Voice Edit   128
Intranet Content Providers   128
How Restrictive Do You Want to Be?   128

Establishing an Online Style Guide   130

9 Building Your Intranet   133
Building a Production Team   133
Where Do You Look for Staff?   135
Creative and Technical People *Can* Work Together   136
    Typical Relationship Issues   137
The Content Function   137
What Is Effective Online Content?   138
    Types of Information   138
Where Do You Find Intranet Content?   139
    Translation Process   140
Typical Development Work Flow   141
    Surveying   141
    Mining   141
    Translating   141
    Converting   141
    Testing   142
    Posting   142
The Technical Function   142
    System Administrator   143
    Programmer   144

10 Marketing Your Intranet   147
Not Just Another Newsletter   147
Educating and Evangelizing   148
    Newbies   148
    Surfers   149
    Power Users   150
Promotion   151

11 Maintaining Your Intranet   153
Involving the Entire Organization   153
    Management Information Systems (MIS)   154
    Strategy Committee   154
    Ad Hoc Content Committee   155
    Users   156

E-mail   156
Online Discussions   156
Automation   156
Provide Online Templates for Content Providers   158
Repurpose Content From Other Online Sources   160
Keeping It Fresh   160
Responding to User Feedback   161
Recruiting and Training Content Providers   162
Recruiting and Training Online Discussion Hosts   163

12 A Model Online Site   165

Structure   165
Home Page (default.htm)   165
Top Page (/section/default.htm)   166
Submenu Page (/section/section/default.htm)   166
Content Page (/section/content.htm)   166
Typical Intranet Elements   167
Animation   167
Audio   168
Backgrounds   169
Copyright   169
E-mail   170
File Names   170
Footers   170
Forums (Online Discussions)   171
Graphics   172
Headers   173
Layouts   174
Navigation   174
Photos   176
Site Structure   176
Text   177
Video   177

13 The Site Dynamics Intranet: A Case Study   179

"Eat Your Own Dogfood"   179
The Need   179

The Process   180
Home Page Features   180
    Major Content Areas   181
Resources   186
Links   186
Tasks   186
Tools   187
    Time Tracker   187
    Lead Tracker   188
    Calendar   189
Bottom Line   189

14 Common Intranet Mistakes   191
1. Failing to Build Initial Support   191
2. Weak Plan of Action   192
3. Setting Unrealistic Goals   193
4. Not Focusing on Users   194
5. Not Knowing the Technology   194
6. Failing to Encourage Interaction   195
7. Information Overload   196
8. Stalling   196
9. Project Leader Doesn't Keep Up with the Technology   197
10. Failing to Keep a Fresh Face   198

15 Intranet Best Practices   199
Communications Objectives   200
Who Is the Audience?   201
Developing Content   202
Structure   203
Measuring Results   204
Style Standards   205
Encouraging Interaction   206
Keeping the Site Fresh and Timely   207
Organizational Issues   207
    Resources   207
    Defining Roles and Responsibilities   208
    User Training   209

Promotion   210
Information Provider Issues   211
　　Controlling Access   211
　　Copyright and Legal Issues   211

Glossary of Electronic Publishing Terms   213

Appendix: Intranet Battle Plan   221

Index   227

1

Introduction

Where Are We Today?

In record numbers, public and private organizations are turning to a relatively new concept called the intranet to gain competitive advantage, expedite information sharing, provide enhanced customer service, conduct online training, improve productivity and quality, and bring the organization to new levels of effectiveness with one stroke.

Simply defined, an intranet is an internal application of technologies developed for the Internet.

And where are you in this feeding frenzy? You may be the one who just inherited the task of bringing this phenomenal new technology to your organization. You are probably involved in the "human" side of your organization, otherwise, you would be reading one of the several hundred books out there on the technology of intranets. Maybe your job title includes the word "communication" or "marketing" or "training" or "development".

You may also be a bit overwhelmed by all you have heard, read, and seen about this new innovation. You may be looking for some help in making sense out of intranets and clarifying your role in rolling one out in your organization.

The authors of this book represent the gamut of skills and backgrounds necessary to create an effective intranet, from the Information Systems (IS) perspective and from the human perspective. Most of the book discusses the human issues involved in producing an effective intranet. We believe that the human side is, by far, the most complex part of this new undertaking.

Challenges and Issues

If our assumptions are correct, you will be playing a key role in designing and developing an intranet for your organization. The popular press is filled with articles and surveys about the topic. More and more those articles are dealing with the human issues associated with intranet implementation.

Under any circumstances, an intranet reflects the overall culture of the organization it serves.

Even under the most favorable circumstances, an intranet is a natural extension of a collaborative culture. It allows for the free flow of information and exchange of ideas among people who are used to an open environment.

Under the least favorable circumstances, an intranet is another outlet for structured and controlled communication within an autocratic organization. It allows for the instantaneous flow of filtered information and may provide some limited potential for user interaction. Your greatest challenge as a member of the intranet development team is to set your own expectation level realistically. To do this requires an absolutely clear and unbiased survey of your current organizational climate. This can be extremely difficult to do from your vantage point inside the organization. This step is nonetheless critical — every other step that follows in the process. Without a clear understanding of your organizational climate, and subsequent decisions about how to structure your intranet, your project — and your job — could be in some jeopardy.

Moving Toward Empowerment

As organizations embrace new management philosophies promoting individual empowerment, intranets become a powerful medium for information sharing and dialoging. Different organizations are on different glide paths toward empowerment. Some have fully embraced it and are moving aggressively toward a collaborative culture. Some have taken a less aggressive approach, allowing it to move through the organization on its own schedule. Still others have only paid lip service to the concept of empowerment and collaboration. For them, intranets an be just another medium for cranking out management directives.

Where your organization is on that continuum will have much to do with how you will plan and build your intranet. Obviously, an intranet can be totally open and collaborative, offering users maximum, real-time exposure to all the information they need to make meaningful decisions about their jobs and work. If, however, you attempt to build such an intranet in a non-collaborative environment, your project may be doomed before it ever begins.

The Promise of Technology

First it was the telephone — interrupting our peaceful, tranquil lives with live, on-demand communication from anyone with a phone. Through the past few decades, technology has

Introduction

taken us for a wild ride, from cellular phones to wireless fax machines, from dial-up local Bulletin Board Services (BBS) to high-speed cable modem access to the World Wide Web, from video teleconferencing to personalized, digital news services.

To keep pace with all this innovation, many have begun to measure technology time in "Web years" (named for the World Wide Web, the multimedia portion of the Internet). Web years are approximately 30 days long. What that means, simply, is that anything over 30 days old is likely to be out-of-date. By the time you read this book, the latest information in it will be about 6 Web years old.

News sites on the Web offer continual updates throughout the day, rendering their print counterparts to the status of the dinosaurs. Modern Web technology enables software agents to watch Web sites you designate and report back to you periodically on what is new, what has changed. Portable Web devices connect even remote workers to a universe of information. Transactions can be completed by field sales people using laptop computers with modems connected to cell phones while driving down Interstate 10!

Technology has kept its promise to revolutionize communication as we know and practice it. The technology trap has always been human. From the form factor of new, portable communication devices (keypads must be large enough to accommodate pudgy human fingers) to the necessity for Graphical User Interfaces (GUIs) on PCs (humanizing the technology), human factors have always affected the rollout of new technology.

Your intranet project will most certainly be shaped by the humans who touch it. It will have management's fingerprints all over it. It will reflect the culture and style of its host organization. It will be as interactive and fluid as its creators can tolerate.

The Purpose of This Book

This book is not an intranet technology book. There are hundreds of technology books already taking up shelf space at your local bookstore. Those books have been out of date since the day they were written. Intranet technology development is accelerating at an astronomical rate. Major, new technology announcements are made almost every day. In an age when most typical software applications are in their 5th, 6th or even 7th complete version, Internet and intranet software tools and applications are being hastily released in their beta (final test before final release) mode. Knowledgeable online citizens (called netizens) measure their relative pecking order by how many beta versions of different software they are testing.

```
Intranets are not about technology, intranets are about people.
```

This book is about the soft side of technology — people. If Rip Van Winkle woke up today, person he would still be very human despite his lack of technological expertise.

Every once in a while, even a seasoned consultant gets a rude reminder of how wide the technology gap can be:

> The publisher of a major business magazine does not own a computer either personally or professionally. She is very proud to tell people that she is totally computer illiterate — never stared into a computer screen, never handled a mouse. She thinks DOS is the Spanish word for two. She wanted the consultant to show her how to "surf the Web". Imagine the learning steps she would have to go through (basic computer operation, hardware, software, etc.) to bring her up to speed with the rest of her peer group.

This publisher is not as unusual as she appears on the surface. She simply has not had a compelling reason to embrace the technology yet. She has been quite successful, thank you very much, in conducting her job responsibilities without a computer.

Your organization may be full of non-technical people who are doing just fine without a computer on their desk. You might not be as computer literate as you wish you were. Especially if you just became part of an intranet development team.

This book will provide you all you need to fully understand both the process of building, launching, and maintaining an intranet, and the outcomes you can expect as a result of your efforts.

The first section of the book (Chapters 1 through 4) are all about organizational issues, communication management in the electronic age, and the benefits of intranets. In other words, they are very much outcome oriented. They are a good foundation upon which to base an effective intranet project.

The middle section of the book (Chapters 5 through 11) are very much process oriented. present the entire cycle, from a brief technology introduction in Chapter 5 (just a primer so you can have a halfway productive conversation with your MIS department) to an example in Chapter 11 of a model intranet site.

The final chapters of the book provide you with a close-up look at a functional intranet site, document examples and a comprehensive glossary of online publishing terms.

Content, Style and Politics

The subtitle of this book was chosen very carefully and represents the three major activities that will occupy your time over the next few months as you move through your intranet process.

Content

What goes on your intranet site? Does it exist now? Where? Who has access to it now? Who will have access to it on your intranet?

Content issues can be daunting because in many organizations, information is power, and those who control the information may not want to share it widely. They are also challenging in that they require someone to exercise some control over what content goes online. These decisions can involve organizational censorship issues, control issues, and security.

Publishing content online puts it into a new category. Any time you convert content to digital form, it is much more transportable. Modern browsers allow users to copy any element contained on a Web page and save it to an internal hard drive. Electronic files can be attached to email or printed out. The best firewall (a device that keeps unwanted users out of your intranet) cannot protect your information once it reaches the browser window.

Content issues are likely to be a large part of your project throughout its development cycle.

Style

Online style is usually called "look and feel". It's more than design. It integrates how the site is structured and how the content is arranged. Much has been written about good interface design.

```
Bruce "Tog" Tognazzini is widely recognized as the interface
design guru. His book, "Tog on Interface" provides a com-
prehensive overview of the elements that combine to create
effective user interfaces. (Addison-Wesley Publishing Com-
pany, Inc. 1992)
```

Unlike print design, online design is seriously limited, at this point, by technology. The speed and amount of traffic on your Local Area Network (LAN) will determine much of your design. Large files (above 50K) take a long time to download. Multimedia files can be very large (up to 500K) and can bring network traffic to a crawl — a situation likely to cause some concern to your network administrator. In fact, since you are, in effect, riding on someone else's highway, network traffic concerns will soon become major issues for you and your intranet committee. You may end up playing referee between your site designer and your network administrator.

Elements of effective online style are covered in detail in Chapter 8, "Designing Your Intranet."

Politics

This is the one that can destroy a project, or even a career.

The advent of the intranet will probably be remembered as one of the most significant organizational developments in history. Intranets represent the final delivery on the promise of open communication. For the first time, every member of an organization can have access to all types of organizational information in real time. The flood gates are beginning to open on the organizational knowledge base. Technology is driving the price of collaboration down to the level where most organizations can afford some type of intranet system.

You and your staff will learn the finer points of online publishing, including effective design and valuable content.

The technology is here (and improving every day), the networks to carry the traffic are there (in most cases) and the publishing tools are there (simple, inexpensive and easy to learn). All the necessary pieces are in place to bring this revolution to your organizational desktop.

The one unknown in all of this good news is how this intranet project will affect the organizational power base. Knowledge is power. Plain and simple. People reach positions of power by the careful manipulation of information, making decisions about what to share, when to share it and with whom.

Make no mistake about it. Politics and organizational intrigue will play a major role in your intranet project. If your management believes in individual empowerment (giving people control over their jobs) and demonstrates those beliefs in practice, your job will be relatively simple. If, however, your organization is autocratic in its approach to management, your task will be much more difficult.

Simple process decisions often become complex issues when they involve politics. Without a firm commitment to your intranet project from the highest management levels, political issues can delay, sidetrack and completely stall your efforts.

We discuss the political implications of intranets more fully in Chapter 4 "Electronic Empowerment."

The Human Side

In reality, all sides of any project involve people. In this book, we have drawn a hard line between the people and the technology. Most intranet books deal almost exclusively with technology issues. We believe that the technology issues are simple compared to the very complex human issues involved with bringing new technology into the organization.

We concentrate on the human side of intranets because that is where most of your efforts will be focused during your project and beyond.

We approach every topic in this book with the understanding that organizations are no more or no less than a collection of people focused on similar goals.

Book Organization

Chapter 2 is a comprehensive overview of today's organizational communication theory and practice and what happens when a new, powerful communication medium — your intranet — is added to the mix.

Chapter 3 presents some very compelling reasons why organizations have adopted intranets with special attention paid to intranet advantages. Case studies of some very successful intranet projects are presented.

Chapter 4 addresses the very political issues associated with empowerment and the sharing of knowledge. Traditional communication concepts — gatekeeper, filter, grapevine — are discussed in light of intranet technology.

Chapter 5 provides an overview of online technology in non-technical terms. It is intended to provide you with a solid foundation (and some useful acronyms) to use when you talk to technical people about your project.

Chapter 6 begins the process segment of the book. This chapter deals with the 40,000 foot view of your project. Topics range from establishing realistic goals to defining roles and responsibilities for your staff.

Chapter 7 provides a complete guide to planning your project once your strategic direction has been set. It presents practical information about intellectual properties, make-buy decisions, identifying internal resources, understanding nonlinear construction, designing interactivity, enlisting management and technical support, security issues, and encouraging feedback.

Chapter 8 covers online design issues ranging from look & feel to site personality. Special attention is paid to the limitations placed on design by the nature of online network issues.

Chapter 9 gets into the nuts and bolts of building your intranet. It deals with the challenges of working with technical people, assembling a development staff, developing content, style and structure.

Chapter 10 covers the continuing challenges associated with promoting your intranet to current and potential new users. Your ultimate success depends on your ability to attract users and to make your intranet an integral part of their worklives.

Chapter 11 deals with one of the most understated issues facing intranet development teams — maintenance. Unlike traditional communication media, an intranet site is never complete. It requires constant updating and expansion to become successful. The chapter deals with ideas to automate much of the routine maintenance so you can spend time developing and refining new content.

Chapter 12 presents a model intranet site with examples of typical content areas.

Chapter 13 is a case study of the Site Dynamics intranet. Site Dynamics is an online applications development company that uses its intranet to conduct almost every aspect of its business. Real-life examples are presented.

Chapter 14 is a compilation of document samples taken from successful intranet projects.

The Glossary is comprehensive list of common electronic publishing terms.

The Appendix presents an intranet battle plan to carry you through the entire planning process.

2

Intranet Benefits

Fear is a powerful motivator.

In today's corporate world fear is compelling a lot of companies to rush into intranet projects because their management fears they will fall behind their competition if they do not.

A chief executive officer attends an industry meeting where the buzz is all about intranets — who has them, how much money they are saving with them, how much more efficient they are by using them, etc.

The Human Resources manager sees a demonstration of how one company has posted all its policies and procedures on their intranet. They even created a way that their employees can calculate the number of sick days they have left in the year, the current balance in their retirement savings account, or the current new car interest rate being offered by the company credit union.

The Communications Administrator just finished reading the *Wall Street Journal's* special edition on Corporate Networks, and she knows that the next phone call she receives will be from the General Manager (who just read the same special edition) asking when she will complete her intranet strategy.

Intranet Springboards

Intranets tend to get started in one of three ways in most organizations. They begin as grass roots movements from who knows where, guerrilla operations, or directives from the chief. Let's look at these beginning spots one at a time.

Grass Roots

One of the more positive benefits of the intranet movement is the ease with which it can be implemented. Some very successful intranets have grown out of a single "evangelist" within the organization. This evangelist may have run a bulletin board system (BBS — the forerunner of the World Wide Web) on a computer in their garage. He could be a corporate trainer who has seen the potential of online instruction. She could be a human resources administrator who has seen a demonstration of online insurance claims filing at a vendor location. He might be a real computer nut who understands and evalgelizes the advantages of publishing company information online.

Guerrilla Operations

Like much of new technological innovation, certain individuals just naturally are drawn to online publishing. After all, the cost of entry into the online world is relatively small. Almost any multimedia-capable computer made within the past few years can be turned into a server — the computer that "serves" files to other computers "clients" that request them. Creating Hypertext Markup Language (HTML) "pages" or documents is now easier than ever. Many popular software applications (including most word processing, page makeup and spreadsheet applications) have HTML filters or converters. In many companies, someone within the MIS department creates some files, buys an inexpensive server software and begins to publish personal pages on the company's Local Area Network (LAN). Word gets out, people discover the "cool" site and a local legend is born.

Directives from the Chief

Many intranets have started as the result of a magazine article, seminar session or staff meeting. Lots of top execs are looking for any competitive advantage possible in today's nimble era. They may have been slow to embrace the Web when it began to pick up steam. They do not want to be left behind by their competitors. Up till now they have been able to follow their competitors' progress on their Web sites (open to all). But now they have no idea what anyone is doing behind the firewalls of intranets. Information about who is doing what is sketchy and hard to find. They may become paranoid about losing out to others who are embracing new technology to competitive advantage. In many cases, that paranoia may be justified.

> From AT&T to Levi Strauss to 3M, hundreds of companies are putting together intranets. At Compaq Computer Corp., employees tap into a Web server to reallocate investments in their 401(k) plans. At Ford Motor Co., an intranet linking design centers in Asia, Europe, and the U.S. helped engineers craft the 1996 Taurus. Scientists working in fields such as genetics and biotechnology credit intranets with allowing them to share information with colleagues and to quickly sift through volumes of data that might have taken days to find in the past.
>
> Across the business world, employees from engineers to office workers are creating their own home pages and sharing details of their projects with the rest of the company. At National Semiconductor Corp., for instance, an engineer rigged a home page that lets his department schedule meetings online. ``It's like a thousand

flowers blooming," says Frank Dietrich, corporate Web systems manager at Silicon Graphics Inc., whose 7,200 employees have access to 144,000 Web pages stored on 800 internal Web sites.

Business Week, February 26, 1996

However, the idea of intranets enters your organization, the challenges are very similar. Those challenges should start with a well-defined and carefully constructed answer to the question: Why are we doing this?

Yes, intranets are very cool. Yes, many companies already have them. Yes, most other companies are planning them. And no, most of them haven't given much thought as to why they want to develop one. Very often, organizations jump on the technology bandwagon so they don't get left at the hitching post. Intranets are a relatively new extension of the Internet phenomenon that has swept the planet during the 1990s. According to industry estimates the market potential for intranets dwarfs the Internet. In human and organizational terms, the growth of corporate intranets looms as one of the most important and powerful changes in history. Intranets have the potential to transform organizations in ways we have just begun to consider. It is because of this powerful potential that organizations should take a long hard look at the reasons for and potential outcomes of embracing real-time, online, interactive communication.

Some reasons are obvious — and compelling.

Of course you can save money by publishing our employee newsletter online and eliminate production costs.

Of course you can offer our employees faster claims filing with online forms.

Of course you can open up our organizational knowledge base to help our employees become more productive.

But is it the right thing to do? Can you justify the necessary resources with any kind of expected ROI? Is online delivery more effective than the delivery methods you are now using?

After all, organizations have been running successfully and communicating for a number of years now without a single Netscape browser, Java applet or HTML tags.

People in many organizations actually talk to each other about important issues. Other people use a telephone in real time to exchange ideas. Recently, many more have learned the benefits of corresponding through electronic mail.

One of the authors of this book, Dr. Jerry Koehler, shared an interesting story regarding his experience with e-mail.

> Jerry is a communication theorist who believes in the value of face-to-face communication with real-time feedback. While on special assignment with the Florida

Department of Labor in Tallahassee, he needed to keep in touch with the XYZ employment offices and staffs located around the state. Jerry had never used e-mail before, but his staff convinced him that that was the best way to keep in touch.

Jerry soon found his electronic mail in-box filled with a great variety of questionably important messages. The staff began to copy him on everything they sent to anyone else. Being somewhat technophobic, Jerry found a way to bridge from his traditional communication background to the new medium. He asked his secretary to review his messages every morning. She determined which were important and which needed responses. In a brief daily session, his secretary read him the messages, and he dictated answers. She closed the loop with the senders and the system worked!

This is a classic example of how people manage new technologies by fitting them into existing paradigms. And that, traditionally, has been the way organizations have evolved over the years.

This chapter takes a look at some of the reasons intranets have become so popular. It also examines some of the organizational case histories in which intranets have been used for organizational and competitive advantage.

Intranet Prerequisites

As is the case with any new organizational initiative, your intranet needs a receptive environment to prosper and grow. The topics below form the basis of a good acid test for the potential success of your intranet project.

Local Area Network (LAN)/Wide Area Network (WAN)

Your intranet needs a highway to travel on. It is much easier to create a new vehicle (intranet) to ride on an existing highway than it is to build both simultaneously. Having an existing network is a good indication that your organization has already embraced the idea of information sharing, and this may make your task a bit easier.

Technology and Tools

How many desks in your company have personal computers (PCs) on them? Hardware is an essential element of your project. It is the gateway through which you and your users will share the intranet. Purchasing needed hardware may increase the cost of your project beyond the company's comfort level.

Collaborative Culture

Open and sharing companies will find the intranet a welcome new tool that can help facilitate the flow of information. Non-collaborative companies may view the new intranet as simply an electronic bulletin board for a collection of mundane and relatively unimportant information. Without a company-wide culture of collaboration, the intranet will never reach its ultimate potential.

Budgetary Buy-In

Intranets are not expensive as new technology goes. They are based on rock-solid technologies that are being made available at very reasonable prices. But they are not without cost. The company must commit to a reasonable budget that should include salaries for an intranet staff. A limited staff (Webmaster, content editor, graphics person, and programmer) can multiply their efforts by drawing on interested individuals in other departments.

An intranet development project that begins without these critical elements may encounter significant difficulties throughout the process.

Online Advantages

> Simply put, companies want the technology of the Web because it makes it easier for computers to finally start doing what we've wanted them to do all along. Surfing an internal corporate Web, employees use hypertext links to search for and access text, graphics, audio, or video, all organized into colorful documents called home pages. At the most basic level, this means being able to easily find and read online internal documents such as policy manuals and phone books. Webs also allow employees to call up internal data such as customer profiles and product inventory, information once hidden in databases that could be tapped only by technicians. The most advanced internal Webs are even getting linked to the proprietary systems that govern a company's business functions.
>
> Alison L. Sprout, "The Internet Inside Your Company" *Fortune* Magazine.

Faster, Cheaper and Easier

These are the three words that keep cropping up as intranet developers talk about why they opted for an intranet over a groupware (Lotus Notes) solution.

Intranets have existed for some time now, if you count shared information across Local Area Networks (LANs) or Wide Area Networks (WANs). Goupware solutions like Lotus Notes made it possible for large numbers of people in lots of locations to share information. These networks tended to be complicated, expensive and slow to implement.

Intranets, on the other hand, since they use rock-solid technologies proven over the past several years on the World Wide Web, tend to be fast, cheap and easy to build and maintain. Platform independence is one of the great advantages of using internet technologies (Hypertext Transfer Protocol and Hypertext Markup Language). The creative staff with their Macintoshes, the engineers with their UNIX platforms and the accountants with their PCs can all access the same information through the same browser and see virtually the same screen display. This universality is what helped the Internet grow exponentially over the past decade.

Faster

Unlike proprietary groupware, intranets are extremely inexpensive to install and maintain. These savings can be realized in both the content and delivery system. For those creating intranets, tools abound. Almost every word processing, page layout, and spreadsheet application has added HTML filters. It is now possible to create a compelling Web page in Microsoft Word — complete with graphics — perform one additional operation at the end, and end up with a finished HTML document ready for your intranet. The race to convert to HTML has been fierce. Over the past two years all major software manufacturers have embraced Web publishing. This rush to the Web has made it faster and faster for content providers to create finished HTML pages. As new Web authoring languages like Java and VRML mature, you can be sure that traditional software manufacturers will find ways to automate the conversion. Training time will also be faster as content providers will only have to learn the use of plug-ins and extensions to existing applications instead of entirely new ones.

> Job listings are updated once a week, and include information on how to fax or e-mail a resume. The company currently has corralled in its database more than 20,000 active resumes from the last six months. Each work day, it receives another 50 to 75 from the Internet. Like its internal counterpart, the external site saves HR time: Resumes are automatically scanned in, and HR can conduct a keyword search, rather than reading through piles of paper. For instance, if the company needs to hire an ATM developer, HR can type "ATM," and the computer will scan for all resumes containing that word or derivatives of it.
>
> Cisco Systems "HR is Wired for Success"
> *Personnel Journal,* January 1996

Cheaper

Groupware solutions (like Lotus Notes) are usually expensive to operate. Browser software, on the other hand, is usually free or sold at a fraction of the cost of groupware clients. The entire software industry is moving away from the era of proprietary, closed systems and software to the age of open standards.

What that means, simply, is that a whole universe of people out there writing new tools and applications every day. Web development technology is in the midst of an exponential explosion that is bringing down the cost of entering the online world.

Web servers and software are neither exotic nor expensive. Improvements are being made constantly in server speed and server software capabilities. More products usually means lower prices.

> Bottom Line: The preliminary results from IDC's return on investment study of Netscape intranets found the typical ROI well over 1000 percent — far higher than usually found with any technology investment. Adding to the benefit, with payback periods ranging from six to twelve weeks, the cost of an intranet is quickly recovered — making the risk associated with an intranet project low. The results to date clearly show that for any company, not just those already contemplating an intranet, the best strategy is to begin an intranet deployment today. The sooner

an intranet becomes a core component of the corporate technology infrastructure, the sooner the company can reap the benefits.

> The Intranet: Slashing the Cost of Business
> Ian Campbell, Director, Collaborative and Intranet Computing
> International Data Corporation
> (http://cgi.netscape.com/comprod/announce/roi.html)

Easier

What could be easier than using familiar software applications while producing Web pages? That's the beauty of HTML publishing. It offers a standardized palette of tags to present a wide variety of information across networks to multiple platforms. Content providers may choose to learn the nuances of creating HTML documents from scratch, or they may take advantage of any of a number of new HTML authoring applications. Following is a partial list of the HTML authoring tools available today:

Internet Assistant	FrontPage
Adobe PageMill	HotDog
Adobe SiteMill	HotMetal Pro
InContext Spider	Claris Homepage
Corel Web Designer	HomeView
HTML Assist	Navigator Gold
HTML Edit	Web Weaver
Wiz Web	Web Publisher
Net Objects	Macromedia Backstage

In addition to these applications designed to create HTML pages from scratch, a host of other traditional word processing, page layout, and spreadsheet programs are now including HTML filters or plug-ins that translate their output into HTML pages.

The bottom line is this: HTML pages are easy to create and change on the fly. Most computer-literate people can master HTML tagging with a little practice and training.

It Makes Everyone a Publisher

Spend a few minutes doing a mental inventory of all the useful information within your organizational walls. Think of the marketing materials, the product sheets, the management presentations, the safety regulations, the employee benefits packages, etc. Now think of the process it took to create those information packages.

```
Creation → Make Ready → Production → Distribution
```

In a typical organization, this process can take anywhere from a few days to a few months to complete, and it can involve a number of internal and external resources. A simple brochure could follow a publication cycle like this:

Traditional Print Production Cycle

1. Sales representative complains that a product sheet is out of date (or doesn't exist).
2. Sales department management agrees to spend the time and money to create the sheet.
3. Sales department orders new sheet from Marketing Communications.
4. Marketing Communications writes new copy and orders new product photography.
5. Brochure is laid out using desk-top publishing tools.
6. Electronic file is sent to production facility to create print negatives.
7. A "blue-line" proof is created and approved.
8. The negatives are sent to a printing facility to create the final product.
9. Brochures are sent out or handed out by sales reps.

Online Production Cycle

1. Sales representative complains that a product sheet is out of date (or doesn't exist).
2. Sales department management agrees to spend the time and money to create the sheet.
3. Sales department orders new sheet from Marketing Communications.
4. Marketing Communications writes new copy and orders new product photography.
5. Web page is laid out using Desk Top Publishing tools.
6. New page is posted on the intranet.

As you can see, the traditional production and distribution steps are eliminated in online publishing. Since you are working in a WYSIWYG (What You See Is What You Get) environment, as soon as you can preview your page and it looks good in the browser window, you are set to "make it live" on your intranet site. In one step, the requested product is completed and available for viewing by anyone with a connection to your site.

If there is a reason your users will want printed copies of the intranet content, there are two choices. They can simply print from the HTML page right off the browser. Or you can offer a high-resolution version of the on-screen content for download and printing from the user's system. Adobe Acrobat and other applications make this a relatively easy process. You may find this particularly valuable with maps and other graphics that have small text. On a low resolution screen, the text under 12 points gets difficult to read. You may decide to offer an on-screen version for a quick look and a high resolution for download and print by the user.

Instant Updating

A Website is never finished. Throw out all the traditional publishing metaphors. Nothing on the Web is ever finished. Updates are continuous. It is the one medium that allows you to present a living, growing and evolving message in real time. Prices change at noon — new prices are online at 12:15. Inventory levels change all day — online inventories are tied to internal documentation. In this era of just in time inventory, intranets offer just in time, all the time information.

One of the perennial problems associated with our typical print production cycle is shelf life. At Honeywell, we printed updated brochures about every two years. We had so many products and services, we could not afford to reprint everything as soon as it needed updating. Our content creation cycle was filled with decisions about the shelf life of the information we were including in the printed piece. We knew that technology was spinning very rapidly, and that technical specifications and performance were likely to change every few months. This left quite a lag between the time we needed to print new literature and the time when we could afford to do it. We tried a two-tiered approach for a while. We created beautiful full-color product brochures with artsy photographs and compelling graphics. We kept text to a minimum and we were sure to avoid any statements that would render the piece out-of-date before its time. Then we created a black-and-white specifications sheet with all the changeable information. This we could update as needed. We printed several thousand of the colorful, high-cost brochures, and only a few hundred of the spec sheets.

Today, we would do things differently. We would create our compelling brochure using HTML. We would animate certain graphics, add video and audio where appropriate, and put the whole thing up on an intranet so our sales and marketing people could access it at any time. We would also create a master, high-resolution version of the piece for download and print. Updates would be instantaneous, simple, and inexpensive. We would ask our customers for instant feedback and we would include their suggestions in later versions. We would time stamp our information and make sure it was reviewed and updated at least every day.

Time online is measured in hours and days, not weeks and months. On-line publishing gives you the flexibility and power to update, revise, and improve your information continuously.

Instant Global Distribution

One of the choices you will make early on in your intranet development process is whether to open your network to the outside world. There are compelling reasons both ways, and they are presented elsewhere in this book in Chapter 6.

If you open your intranet to vendors and customers, you may want to set aside specific, password-protected areas for their use and involvement. It just makes a lot of sense because one of the great challenges of maintaining good vendor and customer relations is communication. Sometimes we assume that our vendors and customers know as much about our organization as we know about theirs — or ours. Why not design and structure a separate area with the particular needs of those two groups in mind.

Even if you opt for an employee-only intranet, you can still decide to provide remote access to your field representatives.

Imagine this. Your sales representative is sitting in the office of your most valuable customer. The customer wants to know if you can produce the product he wants in the amount of time he needs it. She takes out her notebook computer with its built-in modem and cellphone. She accesses your intranet through a password and user I.D. She is able to show the customer this morning's inventory levels and production schedule. Using a data-entry screen she enters the customer information. Her request is entered into an automated production scheduler application for instantaneous processing. In a few minutes she receives an affirmative reply. She's happy because she was able to make a production commitment in a few minutes. She closes the order while sitting in the office, enters the information into the customer order database, prints out a verification for the customer, and leaves the office whistling a happy tune. The customer is happy because he knows now that his order will be produced and delivered in time — and on budget. He likes doing business with your company because your sales representatives have valuable and accurate information at their fingertips. You are happy because all the time and effort that went into the development of your intranet is paying great dividends — in both booked business and customer good will.

The advantages of a 24-hour per day, seven-day per week, instantaneously updateable digital network are only limited by your imagination. Your business and your organization present their own set of challenges and opportunities.

> Eventually the biggest impact of the Web will be how companies use it to stay in close contact with their customers. And it will be an increasingly important way for corporations to stay in touch with investors. Apple, Intel, J.P. Morgan, Microsoft and other companies already publish their annual reports on their Web sites. But over the next 12 or 18 months the real pay-back to the typical business will come from using intranet Web sites to give employees the information they need to be more effective.
>
> ©1996 *New York Times* Syndicate
> (4/24/96), By Bill Gates

Who's Doing What? Case Studies

The following section deals with some examples of other organizations and how they are using their intranets for organizational advantage. These examples are highlighted on Netscape's intranet site:

> **Northrup and the U.S. Air Force** use dedicated, encrypted, high-speed phone lines to review and revise plans for the B-2 Bomber.

Examples of **AT&T's** intranet applications are:

- a system that integrates disparate billing systems from various AT&T business units
- an interface to library services, internal research, and external news feeds
- a system for ordering office supplies (including Netscape software)
- an interface to an employee-contacts database of over 300,000 employees

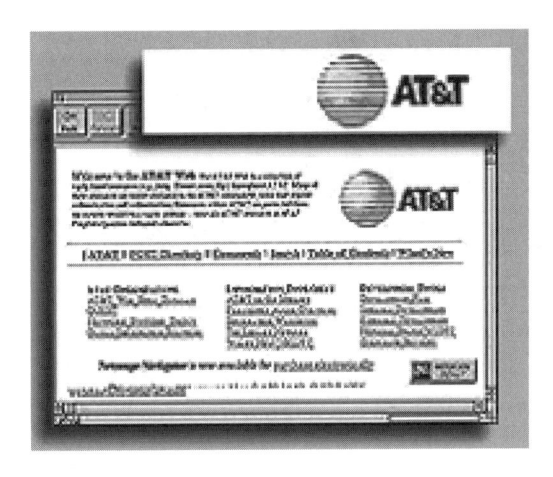

Columbia Healthcare's internet site provides visitors:

- articles about health issues
- downloadable healthy recipes
- a directory of Columbia facilities
- online magazines
- a schedule of physician chats that Columbia holds on an online service

Electronic Arts intranet includes:

- information sharing — employees can find human resources policies, organization charts, and employee and group information in one place
- team collaboration — newsgroups enable "virtual" teams to work together effectively

Departments throughout **Eli Lilly** — engineering, sales and marketing, manufacturing, human resources, information technology, medical — are developing projects on their intranet. Employees can access information such as internal job postings, employee handbooks, benefits information, corporate news bulletins, phone directories, press releases, corporate policies, computing policies, the daily stock price, a daily news feed on the pharmaceutical industry and a weekly newsletter. Additionally, authorized employees can access document management systems containing regulatory data while senior management uses an intranet-based Executive Tracking System.

New **HBO** marketing campaigns are rolled out to the sales force via the intranet. The new system:

- eliminates costs for printing, videocassette duplication, and distribution
- reduces the time needed to find information
- gives the sales force immediate knowledge of new marketing campaigns

Intranet Benefits 21

John Deere's Waterloo Works Division uses an intranet to:

- access an online catalog of equipment that integrates data from multiple sources
- allow company-wide access to results from remote test sites, provide technical documentation to employees
- offer a visual front-end to a parts database
- repurpose otherwise obsolete equipment as Web clients
- integrate corporate information with agricultural data on the World Wide Web

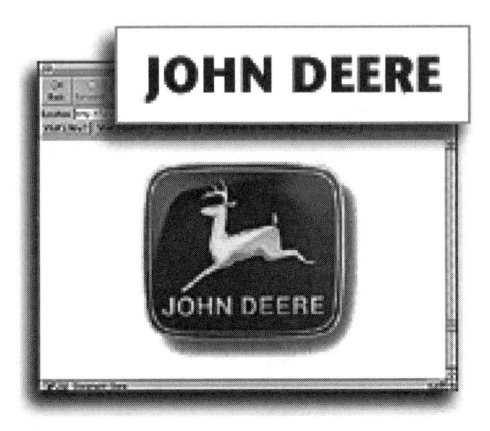

Mobil's internal Web provides employees with three general types of information. The first is employee information such as announcements, reference material, and news posted by individual departments, divisions, and organizations. Second, they post all intranet guidelines and procedures, such as style guides, security guidelines, frequently asked questions, how to get software, how to access the Internet, and how to identify business opportunities to port to a Web server. Third, the internal Web provides a platform for divisions and affiliates to put up their own Web applications, maintain bulletin boards, and collaborate on projects.

Oil exploration is a very collaborative environment. The Exploration Group in New Orleans puts its daily operations status report online for the team to access. Mobil's geophysicists, geologists and reservoir engineers use the Internet to share knowledge on research, software, or to point to where information can be found.

Olivetti's intranet provides researchers with a wealth of information on innovative subjects such as ATM, intelligent agents, new Web developments, and multimedia applications. In each topic area, researchers can find articles, news, bibliographies, and references to relevant Web sites. They also can add information, so the process of collecting and disseminating information is distributed. Before the Web, there was no central repository of information, so researchers often spent time looking for information that was already available in-house. Researchers can also debate topics in dedicated "discussion areas" and share experiences and project results with their colleagues.

Sandia National Labs' intranet provides enterprise-wide access to all corporate information — databases, financial data, policies, engineering and manufacturing data, newsletters, bulletins, and administrative information. Every major department has a home page on their intranet. In addition, corporate applications are loaded into HTML from SQL and other UNIX applications.

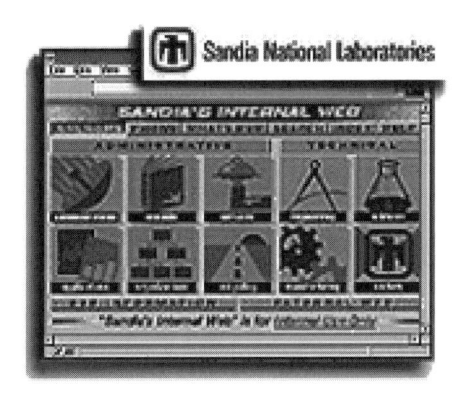

(These and other intranet profiles are found on the Netscape WWW site (www.netscape.com). These particular case summaries are found at: http://home.netscape.com/comprod/at_work/customer_profiles/index.html)

Are You Ready for Real-Time Interaction?

A key decision to make right at the start of your planning process involves your new relationship with your audience. Unlike traditional media, where feedback is often delayed or nonexistent, online media encourage immediate dialog between content provider and user.

Whether it's a standard e-mail form or an HTML form for leaving comments (guest books), your users will probably expect something close to an immediate response.

With online publishing, you won't have the luxury of shuffling through a set of letters to the editor. With online publishing, there is an implied response warranty. Normally, users will expect a 24- to-48-hour response time window. We mentioned earlier that Web usage is a very personal event. It is very much a one-to-one, mass medium. It is one-to-one because each user controls their own online experience. It is a mass medium because multiple users can access basically the same information at the same time. Each user is able to customize their interaction with the information on your intranet. No two user experiences need be the same. That's what makes the online world so compelling. It promises a connection between the user's computer (and by extension, the user) and any other computer (and by extension, any information provider) anywhere on the network. On the Internet, that means millions of computers, all interconnected, all capable of providing a unique, interactive experience for any one of the millions of people using the Internet at any time. It's always on. The entire content is available on-call. The user controls the speed and direction of the interaction.

Is it any wonder, then, that your users will expect the same user control on your intranet? Good intranets ask for and respond to user input. They make it easy for users to record their comments from any page on the site. Many intranets also have forum or newsgroups areas where users can dialog with each other over a wide range of topics. Some of the most valuable information on any intranet comes from these user interactions. That's the upside of instant interaction.

The downside of instant interaction is the expectation that questions and feedback will be acknowledged and acted upon by someone in control of the intranet. Most intranet staffs soon discover that the initial launch was the easy part. That wave of activity that propelled them through the various phases of intranet development were always fueled by the fire of doing something new — of innovation. Typically, the intranet is launched amid a blaze of promotion and hoopla. The staff breathes a collective sigh of relief, much as the newspaper staff who have just put the latest edition on the press.

But, unlike traditional publishing models, the intranet doesn't stop when launched. In fact, the launch is the event that starts the interactive process with the user communities. Unlike a newspaper or magazine, the intranet has no shelf life. It is a living, growing thing. The users begin to add content immediately, through forums, newsgroups or e-mails. And they want to be recognized for their efforts. They want answers to their questions. They want recognition for their input.

A recent *Wall Street Journal* article (October 21, 1996) recounted the woes associated with simple e-mail queries to Internet sites. The Journal reported on a survey of 100 of the 500 largest U.S. Corporate Web sites. About half of the sites provided no e-mail capability. Of the others that did, only 17 sent back responses to the e-mail inquiries. When the Wall Street Journal tried their own survey with two dozen large sites, they found nine made no response at all, two took three weeks to answer, and only three responded adequately the same day.

Why all the problems? Simply, the online planners failed to address the issue of user interaction adequately. In the same article, they report that L.L. Bean, the catalog company, moved nine employees off their 800 phone lines to answer inquiries generated on their Web site. Volume has become so heavy, they may have to add another shift of e-mail responders.

If, after reviewing all your reasons for creating an intranet, you decide that online publishing is the way to go, plan carefully for user interaction. There is an implied warranty of responsiveness associated with the online world — Inter- or intranet. Make sure you are ready to handle all your user interaction. Make sure your Webmaster has time built into their daily schedule for user interaction. Make sure your site is inviting and welcomes user interaction.

You will find a whole group of active, energized users throughout your organization. They will be lively contributors to the company's overall success — that is, if you acknowledge their contribution. If they send you e-mail messages, you must answer them — and you must answer them within 48 hours. If you find the answer difficult or time-consuming to find, send a message that you are working on the problem and give an estimated time to respond. Your users want to know that they have an open channel into your intranet. They don't expect you will adopt every thing they suggest, but they will expect a reply.

Get ready for real-time communication before you find yourself treading water to stay afloat.

Content Providers

If you build it, will they use it? Which departments will be the first to embrace the new paradigm with their content? Building a successful and valuable intranet is a total organization effort. Much of the content needed to create a compelling site resides within individual departments or groups within the organization. Successful intranet projects reach out to include all the various functions within the organization with information to share.

Human Resources

Human Resources, for example, has traditionally been one of the most logical content providers on intranet projects. Much of the information they deal with every day — policies/procedures, benefits, staffing — affects the entire organization. Following are some topic areas within Human Resources that translate easily and effectively to an intranet.

Corporate Policies and Procedures. Keeping these documents current and accessible have been daunting problems within traditional communication channels. Publishing them online allows for instantaneous updating and enterprise-wide distribution.

Health and Safety Regulations. Ignoring these regulations could put the organization and its employees in jeopardy. There's more at stake here than compliance with governmental rules. And, in many cases, these regulations are frequently updated and revised. Add to that the fact that many organizations provide this information only to those most affected by it. Using the intranet, current and correct health and safety information is always available to anyone who needs or wants to know it.

Benefits Information. In some organizations the list of benefits is so extensive that many employees are simply unaware of them all. Using simple Common Gateway Interface (CGI) scripts (programming that attaches some functionality to HTML pages) allows employees to calculate their retirement income, determine their available sick time, enroll in lifestyle improvement classes, print discount coupons, file insurance claims online, change retirement savings plans, and check their 401(k) balance.

Organizational Charts. Talk about updates! These charts showing organizational structure have been the scourge of company graphic artists for years. As organizations reorganize, downsize, rightsize, flatten, decentralize and transform themselves, organizational charts must keep pace. Placing these changeable charts online means saving countless paper versions.

Job Postings.   The entire employment process can be automated online. Postings are current and accurate. Resumes can be standardized using online forms.

Employee Recognition.   On-line recognition is special. Seeing your face or your story on your computer screen, and knowing it's also on every other computer screen in the company, can be heady — and extremely effective — recognition.

> Founded in 1987, Columbia/HCA Healthcare Corporation is the largest health care provider in the world, with 347 hospitals, 180 home health agencies, 125 outpatient surgery centers, and 75,000 affiliated physicians.
>
> Columbia launched its intranet in January 1996. Already it contains content from more than a quarter of the company's departments and two geographical divisions. "We've always communicated very well using paper publications," says J. Tod Fetherling, director of interactive marketing. "We now have 275,000 employees: we needed a more timely and cost-effective method. Paper uses money that would otherwise be spent on improving health care service delivery."
>
> The intranet houses an up-to-date corporate directory, provides reports, posts resumes collected from the Internet site, and trains employees on procedures. Using Netscape News Server software, Columbia offers threaded newsgroups where employees can exchange information about process improvements and other topics.
>
> Online report distribution has significantly decreased costs. "We believe that anything worth doing is worth measuring, so we produce weekly tracking reports," says Fetherling. "By distributing the reports online, we're beginning to save trees. We'll document costs as we move forward, but the potential for our $20 billion corporation is astronomical.
>
> Netscape Web Site
> (http://home.netscape.com/comprod/at_work/customer_profiles/columbia.html)

Communications

Your intranet will probably have its greatest impact on the communication group since communication is their charter. In many organizations the communication group initiates or assumes the intranet project management function. In those cases where project management is elsewhere, the communication group is one of the major content providers.

Newsletters.   On-line versions of this employee communication staple usually take two forms. They may be replicas of the printed version with little or no additional content, or they may be enhanced versions that take advantage of the online possibilities (interaction, instant updating, sound, video and animation). Both can be effective. But an electronic version that offers a video clip of the community event is more effective than the one that shows the same photo that appeared in the printed piece. Adding audio of the CEO's speech at the stockholders' meeting adds enormous impact. Or simply creating a feedback area where employees can comment on and react to company news is a great addition to the traditional print product.

Press Releases.   Why not let your employees see your press releases before you send them to the media? An intranet allows you to archive all previous press releases and have them continually available.

Departmental Information.   Empower your departmental content providers to create their own areas or sections within the intranet exclusively for their news information.

Company Goals.   A nice way to keep the entire organization focused on the guiding strategies throughout the year.

Employee and Community Activities.   No more missed deadlines or incorrect information that cannot be changed in the printed newsletter. These postings can be created and updated by individual content providers.

> Eli Lilly & Company, headquartered in Indianapolis, Indiana, develops, manufactures and sells pharmaceutical products in 150 countries worldwide.
>
> "We have 27,700 employees around the world. It's often difficult to keep people informed about what's going on in the company," says John Swartzendruber of Lilly's Internet Services department. "People often don't know what is happening in other departments because they can't find the information."
>
> With the advent of the World Wide Web, Lilly saw a powerful technology that might help alleviate some communication challenges. The company formed an Internet Services department to use the Web to create an internal virtual information network. The result is ELVIS — the Eli Lilly Virtual Information Service. "The goal of ELVIS is to make information easily available to everyone who needs it," says Swartzendruber. "It's an internal distributed information system based on Internet technology."
>
> Departments throughout Lilly — engineering, sales and marketing, manufacturing, human resources, information technology, medical — are developing projects on the Web. Employees can access information such as internal job postings, employee handbooks, benefits information, corporate news bulletins, phone directories, press releases, corporate policies, computing policies, the daily stock price, a daily news feed on the pharmaceutical industry and a weekly newsletter. Additionally, authorized employees can access document management systems containing regulatory data while seniormanagement uses an intranet-based Executive Tracking System.

Netscape Web Site
http://home.netscape.com/comprod/at_work/customer_profiles/lilly.html

Sales Automation

One of the greatest promises of your intranet is in the area of sales automation. The great curse of the printed world is outdated or incorrect information that is difficult and expensive to change. In today's rapid moving world of product/service and pricing changes the ability to perform real-time publishing can be a tremendous advantage. Your intranet can enable your sales representatives to transact business from a customer's location. Inventory levels, production schedules, pricing information and more can be made available through remote access to your system from a portable computer using a modem and cellphone.

> Cadence Design Systems, based in San Jose, California, supplies electronic design automation (EDA) software and services to leading electronics companies around the world.
>
> The OnTrack system maps out each phase of the sales cycle, including how to work with Cadence's in-house consulting group and other corporate resources. "For example, one section points sales reps to Netscape-based forms that they can submit electronically to request a local seminar. This request is routed to the appropriate group at headquarters and kicks off the planning process for a seminar campaign," Barry Demak, Manager of Worldwide Sales Automation Projects says. "You don't have to be at Cadence for three years to know who to call to get something done."
>
> "The system is especially valuable for new sales reps," Demek adds. "One recent comment summarizes the thoughts of many: 'With OnTrack, I felt that I had learned in hours what otherwise would have taken weeks to learn.'"
>
> The sales process and sales support resources are dynamic and require frequent updates and modifications. "This isn't just a series of Web pages, it's an automated publishing system," says Demak. "Sales specialists at Cadence edit the text files,

put them on the server, the system automatically creates hypertext in the documents, and the changes are immediately propagated around the world. If we need to adapt a process in the sales cycle, or add a new collection of sales tools, we don't need to call a programmer to make changes."

Netscape Web Site
(http://home.netscape.com/comprod/at_work/customer_profiles/cadence.html)

Customer and Vendor Relations/Support

Open up part of your intranet to your customer and vendors (usually called an extranet) and you can extend the value and utility of your information. Just-in-Time processes can gain a tremendous advantage from real-time, interactive communication with your business partners.

Quality

The whole idea behind Total Quality Management and other quality/productivity initiatives is empowering individuals to make decisions about their work. The critical component in intelligent empowerment is providing timely and correct information to make those decisions. Your intranet will make it much easier to track and circulate the latest company, industry and government rules and regulations.

Training and Development

This function has taken on added importance in today's nimble organizations where people must be able to perform a variety of tasks and where they must be kept current on recent innovations. Traditional classroom training has been gradually replaced by more automated methods, computer based training (CBT) for example.

Intranets offer incredibly more diverse avenues for training than have ever been available before. On-line training is self-paced (the student controls the pacing of the training), portable (with remote access authorized the student can participate from virtually anywhere) and dynamic (multimedia expands and enhances the online training with the addition of animation, sound and video).

Your intranet also allows you to keep track of who is participating in the training, how they are doing on tests and where they may need remedial help. As individuals finish training components, the intranet is capable of sending congratulatory messages and filing results into a training database for future reference. Using intranet technologies, training administrators are able to create and maintain a diverse training curriculum, track its usage and effectiveness, gather feedback for future improvements or modifications, recognize individuals who have completed training, and keep track of every employee's progress toward required training and development goals.

3

Electronic Empowerment

In the beginning, humans communicated mostly face to face. There were no communication systems. There was no technology. There were grunts, grimaces and grumbles. Feedback was immediate and usually personal. There were few nuances. Things pretty much meant what they meant. There were no channel issues, no hidden meanings and no political correctness.

Life was simple, though short and usually violent. Today, all that has changed. We have created organizational communication structures that stand like the Great Pyramids. We have lifted hierarchy to the level of science. We have created and documented verbal and nonverbal communication methodologies and strategies. Our organizations are filled with people whose value is measured by how much they know. We have deep pockets of knowledge power entrenched in every organization. The information "haves" usually rule over the rest of the organization. Information is power. Absolute information is absolute power.

That is, until recently. The advent of online publishing has changed the pow structure. Intranets are transforming organizations in substantive and ever unimaginable ways. They are opening up channels to information that never existed before. They are prying open locked filing cabinets and desk drawers. They are burrowing into databases and connecting parts of the organization that have never been connected before. Intranets are powerfully, emphatically and undeniably rewriting the rule book for organizational communication.

Industry analysts say we are in the midst of a communication revolution that dwarfs everything before it. Technology has shrunk the world over the past 40 years; now it is knocking down corporate walls. The Internet has become the model for sharing information across all platforms and all continents. Now, intranets offer the hope of a truly seamless organization with fully empowered employees acting as informed stakeholders in a common enterprise.

We have all heard the early warnings of this organizational transformation for years. We have moved from the "open door policy" to the age of empowerment, from benevolent paternalism to true consensus. Yes, organizations have progressed and transformed significantly over the past few decades. The advent of the corporate intranet signals a shift into high gear. The pace of innovation through information will accelerate dramatically over the next few years.

What Happens to Traditional Communication Functions

The Way It Was

Any person with an MBA or worth their salt will tell you that information is power. Period. Those who control the flow of information in the organization control the organization in very real ways. How many careers have been abruptly ended because critical information was withheld? Conversely, how many careers have been enhanced because someone knew more than someone else? Information is power and, as such, it is carefully guarded, regulated and distributed.

Traditional organizations used a caste information system in the model of the military. "Need to Know" became the overriding factor to how much information each individual was exposed to. Very few people in the organization were privy to organization-wide information. Each department or group communicated with its own set of rules, jargon and networks. Most communication was point-to-point or narrowcast. People either spoke directly to each other over the phone or in person. Wider messages were distributed through memo networks that carefully regulated recipients.

The Gatekeeper

The person who controls access to the king, controls the king. The person who regulates the flow of information in the organization is in a serious power-influencing position. Gatekeepers are defined as people who control the flow of information to decision-makers. They can take the form of the executive secretary who only allows certain individuals to speak to the general manager. They can take the form of the administrative assistant who determines which e-mail messages are important enough to pass along to the executive. Usually gatekeepers are not people with power, rather they are people who can influence power through their influence.

In the electronic organization, the role of the gatekeeper does not go away. But it does change substantially because the communication model changes radically. In the traditional paradigm, the information "have not" must rely on the benevolence of the information owner to share. Usually this sharing is initiated by the information owner, not the information "have not." The reason is simple. People don't know what they don't know. This is especially true across organizational boundaries — like those between functional groups. Each group has its own language, its own communication practices, and usually a well-developed instinct to inhibit the flow of information outside the group. These group gatekeepers only share what is required and worse yet, what they think is required.

While many organizations publicly espouse participatory management and sharing information widely, they tend to practice the old set of communication politics. They view the organization as a collection of varied groups and disciplines, each with their own personality and charter. While acknowledging that the organizational success depends on tight teamwork, they also understand that they are locked into a competition for scarce organizational resources. Besides, what could someone from Production possibly know about Finance and Accounting? They seem to say, "Keep the functions separate, share only what you need to share with others and compete hard for budget money."

Clearly, sharing information with others outside your workgroup or department can be worrisome. However, in today's climate of empowerment, the sharing of organizational knowledge is an absolute necessity. Decision-makers, regardless of their department, group or title, must have a sufficiently wide organizational view to work effectively. Gatekeepers can obstruct that view.

The Trap

Electronic organizations, by the very nature of online communication, seem to be more wide open and information sharing than traditional organizations. Your intranet will provide the vehicle through which your organization can become much more participatory. Just remember that gatekeepers are a hardy lot, steeped in a long tradition of service to the management and dedicated to the preservation of the hierarchy. They won't go away easily.

You may find gatekeepers your biggest single challenge in opening up the organization. Prying information out of their clutching fingers may require some help from the top. You should get a commitment from top management about the kinds of information that are suitable for the intranet. Get them to commit to a certain level of openness with the entire organization. Create a master plan that addresses the way different types of information will be handled online. What information will each department share with the entire organization? What will they hold in a secure area for their people alone?

```
Your challenge, as intranet sponsor, is to convince the or-
ganizational powers to open up as much of their information
vaults as possible.
```

This, of course, is usually easier with top management support. If you sense a strong resistance to total openness, you may opt for a more subtle approach.

One organization found that breaking down barriers was a more formidable task than anyone had realized. This organization had run as a collection of autonomous units for its entire history. Department heads met once a month to give each other status reports. These meetings had degenerated into mutual back-slapping sessions where only good news was discussed. Any negative reports were either neglected or minimized. The message was, loud and clear, that everyone was doing a great job and no one had anything to worry about. Meanwhile, down at the employee level, the view was quite different. The company was in the midst of a substantial workforce reduction and heading toward a complete reorganization. Employees heard the message from the management but they continued to see the reality of their daily worklives. The two messages clashed continually. Finally, one enlightened vice president championed an intranet project. He would build it, staff it and pay for it for the benefit of the entire corporation. He offered to each department a section of their own on the intranet. They could post whatever information they wanted, but the cornerstone would be the electronic publication of those monthly meeting reports. He reasoned that the exposure to the entire workforce and the competitive nature of the senior staff would do much to produce more complete and believable reports.

Your move to online publishing won't guarantee more open and complete communication. Remember, the intranet is only the vehicle. Your organization must make a commitment to sharing that starts at the top.

Create a Plan

A good first step is to create a master plan for content on your intranet. You might start by reviewing some case histories to determine what has worked in similar organizations. More and more organizations are reporting on their intranet projects every day, so the cloak is slowly lifting. The Netscape site **www.netscape.com** is a good place to start. Just remember that Netscape is trying to sell you their products, so take what they say with a grain of salt. More and more case studies are appearing in the periodicals that cover online issues. Check out *WebWeek* at **www.webweek.com**, Information Week at **www.informationweek.com** frequently as they report on successful intranet projects.

```
The content plan should include suggestions for appropriate
content. It should also address information security issues.
Who has access to what information, and how do they access
it? It should also include the process by which information
gets posted on the intranet. Who selects content? Who ap-
proves content? In the absence of such a plan, you are likely
to see new gatekeepers spring up to replace the old ones.
```

A large organization had just made the decision to create an intranet. They took the "ready, fire, aim" approach. They embraced the "if you build it, they will come" philosophy. They did build it and people did come. Dozens of departments and groups came with their content ready to post. Employees came ready to advertise unspeakable things in the classified ads.

The intranet Webmaster had to assume the role of gatekeeper for the entire organization. In the absence of any formal, written guidelines, the Webmaster used common sense and guile to determine what was appropriate for posting.

This is a dangerous situation for two reasons. First, the Webmaster should not be making content decisions on the fly with no formal guidelines to back them up. Second, the organization is opening itself up to challenge and ridicule by making the content approval process so arbitrary. Your plan should address the content issues, and it should also spell out in detail the appeal process for individuals or groups regarding content decisions.

```
Gatekeepers will not fade away easily. Even in the electronic era, someone has to serve that role for your intranet. In most cases, that person is the Webmaster. Just make sure that the Webmaster has a plan and management support for their decisions.
```

The Filter

Like the gatekeeper, the filter plays an important role in traditional organizations. Putting the right "spin" on information has become an art form. Spin doctors are much sought-after commodities, especially in politics. Manufacturing the precise sound bite or photo opportunity is a valuable skill in our world of 15-minute heroes and heroines.

In an organization, filters can be dangerous. It's not that they regulate the flow of information (that's the gatekeeper's job) it's that they change the information that flows through them. They sanitize information so others see a different picture than the one that was intended. The problem with filters is that many people actually value their services. "Bring me only good news," they seem to say.

If you create an intranet that seeks and responds to user feedback, filtering becomes much more difficult. Unlike employee newsletters or other forms of traditional media, feedback online is immediate and visible. Your intranet forums and newsgroups will become the home for "unfiltered" information. Remember, intranets allow everyone to become a publisher. The last thing you want as the intranet operator is for users to perceive "official" information to be filtered.

```
You need to work hard to convince content providers to be as open as they can be with their information. Otherwise the informal employee channels (grapevines) will become more credible than the official organizational line.
```

The Grapevine

In many organizations, employees have established incredibly complex informal communication networks called grapevines. You won't find any formal job descriptions or task lists, but the roles are well defined and the results are usually impressive. Grapevines usually are most active in organizations where there are lots of gatekeepers and filters.

```
Organizational stakeholders want the truth about their
organization — good or bad, happy or sad. It's part of the
overall issue of respect.
```

Does your organization respect its stakeholders enough to share all its information with them. Does your organization have enough faith in its stakeholders to trust that they can handle the truth?

What happens to grapevines in an electronic organization? They become wired. They go online with their truths. Instead of meeting at the water cooler or copy machine, they meet in the newsgroups or forums. Instead of activating the "rumor hotline" over the phone, they bring it to the intranet where information can be shared immediately and universally. They embrace the new technology and find themselves in the media spotlight.

Grapevines can be beneficial. They can serve to verify the truth of your communication. They can become hosts for your forums. If they feel empowered, they can become significant contributors to your intranet and help it grow and prosper.

As you plan your intranet, think about the people in your organization who contribute to the informal information network, and find a way to include them in your intranet as content contributors or forum hosts.

Who Wins, Who Loses?

The electronic revolution sweeping through organizations is sure to leave victims in its wake even as it creates new power brokers.

New media require new paradigms. Just as television grew out of radio to become a new mass medium, online publishing will grow out of traditional internal communication. But just as television was not radio, neither will electronic publishing be the employee newsletter. Recent history shows that it is sometimes easier for new businesses with new ideas to become dominant in new technologies than for older, entrenched businesses. The reasons are simple. Existing organizations became successful by doing things a certain way. New organizations have no preset notions of how things are. They only see things as they should be, and they are small and nimble enough to change and evolve quickly.

Electronic Empowerment

37

One of the great success stories of the World Wide Web is Amazon Books. A couple of people with a bright idea took on all the established book chains and beat them to the online marketplace. The Amazon site features over a million titles to order from and a search and notification service. Amazon encourages independent publishers to place their books on the Amazon site. They also encourage authors to participate in online discussions about their work. Visitors can request a notification when an author releases a new book, or when new titles in a particular topic appear on the site. Amazon built its business and following by embracing the technological capabilities of the Internet and offering services made possible only through those technologies.

What does this imply for the electronic organization? It may indicate that new organizational structures may be the best way to move into the age of new media.

A major American daily newspaper decided to publish an online version of their paper. They hired a new staff, set them up as a semi-autonomous group, and set off to enter the online world. Trouble was, they were a daily newspaper. They thought, planned, and acted in 24-hour cycles. They could rationalize the need for real-time reporting on their Web site, but they couldn't move past their 24-hour imprinting. The Web site became an extension of the core product with a 24-hour cycle of its own. Their Web site is merely an electronic reflection of their newspaper. They have not grown and expanded much beyond the limits of their printed product.

```
Traditional publishers do not necessarily make good online
publishers. It's a different model with different parameters
and different audiences. In many ways, traditional corporate
communication groups are traditional publishers. They think
of projects rather than processes. They think of publication
deadlines rather than interaction possibilities.
```

That is not to say that traditional communication functions cannot embrace the new publishing paradigm and be successful. Many are. But it really depends on how you measure your own success. An important part of the intranet planning process is the establishment of realistic and achievable goals for your new enterprise. Unfortunately, many traditional communication groups tend to think within the existing communication paradigm. Many approach the intranet as an electronic extension of their other media — an electronic version of the employee newsletter, for example.

You may want to consider a totally new group to handle your intranet. Yes, they should have a firm basis in effective communication practices. And yes, you may be able to find good candidates within your traditional organization. But you may also want to consider looking beyond the traditional communication group.

Most important, encourage and reward innovation within your intranet group. Do all you can to stimulate "out of the box" thinking so your new intranet will grow out of your traditional media into something different, something more.

How Much Information Is Too Much?

"I can't read all the stuff that goes across my desk now," is a typical cry heard in the modern organization. We have entered the information age with a vengeance. Everywhere we turn we are confronted with media vying for our attention. Now you are advocating the creation of a new medium into this crowded arena. Not only that, you are placing this medium on everyone's desk so it becomes virtually impossible to ignore.

```
Warning.  Be sensitive to the signs of information overload.
Do everything possible on your intranet to become part of
the solution.
```

The first step is to create order out of chaos. Some have called the Internet "a dumping ground for tons of useless data, with small pockets of brilliance. " It has been suggested that the term "surfing" is appropriate for the Internet because it is a vast ocean of unsorted data. Many of the most successful Internet sites are those that offer some sort of organization to the vastness of the Internet. Yahoo, Excite, AltaVista, and a dozen others, have found success through their ability to categorize Internet content easily and quickly.

Your intranet site should offer its users a very well organized and structured site that contains lots of useful information and makes that information very easy to find. You may want to consider the use of a search engine for your site. There are lots of inexpensive search engine packages available on the market today and their addition to your site will be significant to most users.

Your site structure should be intuitive to the user. For that reason, when planning the site, you should put on your user hat. Don't make content placement decisions based on some organizational chart. Think about where your users would look for the information. In fact, you should ask your users to help you with content placement if you can. User focus groups can be extremely valuable in helping you make the user experience pleasant and rewarding.

We are entering a new era on the Internet. We are moving from a passive environment to an active system. New technologies, like active agents, will open up the Internet and make information much more readily available to users. Agent technology will allow users to be notified when information of interest to them appears on a Web site. Instead of the user having to conduct a search and visit several Web sites to gather and evaluate information, the agent performs that task. Agent technology is in its embryonic stage right now, but its promise for the future of intranets is enormous. Busy executives will empower agents to gather and report information. Instead of spending hours sifting through potentially valuable information, the executive will spend minutes looking over the agent's findings.

However, you choose to structure your intranet, remember how much information there is floating around the organization. Do everything you can to make your intranet play a part in solving the problem of information glut, rather than being a part of it.

Should Everyone Know Everything?

Of course not. If everyone knew everything, the organization would choke under its own weight. In organizations, people need to know enough to do their jobs effectively and to continually improve. Each organization will probably define where those "need to know" guardrails should be placed.

Many organizations place their entire intranets behind "firewalls" that prevent anyone outside the organization network to get into the intranet. Others extend the use of their intranets to customers and vendors. Some allow their employees to remotely access their intranet from home or in the field. There is no universally correct way to construct your intranet.

Decisions about information security need to be made at the beginning of the development process since they involve technology resources. Firewalls are neither inexpensive nor easy to install and maintain. Secure areas require custom programming.

As you make content determinations for your intranet, you should also make simultaneous decisions about content security and user access.

Do we want others outside our organization to have access to this information? Do we want to limit this information to members of this group? Should we place this information behind a tightly controlled password system?

Hanging On To Information Power

Just as surely as you seek to open up as much information as possible, others will try to keep certain information hidden. They will use such terms as "sensitive" and "proprietary" to justify their actions. Most organizations have well-documented guidelines that define these categories of information. As intranet publisher you should push for the universal application of these guidelines to the intranet.

No communication medium is absolutely secure. Documents can be removed from secure storage and circulated. Your intranet makes unauthorized distribution of organizational information easier because it is in digital form, but don't let that fact become a rallying point for those who wish to retain control over potentially troublesome information.

The New Communications Model

Nonlinear Construction

Books, magazines, newspapers, newsletters, etc., are all constructed with a certain user experience in mind. Most people begin at the front of a printed piece and move through to the back. Sometimes they skip pages or articles that don't interest them. Sometimes they start with their favorite section and move around from there. But typically, the printed piece is a front-to-back structure by design.

Intranets are more like spider's webs. Users usually start at one point (home page) from which they can move randomly around the site. In this analogy, the home page is the center of the Web and everything on the site is directly or indirectly connected to it. Users, not publishers, decide what they will access and in what order.

This new model requires new thinking about the relationship between content and structure. As you design your intranet, you should think of its structure in terms of complete, self-standing modules instead of interrelated components. These content modules should be constructed in such a way that they present a complete message on their own. They must also make sense regardless of the order in which they are experienced.

Real-Time Information

The phenomenon of real time is certainly not new to our normal, daily communication. In fact, it is quite the norm when we talk to someone in person or on the phone. It is only when we introduce technology (voice mail and e-mail) that we begin to deal with delayed interaction.

The advent of satellite broadcasting in the 1960s raised the concept of real-time communication to the global stage; events happening half-way across the world could be experienced as they happened in your own home. The effects of witnessing live on television the shooting of Lee Harvey Oswald have been well documented.

Unfortunately, most of our mass media are not interactive. Unlike the phone, our television is immune to our frustrations about repeats or schedule changes. television and radio give us a window on the real-time world, but it is a one-way view-out.

On-line media give us information and interaction in real time. On-line chat allows people all over the world to talk to each other via their computer keyboards. Newsgroups provide a forum for sharing information and ideas with millions of others. Video conferencing and streaming audio add motion and sound to the online experience.

In most organizational settings, the formal communication model is usually top-down with little or no planned interaction. Not so with your intranet. Your users will establish a one-to-one, real-time relationship with you and your intranet. Properly planned and constructed, your intranet will encourage users to offer feedback on current organizational issues, to take part in an online survey about Internet usage, to interact with others about common problems and solutions in your forums, to help you create a participatory environment where they can influence the style and substance of your intranet.

Your users will communicate with you, make no mistake about that. You need to make sure you are ready for the interaction, that you have sufficient resources available to close the real-time loop with your audiences. As mentioned in Chapter 1, getting your intranet planned and launched is relatively easy compared with keeping it responsive and fresh on a continuing basis.

Interactivity

An old rule of organizational communication states: "If you don't plan to change anything, don't ask people for their opinions." One of the worst things you can do as an organizational communicator is ask for feedback and then not act on it. Don't conduct an employee survey about the benefits plan if you cannot afford to offer any alternatives.

When you launch an intranet, you give a pretty clear signal that you welcome user input. Most Internet sites include something like, "Give us your ideas to help us develop a better Web site." It is common to offer suggestions for a site and have them never acknowledged your contribution.

You should take this relationship with your users seriously. They really do have some good ideas about how to make the site better. They really can help you spread the word about this new, valuable communication tool called the intranet. They can become no-cost, motivated and valuable resources that can add significantly to your intranet product.

The New Communications Roles

Webmaster

It's one of the more interesting titles to come out of the online revolution. The Webmaster has overall operational oversight of the intranet. They can be very hands-on or they can supervise a hands-on staff. They can be involved in the strategic direction-setting for the intranet, or they can be focused on the day-to-day operation. They can be highly technical, capable of writing elaborate Perl or C++ scripts to control complex online activities, or they can be non-technical and focused on the site content. They can be a staff of one and do everything, or they can oversee a staff of many.

Typically, they will be somewhat technical and somewhat editorial. They will usually be able to construct HTML pages on the fly and troubleshoot minor technical problems. They will be able to write fluently, edit others' writing, and have some sense of design and balance and color. They may work for the communication group or for the information systems group. They may have a degree in Computer Science or English, or they may have extensive experience in the online world. They may have run a bulletin board system from a computer in their garage. They may spend hours each day surfing the Web for leisure.

Whoever they are and whatever their backgrounds, Webmasters have one attribute in common. They must act as educator as well as administrator. They must do a significant amount of hand-holding as new users attempt to log onto their site for the first time. They must carefully regulate the content of their site so it complies with existing guidelines. They must help others become information providers to and informed consumers of the intranet. Their role is that of the missionary, spreading the interactive, Online word throughout the organization.

Content Provider

Who owns your intranet? Chances are, the answer is more complex than you originally considered. Using the "If you build it, they will come" analogy, be prepared for a flurry of requests from various departments, groups and individuals who want to use your intranet to get their messages out. They are your information or content providers. They are your editorial partners, providing you with the kind of information that will make your intranet a compelling and valuable place. These are the people who own and control almost all of the information within the organization. Whether it's official organizational reports or the scores from last week's intramural softball league, their information is interesting and valuable to someone.

Your challenge as the aggregator of this information is to facilitate the process. You need to locate, cultivate and activate these people to fill out your site. Many will come to you with their content in hand. Others will call or e-mail you to ask what is appropriate content for the intranet. But others will have to be ferreted out and convinced that the effort required to place their information on the intranet is a wise investment.

4

Managing Your Intranet

Most organizations today are experiencing dramatic change. The need to change and to change quickly stems from many sources, including global competition (boundaryless economies), worldwide labor markets, the emergence of new companies and increased customer expectations. During the past couple of decades we have giant corporations fall quickly to competitors who were more effective in meeting the needs of their customers. For example, companies like Westinghouse, Chrysler, IBM, Digital, K-Mart, Sears, General Motors, Continental Airlines, Xerox, RCA, Honeywell, AT&T, U.S. Steel, etc. saw their marketshare rapidly evaporate to companies like Honda, Toyota, Intel, Microsoft, WalMart, Compaq, Home Depot, Southwest Airlines, L.L. Bean, MCI, Nucor. The once mature companies that once controlled most of the marketshare found out the hard way that their management systems were ineffective in a rapidly changing business world. While their new competitors were initiating new management principles, new organization designs and utilizing modern technology (such as intranets and Web sites) to meet or exceed customer expectations, the older and more mature organizations were rapidly falling behind. Therefore, the once prominent organizations had to experience dramatic change and adopted concepts such as reengineering, downsizing, and delayering in an effort to regain their marketshare.

The effect on most people working in many mature organizations was sometimes devastating. Many became stressed, anxious, and even bewildered by the rapid changes swirling all around them. What many people didn't realize is that with rapid change also produces great opportunities. While many people in modern organizations recognize these opportunities, and are eager to embrace them, many top leaders still maintain the philosophy of command and control. They still believe that "they know what is best" and that their organization will be successful "if only people would do what I tell them to do." Concepts such as employee involvement, empowerment, and learning are only buzzwords. To many of these executives believe the intranet is only another technological advancement. Many executives lack the vision to see how the intranet can be the key ingredient in improving the organization . The purpose of this chapter is to provide an understanding of your organization as well as an approach to implementing an effective intranet system.

Managing Communication and Change

Most organizational leaders have long recognized that communication was the glue that held the organization together. They took the position that communication was vitally important and that the channels of communication should remain open from top to bottom. In the past, organizations focused primarily on upward and downward communication. For example, management would dictate the kinds of information it wanted to have communicated upward and through what channels. It believed that it was upper management's role to solicit information primarily for the purposes of decision making. They relied heavily on reports, memos, interviews, telephones, the grapevine, and meetings. On the other hand, management would utilize downward communication channels primarily to inform lower levels about management decisions. They would use various communication channels such as memos, bulletin boards, pamphlets, posters, pay inserts, speeches, training programs, meetings, and house organs to give instructions, orders and directions to employees. Although management gave lip service to horizontal communication it was often ignored primarily because it increased power and authority within the organization.

Massaging Data

In traditional organizations, data was commonly massaged at each management level. The front lines — whether engineering, manufacturing, marketing, quality assurance, finance and accounting, etc. — generated data every day. The data was passed on to the front-line manager who attempted to portray the data to his/her benefit. The data was sent to his/her manager who did the same thing. If you can imagine sixteen levels of management (not uncommon in major organizations a few years ago), you then can understand why top management was so poorly informed and why it would take so long to respond to changing customer or employee needs.

Many managers choose to cling to their old habits for two reasons. First, their positions would become expendable; second, they wouldn't be able to massage the data to their benefit. One of the primary reasons so many organizations have problems implementing an effective intranet communication system is that traditional management and managers are fearful of the consequences. Intranet advocates see the benefit of accurate and timely communication in furthering employee empowerment. What many of these advocates fail to understand is that the more successful they become, the more fear and stress they are likely to produce in traditional managers who work in organizations with numerous levels of management.

We believe that individuals who advocate advances in information technology should also understand that they need to advocate organizational development and change. No longer is it acceptable only to lead technology change. Today's intranet project manager must focus on organization change and all the implications that follow change.

The Clash with Traditional Systems

Too many information systems leaders fail because they specialize in technology and not in systems. They conceive their job as an administrator of a program rather than an overseer of a continual process. Too many times an intranet project takes on the characteristics of a traditional publishing project. In reality, intranet publishing is never complete; your intranet project is always a work in progress. To succeed it requires the support and participation of the entire organization. It cannot flourish in a vacuum.

As intranet project leader (or member of the development team) a key part of your role is to "take the temperature" of your organization with regards to its management style. Over the past few decades, business has witnessed a long parade of management and organizational philosophies, innovations, structures, dynamics and processes. Some have truly advanced the efficiency of organizations. Others have fallen by the wayside as ineffective fads. Every organization's path through these shifting seas of change is different. Every organization's management style is unique. You will be most successful in your new role as technology innovator if you understand where your organization has been in its journeys and where your management falls in the continuum between open and collaborative and closed and autocratic.

Taking the Organization's Temperature

> Not long ago the senior author was asked to review an organization and make suggestions on how the organization could improve their effectiveness. One of the principal problems that emerged immediately was a major conflict between the information systems leader and the division directors. When he interviewed the division directors, they complained about the leader of information systems. They thought he frequently overstepped his bounds and interfered with their division. He conceived of the information systems leader as being "power hungry and out to embarrass them." In fact, five out of the six directors thought it would be better for their organization if they decentralized the information system. Each of these division directors were angry because they were asked to make a significant investment in information systems and were given very little control of their investment. Further, they believe that the leader of the information system only embarrassed them because he frequently reported to top management data that often made the division directors look bad. When the senior author interviewed the Director of Information Systems, he, of course, heard another story. The Information Systems Director was on the verge of quitting because he believed that the most effective way to improve the organization was to generate accurate, reliable and real time information. And even though he was making significant strides towards this

objective, top management did not appreciate his hard work. He stated, "I bust my tail to develop a system that finally details what the organization is really doing and all I get for it is lots of complaints and grief." He obviously thought he was in a "Catch 22." On one hand, top management claimed that they wanted an information system that produced reliable data, but on the other hand when reliable data was produced, top management failed to accept it.

Another complaint frequently made by division directors was that much of the data generated by the information system was doing was only confusing the lower levels in the organization. The senior author felt sorry for the Information Systems Director since he realized that the director was working twelve hours a day implementing technology that was yielding quality data, but at the same time generating complaints and misery. It seems as though no matter what the Information Systems Director did he was bound to lose.

This example illustrates the Catch-22 nature of most effective information systems. The online advantages an intranet brings to the organization (instant dissemination, universal access, interactivity) are the very features that are most likely to cause problems. Instant dissemination of incorrect or highly filtered information will produce instant dissatisfaction. Universal access to questionable data will produce widespread dissatisfaction. Allowing people to interact with your intranet and its content means opening a dialog your management may not be ready to engage in.

One fact is certain. Introducing an intranet into any organization will magnify that organization's management style and communication climate. Placed into an open and collaborative environment, and intranet will promote empowerment by really opening up the available communication channels. Placed into a closed and autocratic environment, an intranet will become a very powerful management tool for control.

In most cases, your organization will fall somewhere in the middle of that continuum. Intranets introduced into more open and collaborative organizations will grow from the grass roots as all members of the organization become energized to participate in the project. The interactive elements (discussion groups, surveys, feedback, forums, chat) will be active and dynamic. Content providers will be easy to find and recruit to help you build the site content. Top management will embrace and endow the project so it can become an integral part of the organization's strategic business process. New content will be posted on a continual basis as more and more elements of the organization become active participants. Employees will begin to rely on the intranet to do their jobs more effectively. They will find large amounts of valuable information they can use to make better decisions. They will begin to think about this online resource as much more than a communication channel. They will embrace it as an integral and valuable part of their work routines. In short, the intranet will grow, prosper, and become fully integrated into every aspect of organizational life.

Intranets introduced into more closed and autocratic organizations will take a much different route. They will likely become a favorite showcase for management information.

Interactive elements will probably be inspected and filtered by management. Content providers will become active participants in building the intranet — probably as a function of their jobs. Top management will embrace and endow the project, but will most likely limit its function to tops-down communication. New content will be posted on a more episodic basis because most content will require some form of pre-posting approval. Employees will find large amounts of valuable information they can use to become better employees. They will tend to think about this new communication channel as a quick and reliable reporter of appropriate organizational information. In short, the intranet will grow, prosper and become a powerful new management medium.

Managing An Effective Intranet Project

Building Initial Support

In your job as intranet project manager, you will assume the role of cheerleader for this new communication medium. This is not like creating a new brochure; this is a whole new thing. The ultimate success of your project will depend on how well you handle this "evangelist" role. Evangelists are usually technology pioneers. They are advocates of new systems and processes. They spend a great deal of their time educating people about a new concept. They provide a continual stream of information about the technology and its advantages. They do this to build support among management and to create a demand among potential users.

Plan of Action

Brief management at all levels. In the very early phases of your project, organizational interest is likely to be higher than at any other time. You probably will discover that some of your management are very computer literate and others are barely able to operate a mouse. Your job is to provide educational information to every level of management that concentrates on the advantages of this new intranet.

You should prepare a basic presentation that covers the broad strokes — what is an intranet? how does it work? why should we build one?

You can then add specific information appropriate to the audience you are addressing. For example, when addressing finance management you will want to cover all the normal financial topics (return on investment, start-up costs, personnel costs, capital costs). Just as important, though, you should include information about how the financial function will benefit from this new intranet (streamlined accounting procedures, accounts payable/receivable online, etc.)

After your initial briefing, you should attempt to keep each management group informed of your progress and any potential problems you may have to overcome. In most cases management is going to be very supportive of your efforts — assuming they are kept in the loop.

Developing an Action Plan

Don't allow the enthusiasm of this new project to distract you from the tasks at hand. Your intranet project is complex and potentially difficult. Remember that you are bringing an entirely new communication medium into your organization. Your project will probably receive lots of attention from various elements of your organization. Management will be watching to see how well the project unfolds. It is up to you as project leader to ensure that this project has every good chance to succeed. An important element in that success is a comprehensive action plan. Chapter 7 provides a detailed description of the process steps.

Plan of Action

Draft a comprehensive action plan and circulate it widely. Your plan should include the elements of any effective action plan — action item, responsible person, due date and status. This plan will become the blueprint by which your project becomes a reality. Make sure its contents are widely circulated so that all necessary elements within the organization have a chance to comment and make suggestions. You will also want to make your plan a living document so that items can be modified, added or deleted as the project unfolds. Each action plan will be different depending on the particular situation. Certain elements, however, are fairly universal and should be addressed in any intranet action plan:

- Obtaining user involvement
- Surveying available resources
- Selecting appropriate content
- Building in interactivity
- Encouraging feedback
- Enlisting management support
- Defining responsibilities
- Protecting your intranet from copyright and libel violations

Finally, it is a good idea to review your action plan regularly. You may want to make it your agenda each time you meet with your planning or implementation team. This will serve to keep everyone focused on the key elements of the process.

Setting Realistic Expectations

Managing expectations is absolutely critical to the success of every intranet project. It is so important because it sets the tone for the rest of the project. It answers the question, "How will we measure our success"?

Plan of Action

Underpromise and overdeliver. Don't get caught up in the hype that always seems to surround the advent of new technology. Yes, intranets can be a wonderful benefit to an organization. Yes, there are incredible reports of astronomical returns on investment for intranets. All of that is true. It is also true, however, that what you are undertaking is full of potential hurdles and roadblocks. You and your staff can make any kind of wild predictions about your potential success. Just make sure that what you publish and promise to the outside world is reasonable given your circumstances.

The best thing to do is to take a very realistic snapshot of your current situation and formulate a best case scenario based on what you see. If you are given a limited budget you may need to start off with a small, pilot program to prove the concept. If you are given limited staff, you may need to limit the amount of content you put up or the frequency of updates. When you have developed this best case scenario, determine what might happen if you encounter delays or unforeseen problems along the way. Look again at your best case scenario in the harsh light of the real world. Just make sure that your published goals are attainable. Remember, no one ever got fired for surpassing their goals.

Keeping a User Focus

Many times the intranet design and development team operates in a vacuum. They may enlist management support and keep the organization informed of what they are doing, but they may not involve the most important group within the organization — the potential users.

Plan of Action

Make a concerted effort to involve your potential users throughout the process as often as possible. Your users will give you invaluable information about what is valuable to them, what they want, how they want it, and how logically to structure the content. Chapter 7 details the use of general employee surveys, focus groups, planning committees, and beta testers. Keeping a continual stream of ideas and feedback from your future users is the best way to ensure that you are building an intranet that will be used and used often. A final note. If you ask for input you need to make sure that the feedback loop is completed. You can do this by acknowledging the input with an e-mail or memo. Make sure you mention their specific input and tell them what you intend to do with it. Even if you do not use the input they provide, your users will feel part of the process if their efforts are recognized.

Understanding the Technology

You may not ever become totally proficient in all the technical aspects of an intranet project. Even so, you should attempt to become sufficiently knowledgeable about the technology to communicate effectively with the technical staff and support people who will be so important to your success. One of the best ways to understand the technology is to immerse yourself in the technology. Daily use of your browser will help you become familiar with the terms and concepts you will encounter as you begin your online experience. On the WWW you will find a wide variety of online publications that deal with the technology. This list was current at the time of publication, but you may discover that some of the listings have changed or ceased to publish.

Click Online Multimedia Magazine   http://click.com.au/
Computer World   http://www.computerworld.com/
Computer-Mediated Communication Magazine
   http://www.december.com/cmc/mag/
ComputerPaper   http://www.tcp.ca
Cyber Culture Magazine
   http://cvp.onramp.net/cyber/
c|net online   http://www.cnet.com/
Family PC   http://www.zdnet.com/familypc/
HomePC   http://techweb.cmp.com/techweb/hpc/current/default.html
Information Week   http://techweb.cmp.com/techweb/iw/current/default.html
Infoworld   http://www.internet.net/cgibin/ehtml?/stores/infoworld/index.html
Interactive Age   http://techweb.cmp.com:80/ia/iad_web_/
Interactive Week   http://www.zdnet.com/intweek/
Internet & Java Advisor Magazine   http://www.advisor.com/ia.htm
Internet Magazine   http://www.emap.com/internet/
Internet Professional   http://www.netline.com/
Internet Week   http://www.phillips.com:3200/
Internet World   http://www.internetworld.com/
Intranet Computing   http://www.apnpc.com.au/intranet/
Intranet Design   http://www.innergy.com/
iWorld   http://www.iworld.com/
Mac Week   http://www.macweek.com/
MacUser   http://zcias3.ziff.com/~macuser
NCT Web Magazine   http://nctweb.com/nct/
Net Business Daily   http://www.iocom.be/nbd/
Net Surfer Digest   http://www.netsurf.com/nsd/
Net Traveler, The Internet Directory   http://www.primenet.com/~ntravel/
NetGuide Magazine   http://techweb.cmp.com/techweb/ng/current/
Network Computing   http://techweb.cmp.com/techweb/nc/current/default.html
Online Magazine   http://www.online-magazine.com/
Online World   http://203.17.138.112/
PC Computing   http://www.zdnet.com/pccomp/
PC Week   http://www.pcweek.com/
PowerPC News   http://power.globalnews.com/
Pulse of the Internet Magazine   http://tvp.com/pin.html
The Intranet Journal   http://www.intranetjournal.com/
UNIX World   http://www.wcmh.com/uworld/
Web Developer Magazine   http://www.webdeveloper.com/
Web Techniques   http://www.WebTechniques.com/
Web Week   http://www.mecklerweb.com/ww-online/
WebMaster Magazine   http://www.cio.com/WebMaster/
WEBSmith   http://www.ssc.com/websmith/
Windows Magazine   http://techweb.cmp.com/techweb/wm/current/default.html
Wired Magazine   http://www.wired.com/
ZD Internet Magazine   http://www.zdimag.com/

Encouraging Interaction

One of the great advantages of online publishing is the interaction it offers. Unlike other forms of mass communication (newsletters, videos, brochures, etc.) your intranet provides the platform upon which you can build an effective, two-way communication channel.

Plan of Action

Your intranet should include an easy way for your users to give you their feedback ideas and comments about the site. Chapter 7 provides an overview of the techniques you can use. At a minimum you will want to include an automatic e-mail form (usually called a "mailto") on each page. These mailtos allow your users to give you specific feedback from any page on your site while their thoughts are fresh on their minds. Discussions (online message posting areas) allow your users to interact with each other about special interests. Discussions can be hosted (using a moderator or host to introduce topics and keep the comments on target) or unhosted. On-line chat (real-time interaction popularized by commercial online services like America Online) is another way (although still technically challenging) to allow your users to interact with each other simultaneously.

Another important aspect of interaction is to keep the site fresh through routine changes so your users will come back often.

Finally, if you ask for feedback and ideas from your users, you should have a well-developed plan in place for dealing with what you get. On the Web, it is expected that people respond to e-mails or online postings within 24 hours. That doesn't always happen, but it is expected. At a minimum you will want to establish a mechanism for acknowledging each message and providing some indication of when they might expect an individual reply. Automatic e-mail responses are relatively easy to set up (for your technical staff or the IS department, that is).

Managing Site Growth

As your project begins to pick up steam you will probably experience what we call the floodgate phenomenon. Whether you decide to start with a small, demonstration project or a full package, you will most likely experience a widespread enthusiasm to get involved as the project rolls out. If you build it, they WILL come! Will you be ready for the onslaught?

Plan of Action

The best way to get ready for the deluge is to plan for it well in advance. Your plan should address the key question of how you will handle requests by various individuals and groups to post their content on your site. The first step is to create a policy that deals with that very issue. Some intranets allow individuals to post personal pages. Others restrict content to strictly organizational issues. Some intranets recruit and train content providers to be their points of contact in the various departments. In some cases, content providers are permitted to post whatever content they feel is appropriate. In other cases, one person or a content committee has the final approval authority over all site content.

As you address each of these issues, you should generate an online content policy that reflects the process. You may want to publish this as a printed piece and circulate it to all interested parties. You may also want to post it on your intranet site as you roll it out. This should go a long way toward reducing potential misunderstandings or unnecessary challenges after you launch the site.

Sustaining Momentum

How will you transition from the euphoria of a new project beginning to the workaday world of project fulfillment? New projects (especially high-visibility ones like an intranet) generally create lots of excitement throughout the organization. A large part of your job is to create ways to sustain that enthusiasm throughout the development cycle, through the launch and beyond.

Plan of Action

Sustaining momentum requires you to sustain your contact with the rest of the organization throughout the development cycle. The euphoria of your new project is likely to diminish as time moves on. While you and your staff are caught up in the day-to-day business of building an intranet, the rest of the organization sees relatively little until your actual project launch. Your action plan should include a series of updates on your project for the rest of the organization. These updates might include some examples of screen elements, a partial site map, actual screens in development, etc. Anything that provides a glimpse of your progress is helpful in sustaining interest in the project.

Keeping a Fresh Face

Your intranet project is never finished. It is a constant work in progress; many times, however, the changes you make to the site are not immediately obvious to your users. To keep your users motivated to return to the site frequently you must commit to a plan of constant site renewal and redevelopment.

Plan of Action

Change something every day. The site Webmaster should have time set aside every day to make cosmetic and content changes to the site. These changes can be as simple as changing a photo or graphic on the home page in some sort of rotation during the week. They can be as complex as providing an entirely new homepage design for each day of the week. Whatever you decide to do, it should be obvious to the user that something is different on the site from visit to visit. This accomplishes a couple of things. First, it communicates to the user that the site is dynamic and interesting, and that if they miss a day they will miss something important. It also conveys the message that someone really is there on the other end of the connection. You may want to include time in the daily maintenance schedule to respond to e-mail messages from the past 24 hours.

Site maintenance is a critical part of your overall site management responsibilities. You should allow ample time in your Webmaster's day to spend on keeping the site fresh and constantly changing. Many of these tasks can be automated, thereby leaving more time for the Webmaster to spend on creating and posting new content.

5

Intranet Technology

In previous chapters you learned the essentials of design, planning, and various other aspects of an intranet. In this chapter you will learn enough technical knowledge to understand the basics and perform well in your role of intranet leader. Although a successful intranet does not need to be a technological marvel, a working one uses various kinds of technology to accomplish the job.

Transmission Control Protocol/Internet Protocol (TCP/IP)

One of the major benefits of the intranet is the fact that it is constructed of open systems. To understand the benefits of open systems, it is important to know how the computers on your network communicate with each other. Intranet technology relies on a protocol called TCP/IP which was created to establish a standardized communication procedure on a wide variety of computer platforms. Every computer on the Internet (as well as your intranet) is assigned a unique number that looks like this: 207.100.78.4. This address is used to identify the machine and the network it is attached to. It is important to note that the IP address identifies the machines connection to the network and not the machine itself. IP (or Internet protocol) addresses must be assigned by the Network Information Center (NIC). If your intranet is not connected to the Internet you can determine your own network numbering scheme.

Domains and URLs

Since most people have a hard enough time memorizing their phone numbers, a system was devised to give connected computers meaningful names. The service that provides this

53

capability to the network is called the "domain name system". Network names typically reflect the name of the organization and the domain name reflects the type of organization. For example: uky.edu is the domain name for the University of Kentucky. The `.edu` denotes that this is an educational organization.

Standards and Concepts

Since intranet technology is progressing at such a fast rate, specific hardware and software guides would be out of date before this book even went to press. However, all intranets are built on a few standards and essential concepts. It is up to you and the creativity of your staff to use these standards and concepts to build your intranet to meet your company's needs.

The standards and concepts are:

    Overview
- Software basics
- Hardware basics
- Browsers
- Servers
- Firewall issues

    How it works
- TCP/IP Network
- DNS Domain Name Server
- URL Universal Resource Locator
- HTML HyperText Markup Language
- HTTP HyperText Transfer Protocol
- Connectionless environment

Intranet Overview

The intranet, or the Internet for that matter, is built upon a few key hardware and software elements: the server, the network, and the browser. The Web server is connected to an ethernet network that is in turn attached to a personal computer running a piece of software called a browser.

The server is commonly called a Web server. This is derived from the Internet being called the World Wide Web. A server is a computer that contains files of information that make up your intranet. It then "serves" these files, or sends them over an ethernet network, to the computers of the people who request them. The browser runs on the user's computer and displays the files that that are sent by the Web server.

In the past few years, many companies that specialize in developing Web-server software have evolved. There is also a great deal of free or shareware software for Web servers. Many times shareware is more difficult to install and lacks the documentation and support of conventional software products. Also, shareware often has to be compiled on the machine on which it will run. When problems occur with the shareware, there is no telephone support line to help you overcome these problems. In fact, you can rarely even contact the developers for help of any kind. While it may be tempting to save a few dollars by using free software, it is generally not advantageous in the long run. By using commercial Web server software you will easily save the purchase price through comprehensive documentation, ease of installation and availability of technical support.

- Web server software should offer a few features that are very important to your intranet effort:
- Support for cgi or common gateway interface
- Support for Server Side Includes or SSI
- Support for image maps
- Support for page security, including Secure Sockets Layer (SSL)
- Remote management and monitoring

cgi

All Web server software supports a programming standard called common gateway interface or cgi for short. cgi is a way to expand the capabilities of the Web server without having to change the server software itself. A typical cgi would process a form that a user fills out. The contents of the form could be e-mailed to a person as in a purchase request, added to a database for a report, or simply added to a "guest book" for feedback. In recent versions of Web server software, many of the capabilities of external cgis have been added to the core server software. This is good because it allows faster implementation of intranet services and simpler maintenance of the site. Look for form processing, image map services, remote management and monitoring and other features built into the Web server software.

SSI

Server Side Includes (SSI) is a standard method by which simple, dynamic data can be included on your Web pages. An example would be a counter that moves forward each time someone requests a page, a date, and time that changes to reflect the current date and time, and the ability to hide and show options depending upon the security level of the user.

Image Mapping

Image mapping allows for the use of graphic images to act as links for navigation. This means that a user can click on a portion of an image (such as a state on a map of the U.S.) and then display information associated with the image (such as vital statistics on that particular state). In newer browser software this function is handled by the browser and not the server. To be compatible with this function, the server must have this capability.

Page Security

There are three levels of security that all Web server software should support. The most basic is access restriction to a page with the use of an ID and a password. This requires every user to be assigned an ID and a password to be able to use the intranet. In small organizations, this can be very effective and very secure. In larger organizations, it can be quite a chore to manage and maintain the list of users.

The second level of security is restriction by IP address. Using this method, you can allow anyone inside your network to browse your intranet while keeping any user with an IP address outside your network from having access to your intranet.

The third level of security is called Secure Sockets Layer (SSL). Your choice of Web server software should include the capability to support SSL transactions. This is a security method where all data transmitted between the Web server and the Browser is encrypted. SSL encryption allows your intranet to be accessed from the Internet by your remote offices or employees and still keep the security you expect from an intranet.

SSL comes in two versions, 64-bit encryption and 128-bit encryption. Currently 64-bit software is allowed to be exported to other countries but 128-bit software is not. This means that if you have overseas or foreign offices, you can't use 128-bit security SSL software, so plan accordingly.

By using a combination of user ID and password, IP addressing, and SSL you can allow only your users access to your intranet, even if your users are spread around the world.

Remote Management and Monitoring

Adding user IDs and passwords, modifying and updating security profiles, monitoring the performance of the server, updating Web pages, and troubleshooting problems are all things that should be able to be accomplished through the browser. This will enable your administrator to manage the system from a computer whether the administrator is in the next room or is hundreds of miles away.

Web server software runs on a variety of hardware platforms: DOS, Windows, UNIX, and Macintosh. While each platform has its fans and detractors, you should avoid using any operating system that requires an eight dot three file name (i.e., DOS). After a very short time the number of files making up your intranet will become nearly unmanageable, especially if they are all required to be variations of eight characters. UNIX is an excellent platform for a server, but it does have two drawbacks. UNIX is very complex and it takes an experienced programmer to manage it correctly. Also, the file names are case sensitive. This means that the name Foo.html is treated as a different file from FOO.html. A lot of time and effort is spent tracking down case errors in the HTML tagging on UNIX systems. Once again, you should pick the platform with which your Information Services department is most comfortable. They will be the final line of support when things go wrong.

Server Guidelines

Web server hardware guidelines are quite simple. Plan on speed, capacity and expansion. Intranet servers complete with software can be purchased for as little as a few thousand dollars for an entry level system to tens of thousands of dollars for a real fire-breathing monster. What you really get for the price difference are speed, capacity, and expandability.

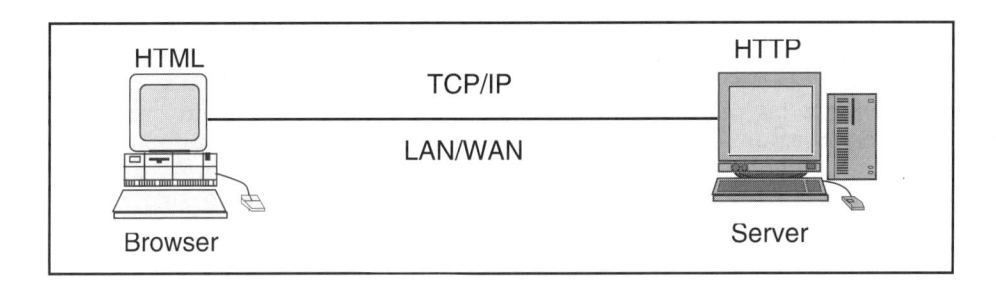

```
HTML                              HTTP
         ───────TCP/IP───────
         ───────LAN/WAN──────
Browser                           Server
```

In the drawing above, notice that the network is signified by a single line. This part is true, the network is a single wire connection that can transfer data at a maximum of 10 megabits a second. The very slowest Web server can easily overwhelm this connection, so there is no network speed advantage gained with faster, more expensive servers.

Imagine you are accessing a database on your intranet for sales analysis. While the database is processing your report request, the server is dividing its processor time between page requests for other users and the database. If your server is too slow, the request could take a long time to finish and the other users will have their requests slowed down as well. It is best to purchase a mid-range performance system at the beginning. The extra capacity you pay for is in the Random Access Memory (RAM) and hard disk storage options. More RAM usually means better overall performance. The larger the hard disk storage, the easier it will be to add large databases, multimedia, video and sound.

Expandability is the last factor. Depending on the platform, you may get all the features you need built-in. If it isn't, make sure you have expansion slots, RAM slots, and SCSI (pronounced skuz'-ey) connections for later hardware add-ons. Your Information Systems department can help you size your intranet server.

LAN/WAN

Originally, personal computers could share information only by physically moving it on a floppy disk from one machine to another. As more computers entered a company, this "sneaker net" became too cumbersome and time consuming. In addition, disk space and printers were expensive resources and it made sense to share them rather than dedicate them to a single computer. So the Local Area Network (LAN) was developed. The most popular one is called ethernet. It connects computers together with a simple wire. It was called a local area network because, due to technical limitations, it could only connect the computers in a single building. Since many companies have multiple buildings and even operate in multiple cities around the world, the Wide Area Network (WAN) was developed. The WAN consists of specialized hardware and software that connect LANs across special telephone lines. In effect, the Internet is nothing more that the largest WAN ever built, connecting thousands of private LANs and WANs into a single globe-spanning network.

```
Your users must be on a LAN or part of a WAN and must be
running a PC, Mac or UNIX computer in order to make use of
an intranet. The PCs must be running a version of Windows.
A central computer such as an IBM mainframe and its termi-
nals can't be part of an intranet. In addition, your network
must be communicating with one of three standard protocols;
TCP/IP, IPX or Appletalk. If your company doesn't have a
LAN/WAN in place, you will have to add it in order to build
an intranet.
```

A browser is a piece of software on the user's computer that communicates with the Web server and displays the files sent to it. Browsers will organize the text and graphics according to the HTML code sent to them. The more recent browsers will allow for expansion by way of plug-ins. The plug-ins allow the user to add additional capabilities such as sound, music, animations, etc.

Like Web server software, there are both commercial browsers and free browsers available. Commercially developed browsers are made by Netscape, Microsoft, and others. Please don't cut corners here by using free browser software. Pick a single vendor for all of your users' computers. You will find the overall support will be better and the deployment of your intranet will be faster with a standard browser.

Browser Standards

Once again, the technology of browsers is changing so quickly that trying to discuss them in anything but general terms is difficult. When choosing a browser, you should consider these standard support requirements:

HTML 2.0

This standard means that simple page formatting commands like centering of text is recognized by the browser and displayed properly. Unfortunately many browsers, Netscape and Microsoft for example, add commands that are not standardized or in the 2.0 standard. You can get around this issue by standardizing on a specific browser to the exclusion of all others on the network.

Java Programming Language

Java allows for the extension of the browser to interact with other portions of the computer and add capabilities that take advantage of the power of the desktop computer. Java is an open standard and is in competition with the system Microsoft is marketing called ActiveX. Java is better since it is implemented on every operating system used in business and ActiveX is not.

Intranet Technology

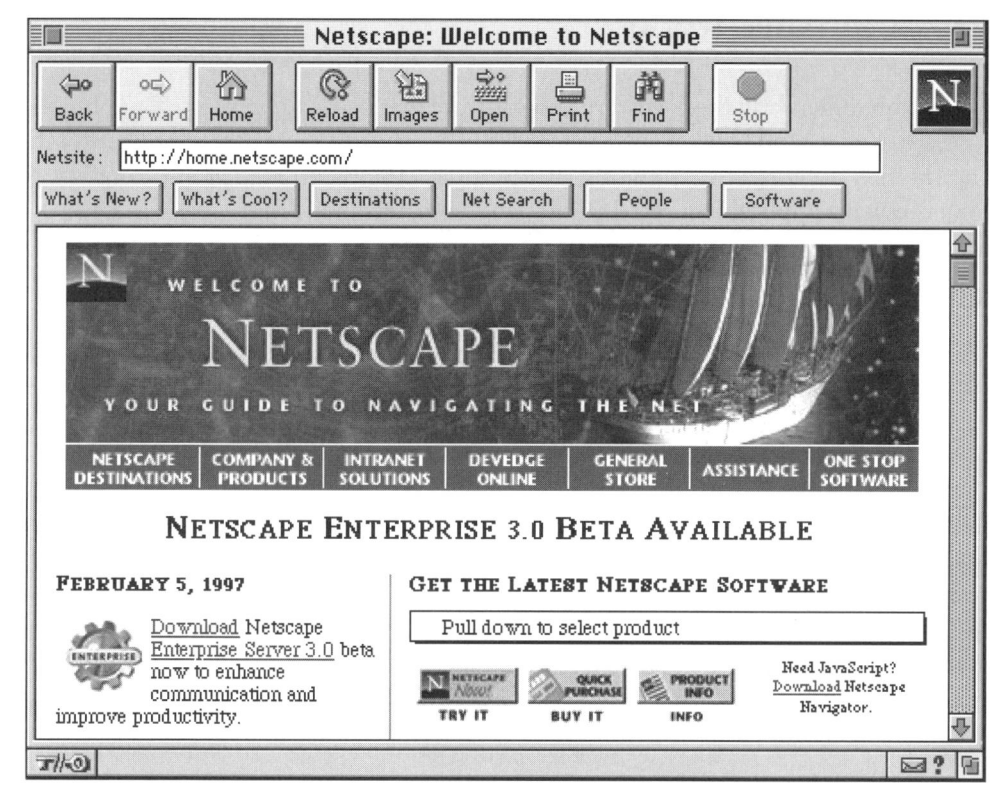

The Netscape browser

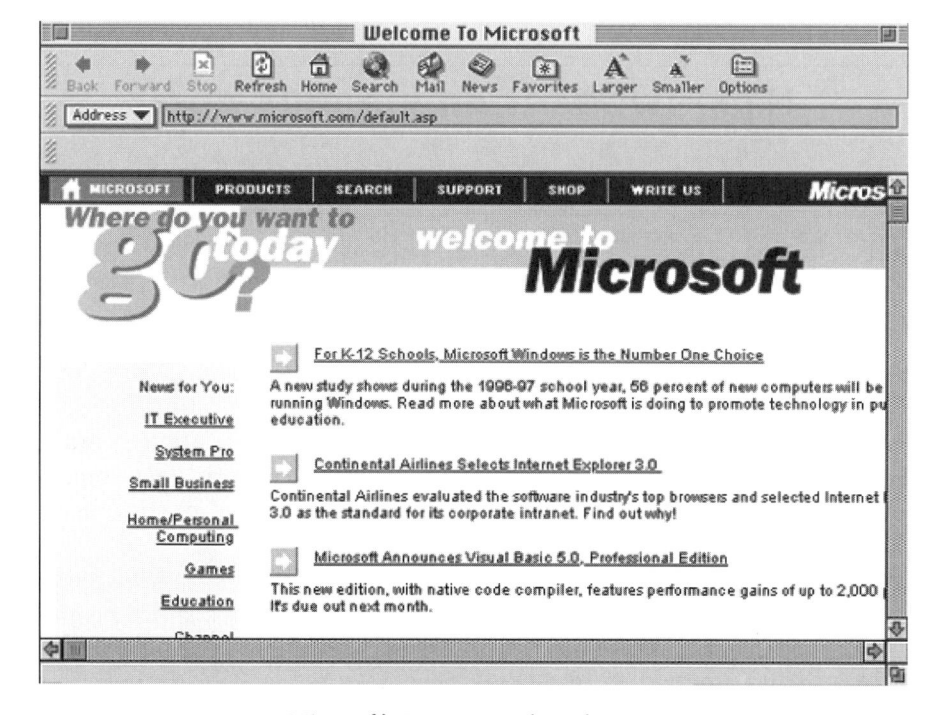

Microsoft's Internet Explorer browser.

How an Intranet Works

Now that you understand the hardware and software that needs to be selected and installed, you need to understand how the intranet works. Since the intranet is based on the structure of the Internet, a basic understanding of the Internet is required. The information that follows is equally applicable to the Internet and your intranet.

Uniform Resource Locator (URL)

The Uniform Resource Locator (URL) is what is entered into the user's computer to access a specific file of information from the intranet. It is made up of several components: the communication protocol, the DNS name of the computer, the domain name, the root domain, and the optional path and file name requested.

Each computer on the network has a unique identity number, very much like a telephone. In order to have one computer "call" another one, it needs the number, or address in technical talk, of the computer it is trying to access. Generally speaking, people have a hard time remembering long strings of numbers. As the Internet grew, some very smart people decided to let the computers do the hard memorizing of the numbers and let the user just remember names. This became the Domain Name System in use today. It is also the standard used in intranets.

Each Web server has a name that is built up from basic elements. The trick is to read the name from right to left.

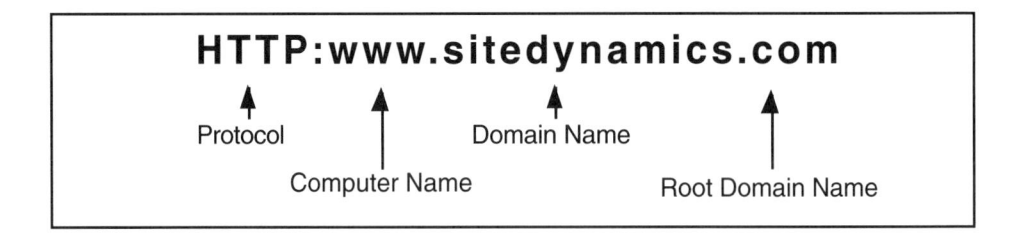

```
HTTP:www.sitedynamics.com
  ↑       ↑           ↑        ↑
Protocol  |      Domain Name   |
      Computer Name      Root Domain Name
```

There are many root domains with names like "com" for commercial, "org" for organization, "gov" for government, "mil" for military, and "edu" for education. In addition, all countries have a root domain name, usually a two character abbreviation of the country. However, it's not required to be used. Accessing a server with a "com" root domain could mean you are accessing a server in the United States, England, France, or any other country in which a Web server has been set up with that root domain.

Next, the domain name is added to the root domain to identify a specific company or organization. A simple example is sitedynamics.com. Notice that the root domain "com" indicates that Site Dynamics is a commercial name.

Intranet Technology 61

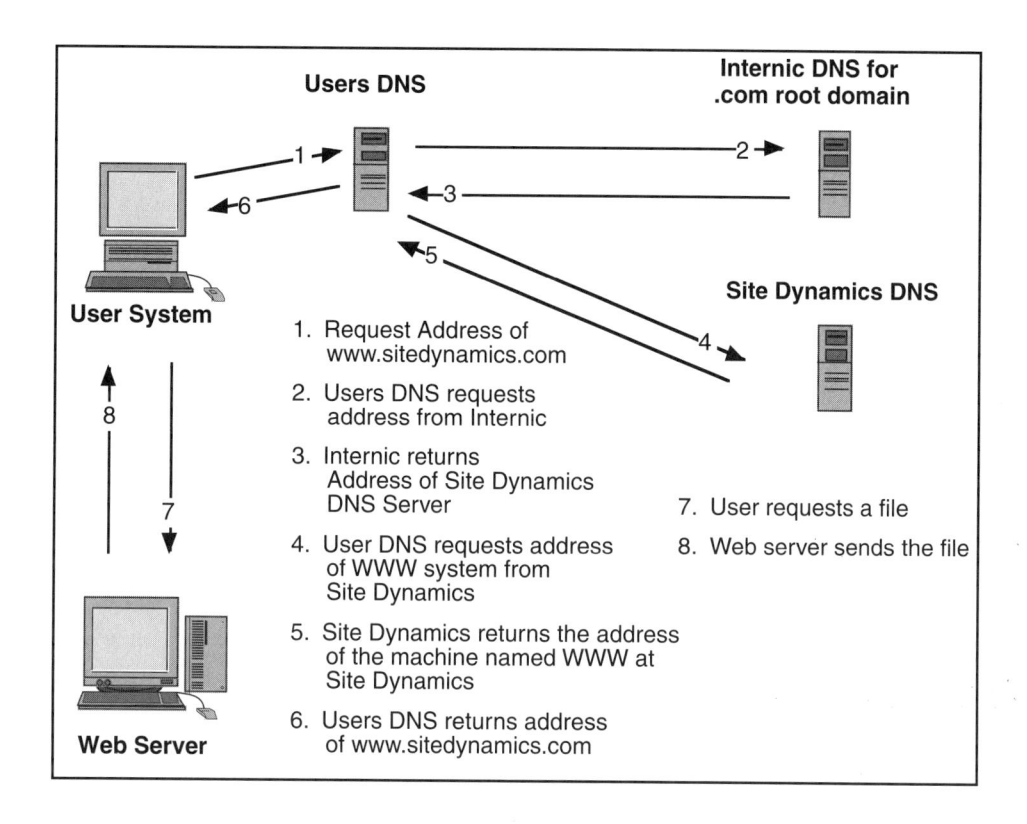

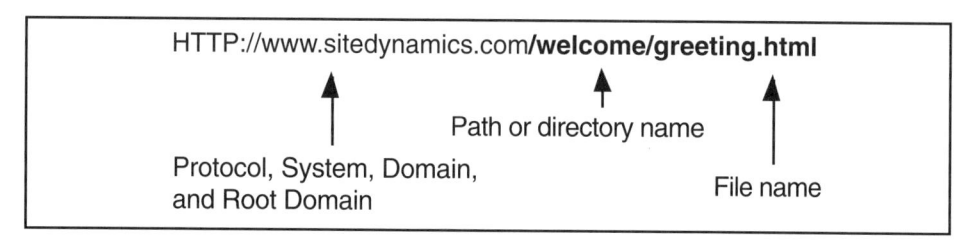

```
                    Users DNS              Internic DNS for
                                           .com root domain
                        ──1──▶     ──────2──▶
                        ◀─6──     ◀────3─────
                                    ◀─5
                                           Site Dynamics DNS
User System                          ──4─▶

            1. Request Address of
               www.sitedynamics.com
            2. Users DNS requests
               address from Internic
            3. Internic returns
               Address of Site Dynamics
               DNS Server                  7. User requests a file
            4. User DNS requests address   8. Web server sends the file
               of WWW system from
               Site Dynamics
            5. Site Dynamics returns the address
               of the machine named WWW at
               Site Dynamics
            6. Users DNS returns address
Web Server     of www.sitedynamics.com
```

```
        HTTP://www.sitedynamics.com/welcome/greeting.html
              ▲                    ▲                ▲
              │           Path or directory name    │
              │                                     │
        Protocol, System, Domain,              File name
        and Root Domain
```

On occasion the full path and name of a file is included in the URL. This is the information following the root domain name.

Each of the Web servers at Site Dynamics has a specific computer name, like www.sitedynamics.com. This name is stored in a database called the Domain Name System, or DNS for short, and contains the number address of the Web server. When a user wants to access the Web Site at Site Dynamics, the user types in **www.sitedynamics.com.** The calling computer asks the com database where the Site Dynamics database is. It then asks the Site Dynamics database for the WWW numerical address and makes the connection. For this reason you must have a DNS system in order to have an intranet.

Some computers are case sensitive. This only applies to the path and file name. The protocol, computer name, domain name and root domain are not case sensitive.

The next two pieces in this puzzle are Hyper Text Transfer Protocol (HTTP) and Hyper Text Mark-up Language (HTML). These items are part of the browser and are not purchased separately.

Hyper Text Transfer Protocol (HTTP)

HTTP is the protocol or method the browser and server use to talk to each other. It defines the way information is sent back and forth. Most importantly, it handles the transfer of text, graphics, sounds, and even video without having to change software or configure for special downloads. When a URL is typed in (for example `HTTP://www.server.com`), the leading HTTP tells the Web server that you will be using the Hyper Text Transfer Protocol.

Hyper Text Markup Language (HTML)

Once the information is sent to the browser from the Web server it must be interpreted to create the image you see on the screen. That is the function of Hyper Text Markup Language (HTML). It is a simple set of tags that are placed around the text to inform the browser how to display it. For instance, <B>Title</B> tells the browser that the text between the HTML tags (<B> and </B>) should be displayed on the screen as bold. The/tag is the end of the command. Sometimes HTML tagging is referred to as programming, but it isn't nearly as complex. Most people can learn HTML tagging in a few hours. However, with over thirty different HTML page layout software tools available on the market today, it is possible to convert a document to HTML without working with the actual tag commands.

```
Your user controls the appearance of the finished product.
Unlike a paper based product, the intranet and the viewing
technology, the browser, are under the control of the user.
After you spend countless hours making everything look just
right on a finished page, if the user decides to use a dif-
ferent font size, your carefully thought out formatting will
look differently than you had originally intended
```

Part of the function of HTML is to tell the browser about the many different elements that make up a page. Each page can hold text, graphics, sound, video, animations, and, most importantly, one or more links to another page. Each item of a page is downloaded separately and is called a "hit". Look at the sample page below.

This page is made up of five separate graphic elements and a small text file. As this page is accessed on the network, the text file is served first. Then all of the graphic elements are downloaded one at a time. When you add them up, this page has six hits on it. As you can see, using the number of hits to understand what is happening on your intranet is not very useful in showing traffic activity.

Intranet Technology 63

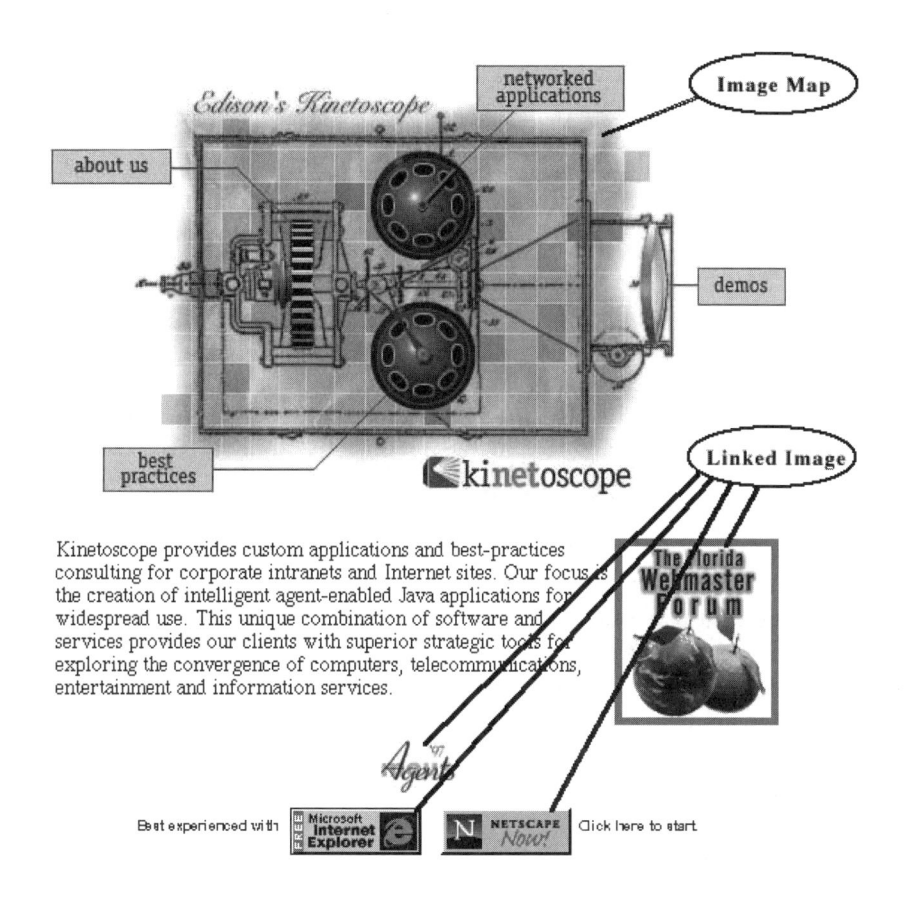

Connectionless Environment

The intranet is a connectionless environment. The only time your users are connected to your Web server are when they download a page or graphic. As soon as all of the elements of the page are downloaded, the connection is completely dropped. Unlike a persistent connection with a mainframe computer, there are no more communication occurring between the intranet Web server and the browser. The Web server does not track the connections made to it. If the intranet server wanted to update information on the page that was just downloaded, there is no way it can send it to the browser. The connection has been dropped and the computer may have even been turned off. All requests for pages, graphics, and any updates must be generated by the browser.

Because of the connectionless environment of the intranet, it becomes difficult if not impossible to track a user's path around your site. Since the user can request the first page from your site, jump to a bookmarked page on another site, then jump to a bookmarked page (page 15) on your site, your log will only show that the user went from page 1 to page 15. You have no way to determine that he had jumped to other pages in between pages 1 and 15.

This makes it very difficult to create multiple pages that carry information along with them. An example is a electronic catalog or information entry form. Going from page to page to select merchandise and add them to an order is simple on a connection based system. With the connectionless based intranet it is difficult, if not almost impossible. The techniques to create a "shopping cart" are complex and very breakable. Unless this capability is essential to your initial intranet, it is best to design around it or put it off until more expertise is developed in your technical staff.

Firewall Issues

One of the major benefits of intranet technology is the ability to share critical company information. One of the major drawbacks of intranet technology is the ability to share critical company information. If your intranet were connected directly to the Internet it is possible for anyone who knew either the name or TCP/IP address of a particular computer to access your intranet from anywhere on the Internet. If this is your company's marketing Web site this is a good thing. However, if this computer contains sensitive financial information, this would be a bad thing. To prevent this from occurring special software and hardware devices known as firewalls can be installed. This name may have come from the automobile world where your car has a firewall that keeps the heat from your engine from reaching inside the car. The same is true of network firewalls.

Putting It All Together

Let's walk through a typical intranet session and look at the magic technology that makes it all so easy. A user starts up their browser and types in or selects a previously saved URL. The user's computer asks its local DNS server if it knows the network number of the URL the user typed in or selected. If it doesn't know the number, the user's DNS server will ask the Internic or master DNS server for the DNS server of the domain requested. The local DNS server then asks the Domain DNS server for the address of the computer name included in the URL. Now the user's browser connects to the Web server and asks it for the first file. The Web server looks at the request which includes not only the file name but how the two systems will talk to each other and then sends the requested file and disconnects. The browser receives the file and starts to display it. Part way through the file is a reference to an image. The browser takes the reference from the first file, reconnects to the Web server and requests the image file. The Web server sends the image file and disconnects. This sequence continues until the entire page is displayed.

As you can see there is quite a bit of technology behind a simple click on the screen. The wonderful part is that it really is as simple as a click for the user.

6

Intranet Strategies

The intranet hype has been unrelenting since the term was first thrust into the public scene in 1996. It has been virtually impossible to pick up a business magazine or visit a publication's Website without seeing some incredible evidence of how glorious intranets really are. And all the while you're thinking, "This sounds too good to be true."

You may very well be right. In the recent past, many new technologies have been overhyped and failed to live up to their advance billings. However, intranets have promised paperless offices and this promise very well be realized. If the growth of the World Wide Web in the past few years is any indication, online publishing (including the Internet, intranets and extranets) has a bright future.

So here you are, hanging your career on a technological innovation you don't fully understand. All those around you are treating the project like some kind of mystical transformer that will cure all the organization's ills. What do you do? How can your project possibly live up to the advanced billing?

Establishing Realistic Goals

The first step as a project manager is to get your arms around the various expectations for your intranet project. This may be difficult to do since nothing like the intranet has ever happend to organizations in the past. It's almost like the advent of the first personal computer all over again. Predictions abounded that the computer would soon become ubiquitous and would certainly dominate every aspect of our lives. Today those predictions have come true with a vengeance. Computers are everywhere. It is difficult to imagine our complex world without them. It is also difficult to grasp the concept that the processing speed of modern computers doubles about every six months. This phenomenon has created a new concept called "webtime" to try to explain the extremely accelerated pace at which online technology is evolving.

So what does all this mean for you, the intranet project manager (or content provider)? It means you need to begin a concerted and comprehensive campaign to control the expectations of your management concerning your project. Sure, there are documented cases of companies realizing returns on their intranet investment of well over 1000 percent. Sure, there are documented cases of companies using intranet technology to save hundreds and thousands of hours by eliminating repetitive functions through smart online publishing. And, sure there are documented cases of intranet webmasters getting huge raises as a direct result of their efforts to produce those stellar intranet sites.

The reality is that your organization will not necessarily parallel those case studies. The intranets we are hearing and reading about today were those undertaken by "pioneers" in the field. Pioneers are defined as individuals or companies that keep up with the latest technological innovations and are among the first to embrace and implement them.

```
Pioneering companies are usually predisposed to change.
They seem to thrive on innovation and "out-of-the-box"
thinking. They use every technological tool to gain compet-
itive advantage in their marketplaces, and they are proud
of that fact. Just as important, they are willing to assume
the risks involved with pioneering efforts. They will endure
the occasional failure to enjoy the glow of high-profile
success. They are able to embrace change and innovation due
to some overall organizational commitment that starts from
the top.
```

Consider Amdahl Corp., a developer of enterprise systems and software, which began adopting Web technologies two years ago and now has 5,000 people on its intranet.

> Early on, a big problem for Amdahl was winning support from senior managers, said Curt Helvey, manager of architecture and infrastructure at Sunnyvale, Calif.-based Amdahl. "Every time I'd walk by the controller of our data center, he'd say, 'Boy, this Web stuff is a waste of time,'" Helvey recalled. Helvey finally sat down with the contrarian and demonstrated how information that could be obtained from the Internet and intranet would make him more effective.
>
> Amdahl also set up a Web council, a group of managers and content providers from across the company that meets every other week to discuss intranet and Internet policies, technologies and implementation issues.
>
> "Intranet influence Internal Webs Drive Changes In Culture"
> By Bill Roberts
> *Web Week*, Volume 2, Issue 18, November 18, 1996.

Politics

Of course the downside to wide organizational involvement usually involves the concensus-building process. Often it is easier to allow the "experts" to dictate the parameters of your intranet project. While speeding decision-making, this can really slow down acceptance of your new product.

```
One great way to manage expectations about your intranet
project is to involve as many levels of the organization as
possible in its rollout. The more involved they become, the
more they understand the complexity of the task. The more
ownership they take over the end product, the more likely
they are to defend that product to any potential detractors.
```

What Will Your Intranet Add to What Exists Now?

Chapter 3 dealt with the compelling reasons to create an intranet in the first place. This question involves an in-depth look at how you are communicating as an organization now and what might be different in the online world of tomorrow. This is not an insignificant question. In fact, it may be the most important question you will answer as you put your intranet together. Consider two possible scenarios.

One involves a company that is doing a really good job of communicating. Management is eager to share important company information right down to the lowest levels of the company. Coworkers are open and honest with each other about all aspects of their worklives. Employees feel encouraged and rewarded for bringing bad news to light. In general, the organization does a good job of keeping people informed about all aspects of the company.

Enter the intranet. A healthy company will embrace such an innovation because it will make it easier for them to share what's important to everyone. It will reduce lag time between events and their dissemination. It will give users an instant feedback channel through which management can monitor their effectiveness. A healthy organization will view its intranet as a technological innovation that improves their effectiveness and gives them a distinct competitive advantage over competitors without intranets.

The second scenario involves a company that is not so open with its communication. Maybe its management shares information, but that information is carefully filtered and sanitized before it is released. This organization has lots of information flowing, but most of it is downhill. Employees feel cut out of the information loop. They read more about their company in the local newspaper than they hear at work. Good news flows easily and well. Bad news is choked off by information gatekeepers at various levels of the company. Rumors abound.

Enter the intranet. An autocratic, hierarchal company will not openly embrace this new methodology used for widely disseminating unfiltered information. It will reduce lag time between events and their dissemination — and that means less time to put a "spin" on bad news. It will give users an instant feedback channel — and that is likely to focus more attention on the inadequacy of current management information strategies. An intranet will have far-reaching effects on an information-challenged organization — and most of those effects will be negative. Perceived problems will now become obvious problems.

Which scenario most closely matches your company?

```
Most companies will probably fall somewhere between the two
extremes on this continuum. Most companies spend considerable
time and resources trying to communicate effectively among
their various audiences. But most companies also realize that
there is still room to improve communication processes.
```

Your intranet project is likely to focus attention on organizational communication issues. How well you handle those issues, and how well the company responds to this opportunity to improve will do much to set the course for your overall project.

One thing is clear. Placing ineffective or marginally effective communication online will only serve to focus more attention on their inadequacies.

Your intranet certainly will bring new dimensions to your existing communication. It may even allow you to bring the state of organizational communication within your company to a new level. With appropriate management support you can use the intranet project as a starting point for a dialog about how your organization communicates — or more importantly, how it will communicate in the future using this new technology.

Begin with a thorough analysis of existing communication strategies and procedures. Does your organization have any? You may start by looking for documents called, "Corporate Identity Guidelines" or "Corporate Communications Guidelines." This can be a daunting task because most effective organizations decentralize their communication function. Progressive organizations make effective communication a prime responsibility of supervision. So as you inventory existing organizational communication, you may have to look beyond the traditional communication function to get an accurate picture.

Following is a battery of questions you might ask as you perform your communication inventory:

> What information is communicated?
> How is the information communicated?
> Who gets the information?
> What do they do with it?
> Do they provide feedback to the originator? How?
> What happens if they don't get the information?

Using the answers to these questions you will be better able to determine what information should become part of the intranet.

How Will the Site Grow?

Your intranet project is never complete. In fact, traditional talk about publication dates loses its meaning online. Your intranet is an ever-evolving, ever-growing, ever-changing communication medium. One of the key features of the World Wide Web is its willingness to ask for and respond to user ideas about how sites can be improved. This carries over to your intranet.

Interactivity — the ability to carry on two way conversations online — will help keep you in constant touch with your users throughout the organization. This direct connection with your audience is a powerful feature of your intranet. Make sure you encourage user feedback right from the day you launch your intranet. Let your users help shape and sustain this company resource.

Typical Site Rollout Plan

Step One — Blue Sky It!

As you plan your intranet project you should build in a significant amount of maintenance time for your intranet development and production team. Your planning process should begin with a grand vision of what your intranet ultimately can be. Make sure you build in input from lots of different groups and individuals. Don't be concerned that what you are modeling can never be built due to time or resource constraints. Assume that everything worthwhile can be accomplished — and add it to the list. This grand vision will become the blueprint for how you develop and roll out your intranet site. You may want to consider some of the following in your Blue Sky plan:

- Multimedia presentations (marketing and sales presentations, plant tours, product demos)
- Video (product videos, plant tours, executive briefings)
- Audio (executive speeches)
- Active Notification Agents (breaking news)
- Personalized Home Pages (display-only, user-requested items)
- Video teleconferencing

Step Two — Deadline It

Now come back down to reality. Take your grand vision and apply the necessary constraints of time and budget. Draw a line in the sand and commit to a Phase One launch for your site. Make sure your deadline is reasonable. Most intranet rollouts average about 180 days (6 months). Some have been pulled together in half that time. Others take well over a year.

It is important to pick a date somewhere within that six months window for a couple of reasons. First, it adds a certain element of immediacy to the project. It concentrates the creative process within a short period of time and tends to energize the participants. Next, it focuses corporate attention on this vital, new project. Last, it says, "We're really going to do this...soon." Sixty to ninety days is long enough to let anticipation grow and short enough to sustain interest.

Step Three — Phase It

You will probably find that you are not able to roll out your blue sky vision of your intranet within the deadline you have established. The most important thing is to be able to roll out a representative intranet with enough content to grab and hold the attention and interest of the users. To make sure that happens, your planning group should decide which of the content items identified in the Blue Sky plan are the most important to the widest possible variety of users. With projects of this magnitude, it is a good idea to think of them in three phases. Phase One is the rollout phase and will usually require the greatest amount of time and resources to accomplish. Phase One takes such a great amount of effort because it is new, and anything new requires new ways of thinking about and doing things. Phase One should contain as many of the top priority items as possible within the production time contraints.

Phase Two is usually rolled out completely within six months of Phase One. Phase Two incorporates many of the items left out of Phase One because of resource constraints. But, more importantly, it incorporates feedback from the initial user group during Phase One. Remember, interactivity — real time feedback — is critical to the success of any intranet. Your ability to collect, analyze and incorporate user feedback into Phase Two signals your users that you are serious about involving them in the developmental process and that their input is valuable. In reality, Phase Two begins the day after the Phase One rollout. You may want to incorporate a feedback form as part of the initial intranet site for the express purpose of encouraging such interaction. Even if you don't use someone's feedback or suggestions to improve the site, make sure you close the feedback loop with them through e-mail or some other direct means.

Phase Three should define your long-range improvements, such as incorporating new technologies (Java or Shockwave) or page formats (frames). See Chapter 5 for an overview of technologies. Phase Three improvements can be made anytime the technology is deemed ready. Since these changes will almost always involve system issues, your technical staff must take a leadership role in their development and implementation.

Step Four — Check It

Make sure you build in methods to check its effectiveness. Use your intranet and other communication media to determine how well your new intranet is performing measured against your expectations. Never be afraid to abandon an idea or content area that simply does not take off. If you maintain a level of flexibility and a minimal pride of authorship about your site, you will be able to read and react to constructive feedback from all sources.

The more you involve your users in the future of your intranet, the more your users will ensure a successful future for your intranet.

```
You should always remember that your intranet is never fin-
ished. The only intranet projects that are doomed to fail
from the start are those that did not include comprehensive
plans to maintain and evolve the site.
```

Site maintenance and evolution is not a one-person show. Just as it takes a concerted effort by various parts of the organization to complete the initial intranet rollout, it takes the same kind of effort to keep the project living and growing.

The problem is with most organizations, after the initial push to launch the site, there is little enthusiasm for the long haul. After the euphoria of launching this sparkling, new technology marvel, there is little appetite for the mundane chore of maintenance. Recognizing this up front may help you and your planning group to work around it when it actually happens.

Just as with the World Wide Web, you must give your intranet users a reason to come back often. If your site does not grow and evolve, your users will soon feel that they have seen everything there is to see and become disinterested. There are many ways to keep your site fresh and interesting; see Chapter 11, "Maintaining Your Intranet."

Determining Audiences

One of the distinct advantages intranets have over the Internet is the ability to know and understand the audience. Current estimates put the online population of the Internet at more than 50 million users in more than 150 countries. That's quite a diverse group! And since audience research and analysis techniques on the Web have just begun to emerge, demographics about particular audiences attracted to particular sites are sketchy at best. Simply, not much is known about the people who visit a Web site except what they are willing to leave behind voluntarily.

Your intranet is different. One look at the coporate phone book tells you who your potential audience is, in its entirety, and by name.

Who Are Primary Users and What Do They Want?

Your primary audience for your intranet is the same as for all your general company communication — your fellow employees. And what do they want? In a word, everything.

As your intranet project unfolds you may find that there are actually three different subgroups within your primary employee audience, divided by the kind of information and services they want and need.

The first group is looking for general organizational information — things like annual goals, organizational charts, company news, press releases and the like. This information is usually open to anyone within the organization and typically has a long shelf life.

General Information seekers want a vast wealth of information across very broad topic areas. They look to your intranet as a "one-stop" source for information they might need to finish a report, respond to a request, prepare a proposal, or any number of other activities. For this group, your intranet must be extremely well organized making information easy to locate and use. Typical general content includes:

- Benefits information
- Claims forms
- General policies and procedures
- Organizational goals
- General employee news
- Mass transit schedules
- Community events calendar
- Company sports news/results
- Carpooling information
- Company financial information
- Company organizational charts

The second group is looking for more focused information — things like departmental memos, project status reports and financial summaries. This information is normally placed behind some security system (usually password protected) within the intranet and is not available to the general population.

Focused Information seekers want lots of information about particular topics of intense interest to them. They look to your intranet as a real-time resource for information they need in their daily activities. In many cases, this information is extremely valuable, but only to a limited number of users. Many intranets place this focused information in a secure area (requiring a password and user ID to gain access) to make sure any sensitive information is protected from unauthorized usage. Quite often this information is departmental by nature and is intended for use only by members of that particular department. Typical focused information includes:

- Project budgets
- Project schedules
- Product build plans
- Online time sheets
- Concurrent engineering
- Quality documents
- Inspection records

The last group is looking for intensely personal information on the intranet. This could range from the status of their retirement savings account to the number of sick days remaining in the year. Again, this information is available only to the specific employee making the request and is usually password protected.

Personal Information seekers look to your intranet as a ready resource for sensitive, individual information. Much of this information is likely to come from personnel files or other areas within the Human Resources Department. Your intranet offers an attractive option to visiting or calling the appropriate human resource. Many times, people are hesitant to talk to anyone else about sensitive personal issues. The intranet adds an element of anonymity to the normal transaction. It also adds considerable flexibility because the information is available at the desktop 24 hours a day, seven days a week. The HR office doesn't even have to be open to get it. Typical personal information includes:

- Vacation information
- Personal time information
- Savings plan balance and availability
- Retirement information

Secondary Users

Just as with other corporate communication, such as newsletters, information on your intranet is likely to be seen by people beyond your corporate walls. One of the advantages of digital information is the ease with which it can be transferred and copied. That also happens to be one of the disadvantages as well. Publishing-sensitive information in a digital form on your intranet makes it very easy for users to capture content on their desktops. Once they have captured it, they can print it, attach it to e-mail or use it in other documents. In other words, no matter how well you secure the information by hiding it behind passwords, you can never be really sure who is going to see it eventually.

Disgruntled employees have been known to capture available sensitive corporate information and circulate it widely beyond corporate walls — to competitors, the press or others. For this reason you must treat everything on your intranet as if it will be seen by everyone.

There simply are no fail-safe methods for protecting your information. About the best you can do is post warnings and disclaimers throughout the site instructing users on the appropriate handling and care of sensitive information. You must make employees aware of the risks involved with sharing sensitive information. You may even ask your users to read and agree to terms of intranet usage before they are permitted to access your intranet system.

To build a truly effective and valuable intranet project, you should consider including robust content for each of the three audiences.

What Do They Want?

If the World Wide Web is any indication of what users want, it's "everything, right now." The online world has provided a sneak preview of how things will be in the near future with virtually unlimited amounts of information available to people all over the world at the click of a mouse. If this model translates to the world of corporate intranets, users might expect to be able to find a comprehensive depository of corporate information available on their desktops.

They Want Everything That Is of Value to Them

Every communication situation is plagued by conflicting desires. Those who own the information usually want to disseminate it in the way that is most advantageous to them. They want other people to know and understand all the good things about them, their department, function or product/service. They may even be selective about what information is chosen depending on its relative value to them as the information provider.

On the other side of the equation, the information consumer wants access to information that is most advantageous to their needs. They want to be able to review everything of potential value and make their own decisions about what to use. They want a minimum of pre-filtering and pre-selection.

As you frame your intranet project, you must convince your information providers to give users what users want. The real question is this: How do you know exactly what your users want? The answer is so simple it may astonish you: Ask them. Many successful intranet projects have started with one or more sessions with potential users talking about expectations. These discussions can be very formal — with a set agenda and structured questions — or very informal with lots of opportunities for free-form discussion and ideas. Regardless of how they are structured, one thing is clear — they are valuable in determining what your users want and expect from the new project. Meeting with your users will also do a lot to keep you oriented on what they want instead of what you want them to have.

They Want It Reworked for Online Delivery

What is good online content? What makes it good? The answers to these questions are simple, and yet complex. Good content is good content without respect to the medium of delivery. Good content is giving people what they are interested in and what they need. If something makes a good brochure, or a good article in the employee newsletter, it will also make good online content.

Having said that, good content must be reworked to make it good online content. For your intranet truly to be effective its content should be presented in a way that takes advantage of online technology. If, for example, your newsletter article contains excerpts from the CEO's year end address (due to space limitations), you may want to include the complete text as a link from the article (there are no space limitations online). You may also want to give your users a forum in which to voice their reactions to and opinions about the speech. Finally, if your system supports multimedia, you may want to include a QuickTime movie of a short segment of the speech, or maybe streaming audio that would allow users to actually hear the speech on their PCs.

> Online users also like to be presented with short summaries
> of key content so they can decide what is important in a
> relatively short time. Especially in the case of long text
> documents, giving the user a brief synopsis allows them to
> decide whether or not they want to invest the time in read-
> ing the entire document.

They Want It Easy To Find

Have you ever gone looking for something in someone else's kitchen? While things are generally placed in similar locations in most houses, their exact location can be a matter of personal preference or some entrenched tradition. Items can be stored according to function or application. For example, cutlery can be stored in with the rest of the flatware or it can reside on the countertop where it is close to the cutting block where it is used. It can also be hung on the wall with the food preparation items. Electric cutlery may be stored with its manual cousins or with all the other electrical appliances.

The point is, different people have different methodologies to organize their world — including their cutlery collection. And just as predictably, people arrange their stuff in their lives to suit their own personal requirements and predispositions. This seems logical because they are the user of their stuff in the vast majority of cases. Visitors and infrequent users are probably going to have to ask for location information.

Your intranet is not being designed for a single user with a known set of location expectations. Your intranet is being designed for multiple users and multiple types of users who may each have their own ideas about how things should be organized and where things should be found.

> The rule of thumb in designing a useful and intuitive site
> is to find out as much about how your users tend to catego-
> rize your content. Put yourself in your users' chairs as you
> ask yourself, "Where would I expect to find THIS on this
> intranet site?" And don't forget to ask them!

Where would someone logically look for information on their retirement savings plan? How about build plans for the new widget in production? Where is information about how to handle cleaning solvents on the factory floor? Where would I find an employee phone number?

Many intranets (and WWW sites as well) have fallen into the "cute" trap. They become very creative in how they structure and name the various elements of their site. The more esoteric and "cute" they become, the more difficult (and frustrating) it is for users to find what they are looking for. Remember, your intranet site must be functional first. You may have technology negatives to overcome — like slow downloads over crowded networks.

Don't make a bad situation worse by making it difficult for your users to find their targets of interest. (More about good site navigation later in Chapter 8).

They Want Some Control Over It

The world is filled with one-way communication media. People are bombarded throughout their personal and professional lives by communication that neither ask for nor respond to feedback. When was the last time you talked back to the local anchor after a particularly biased story was presented on the local six o'clock news? When was the last time you wrote a letter to the editor of your daily newspaper? Was it published? Did it change anything?

Television, movies, radio, newspapers, newsletters, snail mail, pagers, voicemail — these media command much of our attention. None of these allow us to participate. The most control we ever have is the on/off switch, the volume control (mute button) and the channel/station changer.

Your intranet is different, both by design and definition. As its principal architect, you must find frequent and easy ways for your users to participate in the process. This interaction can be as easy as an e-mail form at the bottom of each content page on the site, or as elaborate as a threaded discussion group or live CHAT (real-time keyboard interation among multiple users).

Surveying Communications Resources

On the surface, it appears that you are simply creating a new communication medium for information dissemination. Below the surface, you are actually changing the way the company communicates, and eventually, conducts its business. You are asking these knowledge brokers to share what they know with the entire organization (or a major portion of it). In some very real ways, your intranet represents a clear and present danger to the communication status quo in your organization. You are asking to make substantive changes within the very core of power within your company. These changes will not come easily.

```
Make no mistake about this fact: Knowledge is Power. Those
who control knowledge in the company in some very real ways
control the company. Even those knowledge workers who have
little actual power usually are able to influence decisions
by the appropriate application of their information.
```

One major corporation decided to use their intranet as a way to pry open the communication floodgates. The company had been going through substantial industry and organizational changes over the past several years. Part of that process was a fairly radical downsizing of the workforce (more than 30 percent reduction). During this time the company was not very forthcoming with information about the layoffs. In fact, lots of the communication during that period was focused on the "good news" with precious little being said about the way things really were. A common refrain around the water coolers was, "We find out more about our company in the newspaper than we do from the company." The official company line was that things were going well, that the company was turning the corner and that bright times were ahead. What employees saw was dwindling morale caused by heavy layoffs and precious little information about when the bloodletting would stop. Employee scouts would take mid-morning runs through the company's corridors looking for dark offices with names removed from the doors. Betting pools began to circulate about who might be next on the block. Gallows humor was rampant. Employees spent more time speculating about the company's future than they did performing their own jobs. Everyone had become a communicator, but the entire process was spoiled.

Enter the intranet. The communication manager used the advent of this new tool and the excitement it had caused around management circles to create a new system of real-time, unfiltered information. She was able to convince senior management to let her communication representatives throughout the company act as information providers for the intranet project. These representatives were tasked with content responsibilites for the new intranet project. This group was highly motivated about the new project and their role in it. They understood the new medium and its potential. They also understood the politics of their own departments and how far they could push.

The result was powerful — and predictable. Some departments did a much better job than others at assembling their content. Interdepartmental competition soon took over. Good ideas from one department generated better ideas from another. This new intranet had become an important element in the company's new communication process. It is credited with helping turn around employee attitudes toward the company. Employees participate in online discussion groups and forums aimed at creating concensus on important issues.

Make no mistake about it. You are introducing a COMMUNICATION system within your company or organization that will fundamentally alter the way you communicate in the near term and the way you conduct business in the longer term. What you are beginning now will have ripples and repurcussions throughout the organization for the foreseeable future. Your intranet project is not a product but rather a process. And that process begins with a thorough understanding of what is at stake, and who stands to gain or lose as a result.

What Is At Stake?

Depending on who you ask, the answer to this question may range from "not very much" to "everything." The most obvious things at stake are power and influence.

The best example of an indispensable employee we ever saw was at a New England mail order art supplies company. This company had built its loyal customer base by providing quick and courteous customer service through a battery of phone operators. For the most part, the phone operators were fairly knowledgeable about the products they sold and the various applications for those products. The company had done a fairly good job of cataloging its inventory (manually) and providing this information to its phone operators. But there absolute secret weapon was Charley. Charley knew everything about the intricacies and interdependencies of the art supply business. He knew which plotter pens were compatible with which plotters. He knew workarounds for obsolete equipment in need of new parts. In short, Charley knew everything. In a two hour period one day, Charley was called upon at least a dozen times by various operators who needed specific information. Invariably, Charley provided it immediately and correctly. It was something to behold. Charley was the ultimate knowledge worker, and Charley's place in the company was ensured until Charley decided to leave.

We asked the business owner what happens when Charley is out sick or on vacation. "We get back to people," was the quick response. Charley was their information system. He was the value added dimension that made customers want to buy their art supplies from this small New England company. Now imagine how much more valuable Charley's knowledge would be if they ever found a way to get inside his head and transfer that information so everyone had access to it. How much more successful could the company become with that kind of shared knowledge? And how willing do you think Charley would be to share his knowledge?

There are Charleys throughout the corporate landscape, ready to tell you why it's a good idea to maintain the status quo when it comes to what they know. After all, Charley knows who needs what information and who doesn't. Why mess with a system that already works so well!

In a recent *WebWeek* article, the author, Bill Roberts, talks about the "Four Unnatural Acts" associated with building a successful intranet project.

"Four Unnatural Acts"

Aron Dutta spent several years wrestling with culture change at Booz Allen & Hamilton, where he led an effort to create the global consulting firm's knowledge program, an expert skills repository and client-information system on an intranet. "The technology is only 10 percent of the program," said Dutta, who is now vice-president of Silicon Valley Internet Partners, a consulting firm based in New York City and Foster City, California.

While moving toward the collaborative environment, Dutta said Booz Allen staffers discovered "four unnatural acts" that must be overcome.

1. Sharing Information

Most companies are structured on the command-and-control model dating to the early part of the century. In these organizations, knowledge is a competitive advantage to be used to get ahead. But even the success of simple document sharing on the intranet depends on "making your best thinking — which is an important part of your personal competitive advantage — available to others."

In your organization are your knowledge workers and management willing to make their best thinking available to others? Are they willing to give up the absolute or perceived power inherent in knowing something no one else knows? In our American culture people have learned that they get ahead by knowing more than the other person.

2. Using Information Someone Else Invented

It goes against corporate nature for Worker No. 2 to take the knowledge offered by Worker No. 1 and use it. Worker No. 2 figures she's smarter than her colleague, so why use the information provided? The Booz Allen folks labeled this the "Not Invented Here" syndrome.

You get what you pay for. If something is free, it must not be worth much. Besides, why would Worker #1 be so willing to share her idea? Is she setting someone up for something? Obviously, no one in the world knows or understands our situation like we do. One of the basic tenets of a quality organization is that decisions are pushed down to the lowest levels possible — where the people are closest to the work. We Americans have always prided ourselves on our own self-sufficiency. We may very well ask for advice or counsel from others, but only rarely do we accept it. It is rarer still that we incorporate someone else's advice into our plans. Getting your organization to share its information in the first place is a daunting task. Getting your organization to believe in the value of such sharing of information is something else altogether.

3. Harnessing Teams

Companies that can get beyond the first two often stumble on this one. Groups need to collaborate "in a way where these people are building on the ideas of other experts and aren't killing each other," said Dutta.

The successful adopters of collaborative technologies, Dutta believes, will learn to harness teams of people in ways that let them contribute to each other's growth and advancement.

Individual achievement is revered in this culture of athletic and business superheroes. In those rare instances where team achievement is applauded, many times the individual members of the team go on to starring individual roles. The best example of that is the 1994 World Cup Soccer team from the United States. Their success in reaching the final rounds of the tournament was attributed to the fact that a bunch of relative unknowns laboring in a secondary sport were able to form a highly successful team effort. That team success led to individual careers for a half dozen or so members of that team as they were able to parlay their team success into multimillion dollar contracts playing for some of the best-known soccer clubs in the world. Sharing what you know with others is not highly rewarded in American industry, unless you are a highly paid consultant.

4. Keeping It Alive

With increasingly mobile work forces, "if we get this far, no one stays around long enough to manage the process," Dutta said. "You can very quickly shove a lot of information someplace, but everyone forgets how to track it. You have to keep this alive. You have to figure out ways to improve and synthesize new ideas while purging yesterday's ideas."

To overcome these obstacles, Dutta and colleagues had to rethink what motivated their staff and how they valued people. "How you design a program around these unnatural acts," said Dutta, "is going to be different in a bank than it is in a consulting firm. You have to figure what is important to the company."

One of the most popular misconceptions about intranets is that launching the initial site is the biggest project challenge. It isn't. Sure, there are challenges associated with any new venture, but those are measurable and manageable. Keeping the site alive and interesting is a continuing and daunting challenge. It is doubly difficult because maintaining a site is a daily grind that requires lots of attention to detail, lots of care and handling and most of all, lots of tenacity.

Your intranet is no different from any other communication medium in that your users want something new and fresh on a regular basis. Imagine how motivated you would be to watch television is you had already seen everything they offered several times. Imagine continuing reruns of one Gilligan's Island episode and nothing else. It wouldn't be long before you declared the activity a waste of your time and moved onto better things.

The same is true of your intranet. The user must get a sense of something new and alive each and every time they log on. It can be as simple and automated as a software application that rotates graphics or special announcement banners (instead of advertising banners) on your home page throughout the day. It can also be a manual process of creating new content, graphics or "New" tags for your home page on a regular schedule. Keeping the site alive should be a primary consideration as you move through your intranet planning process.

If you and your organization can turn these "Unnatural Acts" into accepted standards of communication behavior, your intranet project will be wildly successful. If, however, you and your organization cannot move past the communication status quo, your project is doomed at worst and severely limited at best.

Who Stands To Lose?

In traditional hierarchal, autocratic organizations, knowledge is concentrated at the top of the organizational structure. Information is treated as a valuable management asset to be guarded and protected at all costs. Employees are provided with only that information absolutely required for the performance of their jobs.

As you plan your intranet project you must be able to identify those individuals and groups within your organization who are likely to be most negatively affected by the new communication medium. In most cases these "losers" will closely resemble the Charleys of the world. Some Charleys may not mind losing their positions as key information provider, but many more will hang onto it with white knuckles as you try to pry it out of their grasp.

Reworking Strategic Communications Policies and Practices

The key, then, to developing a new and valuable communication resource — your intranet — is to rework your organization's strategic communication focus to embrace new media. This is no small task.

Reworking any strategic direction is full of challenges. Communications is especially challenging since it is fully intertwined into every element and aspect of the organization. It is the lifeblood of every successful organization. It is the top problem area in unsuccessful organizations.

The first step toward incorporating your new intranet into the organization's strategic communication policies and practices is to review what exists now. Some organizations have extensive and well-documented communication policies, practices and procedures already in place. These will normally address a wide variety of audience, media and message issues. If that is the case in your organization, your job should be fairly easy. In such cases there is usually an established process in place for expanding and refining the policy. You need to find out how that process works and begin your efforts.

In organizations where communication policies may not be so well documented, you may have more of a challenge. If you feel energized, you may want to use the intranet project as a rallying point to constuct a strategic communication policy for the organization. If you are not that energetic, you may simply draft your own ideas about how the intranet fits into the family of communication media.

Your intranet policy should address the following topics — audience, content, and conduct.

The audience section should describe every audience you seek to serve with the intranet. The content section should describe:

- Appropriate online content (subject matter, target audience, intended outcomes)
- Content approval process
- Ownership and copyright
- Content challenge and appeal process

The conduct section should describe appropriate online behavior by users and content providers. Remember, this is an interactive medium and people will use it to exchange ideas. Any time you invite a free exchange of ideas, you run the risk of alienating some people. A good policy on appropriate online behavior will go a long way toward helping you manage online content issues.

You may also want to consider a "code of online conduct" in a prominent place on your site. You may even choose to have your users agree to its terms before they are allowed into online discussion areas. Following is an example of such an agreement.

Posting Rules

The following is an example of how one organization spelled out its posting rules online.

> The XYZ company intranet site is a cyber-location open to XYZers of all ages, backgrounds, and beliefs. We intend to provide an entertaining, educational and non-threatening place for all visitors. The use of vulgar, obscene, pejorative, or hateful language is contrary to our vision and is not allowed. We reserve the right to remove any material that violates these rules. Please conduct yourself accordingly. Because of the very nature of the intranet, it is impossible to monitor all postings. But, if you see something that offends you, let us know.
>
> XYZ provides this platform for its visitors' use. We do not in any way guarantee the accuracy, truthfulness, or quality of the postings made by visitors to this site. Any concern over the truthfulness or quality of these postings should be addressed to the author of the material in question.

It is important to the future of your intranet project that everyone in the organization understands its relationship to other communication media. Without this clear vision and definition, your project may not receive the proper support from various elements of the organization. A successful intranet development project starts with a clear understanding about how all the communication media work together to promote the free exchange of information within the organiztion.

Project Parameters

Finally, you must define the scope of your intranet project.

How much information will be posted? Who will be involved as content providers? How does the approval process work?

Answering these questions will help you define the size and scope of your project right from the beginnning. It will also help you determine technical issues, like how much electronic storage is required, what type and how many servers are needed, how much traffic will be placed on your existing network.

Intranet projects mirror what is happening on the World Wide Web. There are intranets with just a few pages containing basic organizational information with no interactivity. There are others with thousands of pages and interactive areas where people are concurrently working on documents, holding video teleconferences, participating in forums and discussions, and interacting with customers and suppliers. Elizabeth Gardner's article, "Survey Reveals Scope of Intranet Use," published in a recent edition of *Web Week*, offers some insight into the dynamics of intranet usage:

> Bill Labate, a computer resource center manager at TRW Inc., said his departmental intranet gets 3,500 users a month, which includes virtually all 3,200 people in his division, plus several hundred from other divisions.

"I'm pretty amazed," he said. "People here are a diverse group, but about 75 percent tend to be low-end computer users. Computers are like outer space to them, and the Web is even more so." TRW began intranet development in the first half of 1994, and Labate's section of it provides computer technical support, as well as links to external news sources most relevant to the company's business.

But heavy intranet use doesn't necessarily translate to a large corporate investment. A third of the respondents said there's only one full-time employee assigned to the intranet, and another third said between two and five full-time equivalents worked on it. A third of the respondents have spent less than $50,000 on intranet-related equipment in the past year, and more than half have spent $100,000 or less. Only about 5 percent of those interviewed said they had spent more than $1 million.

About 70 percent of respondents reported using fewer than 10 intranet servers. A third of the respondents expect no change in the number of servers by the end of this year, and another 35 percent anticipate less than a 25 percent increase in the number of servers. Only 11 percent expect the number of servers to double or more.

"Survey Reveals Scope of Intranet Use"
By Elizabeth Gardner
Web Week, January 6, 1997

The scope of your intranet probably will be determined by your budget, staff resources and organizational culture.

But whatever the scope of your project, you should make sure that you do not overextend yourself or overpromise and underdeliver. Managing expectations is critical to your success. Make sure that everyone with a vested interest in the intranet project buys into a realistic view of what can be done for the resources committed to the project.

```
Bottom line — create the best possible site for the avail-
able resources. Begin your development strategy with a clear
idea of what is possible within the parameters you have been
given. After you have communicated that vision to the rest
of the organization, you should commit to designing and pro-
ducing the highest quality site possible. Time spent lament-
ing limited budgets or small staffs is time wasted. It is
better to build one small intranet than to curse the budget.
```

Take whatever your management is willing to commit and build on it. Demonstrate the utility and value of the intranet. Get people excited about using it and motivated about posting information. Success with a limited-scale intranet can lead to more support, more investment and better things tomorrow.

7

Planning Your Intranet

When surveying such a monumental task as an organizational intranet, there is a tendency to believe that the technical aspects — hardware, software, systems, servers, clients, etc. — will be the most difficult. In reality, there are only a few technical options for your intranet. Your technical staff will be able to make suitable choices within almost any budget and schedule.

This chapter deals with the complex and very human tasks of creating concensus within your organization for this new project. It presents the framework around which you can construct your own organizational systems to ensure a successful intranet project.

Inside or Outside — The Eternal Question

Do you make it or buy it? This has been a key question ever since corporations began looking at their charters and making hard decisions about which activities were central to the core mission of the company and which were not. Your intranet project is no different. One of the most critical decisions you will make as you plan your intranet is whether you will build it with an internal staff or hire an outside company to do all or part of it.

There are pros and cons to either decision, and very successful intranet projects have been created both ways. The decision hinges on a number of factors.

Allocation of Resources

Hardware

Intranet hardware is not enormously expensive. Many intranets work very well using off-the-shelf, fairly inexpensive systems. See Chapter 5 for a complete technology rundown.

Hardware costs begin to mount with the addition of back-up servers (to provide interruption-free service), a test servers (for staging and testing new content before it goes "live") and storage space — especially if you plan to offer an FTP (File Transfer Protocol) option for large-file transfer over your network.

Most hardware (whether leased or purchased) falls under capital expenditures in most companies. In many organizations, authorization for capital purchases (or leases) can to be very difficult. If this is the case in your company, you may find it a lot easier to hire an Internet Service Provider (ISP) to host your site on their equipment. Monthy maintenance charges may be easier for you to justify than large capital expenditures. Another factor to consider is the rapid obsolescence of computer hardware (including servers). If your organization is hesitant to purchase (or lease) computer equipment due to amortization and tax issues, you may decide to outsource your site hosting.

People

Adding staff is usually very expensive. Creating new, permanent positions involves more than just salary and benefits costs. It involves floorspace, furniture, computer systems (hardware and software), support services, and an implied commitment to some sort of job security. New staff must be hired (unless they are promoted from within), oriented, and trained. Job descriptions must be created. The most difficult part of assembling any staff is finding people with the necessary skills and complementary personalities to meld into an effective team. Creative and technical people can work together to produce very successful projects, but the synergy takes a lot of work.

You should also consider the long-range implications of adding headcount to the organization. You may discover it is best to keep a small, full-time staff who are supported on an as-needed basis by outside vendors. Using outside vendors is particularly useful when you are developing complex systems (like database connectivity or transactions) on the site.

Security Issues

Running an intranet poses substantive questions about network security. If your intranet project includes e-mail and the possibility of links to outside online resources, security will be an issue. You have probably already heard about firewalls and network security from your MIS department. Most existing Local Area Networks (LANs) operate as closed, secure systems that provide no access outside the LAN. This enables the LAN operator to make sure that sensitive information cannot be viewed by anyone outside the network.

Your intranet should be connected to the larger Internet for maximum utility. New technologies, such as active agent notification systems require access outside your firewall. Any open connection into your firewall poses a potential security problem for your network administrator.

If security is a vital concern, and outside connectivity is essential, you may have no choice but to have your site hosted by an Internet Service Provider (ISP). This will preserve your firewall (the site is totally outside your firewall) while still giving your users access to the World Wide Web.

Remote Access

Some of your users will almost certainly ask for remote access to the intranet site — either from their homes or from portable systems in the field. You may also want to consider giving trusted vendors and customers access to certain areas within your intranet. This remote access requires access through the firewall, or the creation of a "mirror" site (one that contains the same information as the host server) located outside the firewall.

Whatever your decision about who will actually build your intranet site, building good site content is your primary responsibility.

Obtaining User Involvement

Nothing you do during your preparation phase will be more important than involving your future users in the development of your intranet. This prework before launch will go a long way toward creating a feeling of ownership among the users. The several approaches listed below have been used successfully as stand-alone activities or in combination with each other.

Surveys

Surveys are quick and easy instruments to get focused ideas from your potential users. On the down side, all of us feel at times that we spend too much time taking too many surveys. The keys to a successful survey are brevity and simplicity.

Brevity. Design your survey so it takes no more than 2 to 3 minutes to complete. Make your instructions brief and clear. Questions should be unambiguous and easy to understand. Remember you are asking people to take time out of their work day to help you.

Simplicity. Use yes–no, true–false questions wherever possible. Limit your use of open-ended questions that call for your subject to compose an answer. Do, however, leave space at the end of the form for additional comments.

One of the best ways to conduct a user survey is through one of your other communication media. You may choose to insert your survey into the employee newsletter, or place it in literature racks as a stand-alone piece. Where possible, you may want to use the normal organizational communication network to get the surveys out and back again. If you have management forums or regular supervisory meetings, you can make your survey an agenda item. In any case, you want to make sure you get sufficient response from your potential users. You should certainly shoot for more than half of your work force. To encourage participation, you may offer a prize to be raffled off from a list of all those who responded.

Focus Groups

Focus groups can be highly beneficial if they are properly structured and conducted. These meetings are usually held toward the end of the planning cycle when you have portions of your intranet site already developed. If you want to hold them earlier in the process, you may opt to use drawings and charts instead of real online material.

Focus groups are more productive when kept to a small number of participants, usually fewer than 12. We have found the most success with groups of six. These smaller groups tend to promote more and higher-quality interaction among the group members and with the group leader.

For maximum results, set an agenda for each meeting and stick to it. You may want to have a trial run among your development staff to make sure your sessions will produce the desired results. Try to keep the sessions focused, but not directed. Your agenda should leave lots of room for unplanned tangents. In many cases, your best feedback will come from these wild trips down seemingly blind alleys.

Make sure your attendees are representative of the entire organization. Recruit from all departments, groups, disciplines, ages, technical competencies, levels. You may want to recruit the help of the human resources department to help with your selections. If there are key people within the organization whose help and support you deem critical, by all means invite them. You will probably want to mix your groups to encourage free interaction. One warning, however. If you are going to invite people with extremely limited computer skills, you may want to keep this group together. Their input is valuable because your intranet must be intuitive enough for them to be able to use. They might, however, be hesitant to provide any useful input if they are surrounded by others who are computer proficient.

```
Plan your sessions to last no more than 60 minutes. Longer
meetings are difficult to fit into individual's schedules.
The one-hour meeting has become the staple of organizations.
You may, however, allow for extra time at the end for anyone
wishing to stay and continue.
```

If you are able, videotape the sessions, and be sure to tell the participants they will be taped when you invite them at the beginning of the meeting. These video records provide much more feedback than notes or recollections. By viewing the video you can pick up on the nonverbal dimension of the comments. Observing facial expressions as the group members navigate through your test site will tell you much about the quality of their experience.

After the session, send thank you notes to all participants. If possible, summarize for them the feedback you took from the sessions and how you plan to use it.

Ad Hoc Committee

One of the best things you can do during your formative phase is to involve representatives from each major department or group within your organization to be a part of your Ad

Hoc Committee. This group should be empowered to help decide content and structural issues pertaining to your intranet project. During the formative phase, they should be able to speak for the groups they represent. This is a real action committee, not a policies and procedures group. They should meet about every two weeks to discuss their progress in identifying, gathering and preparing information for the intranet. They should be willing to share with each other their successes and frustrations. In some cases, you may find it valuable to have certain committee members who are farther along in their process give a detailed report to the larger group.

This group can be an incredibly valuable resource to any intranet project manager. They will be your eyes and ears throughout the organization, helping evangelize the project. You may also want to use this group to help test and evaluate new sections before they are officially launched. As these members begin to work through the process of building their own intranet sites, you may find their enthusiasm and methods spreading to the rest of the organization. They will come out of the development process feeling a keen sense of intranet ownership. You may find that they challenge and encourage each other to produce compelling and innovative content instead of flat (HTML) pages.

The committee should be chartered only through the launch of the intranet. Their specific job is to help create the intranet, not maintain it. You will probably want to empower another group to deal with the day-to-day functional issues of maintaining the intranet.

Soft Launch

Before you launch your intranet you might consider a "soft launch" among a small group of potential users. In the software development world, products proceed through developmental phases — alpha, beta, and gold. On-line projects also roll out in three phases, development, soft launch and hard launch. During development, a small group (usually made up of content providers) is able to "look over the shoulder" of the developers and see the site as it is built.

In the online world a soft launch is the rough equivalent to the beta test. Just before the online product is ready for full deployment, a larger group of potential users is recruited to navigate through the site and find any broken links, missing graphics, etc. Your testers may be recruited from your recent focus groups attendees. They can be selected at random from the workforce. They can be you and your staff, if time is tight. You will want to keep the number of testers small — certainly no more than 20. This is also an excellent place to collect their input about content and structural issues so they can be worked through before the rest of the organization sees it.

You should devise an easy way for your testers to report any problems to you by using an online "bug report".

BUG BLASTER
EXTERMINATION, ERADICATION, ELIMINATION.

Please use this form for reporting any problems you have experienced while using Kinetoscope products. The information you provide is very significant and will help us continue to make our products even better.

Product: (select a product)

Platform: (select a platform)

Problem: (select a type)

Severity: (select a severity)

Consistency: (select a consistency)

Summary:

Description:

[Clear] [Submit]

Surveying Available Resources

IT/IS Resources

You will need someone who knows how an online publishing system works. They need to know hardware (servers and clients), software (operating systems, server software and client browsers), computer networks, and something about telecommunication.

Normally, your intranet will ride on an existing Local Area Network (LAN) or Wide Area Network (WAN). You will be producing extra network traffic over a system that was built for other purposes. In most organizations, this system is owned and operated by the Information Technology or Information Systems Group. These people take a lot of pride in their networks, and the thought of you coming in with this intranet may make them uneasy. In many cases the IT/IS departments are somewhat behind the technology curve as it applies to intranets. They may have already embraced a groupware solution for sharing information across the organization. Some may question the need for an intranet when a Lotus Notes (or other similar) system already exists.

You should look for a systems person with some online experience. Who out there spends a lot of time surfing the Internet? Who runs a WWW server in their family room? Who has an America Online account? Chances are these people are excited about online publishing and can help you sell the concept and smooth the way with their contemporaries within IT/IS.

You will also need to locate someone within this group who can step forward and help create the "back-end" resources necessary to run an intranet. These are the special coding resources that allow you to connect to databases, perform online surveys and many other online activities. These products are written in such software authoring languages as Perl, C++ and Java.

Content Resources

Every person within your organization is a potential content provider, whether as a direct contributor, a forum participant or simply someone who posts a classified ad for a 1964 Chevy Impala. As you plan your intranet, plan to involve as many parts of the organization as make sense. You can recruit content providers in a number of ways, but they all fall into two general categories — recruits or volunteers.

Recruits

These are the folks who find out about your intranet project at a staff meeting. The boss knows they have an AOL account at home. Without a word of discussion, this person is made the "online content provider" for the department or group. Awash in the excitement of the moment, they call you on the phone and express their heart-felt thanks at being given this high-profile, labor intensive, new assignment.

Volunteers

These people will find you. They already know and understand the online world and will become your advocates throughout the organization. They are highly energized, highly motivated people who will make your job a lot easier.

Regardless of their point of origin, or amount of buy-in to the intranet project, your content resources will either make or break your intranet. It is nearly impossible for one person, or even one intranet staff, to find and create enough compelling information to fill an intranet. You want your system to have something of value for every potential user. The ultimate goal of your system is improved organizational effectiveness. Content is the critical element in achieving your goal.

```
It is usually a good idea to have each major department or
group within the organization appoint one person to act as
your liaison for all online content. This point person will
work closely with you to define their own section of your
intranet. Ideally, they should have a broad overview of the
department or group so they can determine what content is
appropriate for the intranet, where it is and how to get it
ready for online publishing.
```

You may decide to allow individuals within your organization to create "personal pages" within the intranet. In this case, it is a good idea to publish a set of content guidelines so you and your users are not unpleasantly surprised by some questionable content on these pages.

Inherent in your job is the overall content responsibility for the intranet. You should work with your staff and content providers to create a complete content plan that will result in a universally useful intranet site.

Design and Production Resources

Who designs and produces your corporate communication now? Chances are you have a competent media design and production group somewhere within your organization. You will want to recruit their help in graphically designing your intranet.

```
Be careful. Print designers do not necessarily make good on-
line designers. The two worlds are very far apart. On-line
design requires some knowledge of file sizes, graphic com-
pression algorithms, a universal color palette and other on-
line peculiarities.
```

This is an area where technology and design must co-exist side by side. For example, it is a good idea to have your design staff learn the basics of HTML tagging. Understanding the limitations of this restrictive authoring language will do much to help the designer create beautiful and functional pages.

The online environment is a strange one for designers used to the high-resolution world. On-line designers work with a 72 dots per inch (DPI) medium. That's the normal screen resolution for a 640 × 480 monitor. And that's probably more than you wanted to know

Planning Your Intranet 93

about computer screen resolutions. The point is it takes a special combination of creativity and an understanding of the limits of the technology to create beautiful online pages for your intranet. You may not find someone who fits that bill right away. You may have to invest some time and training into one of your print designers.

Producing the actual HTML pages is not brain surgery, but it's not simple either. The process requires a thorough understanding of computer operation, knowledge of a host of software applications, and most of all, a lot of patience. HTML is an unforgiving language. It is not intuitive, nor is it user friendly. Some HTML conversion applications (PageMill, FrontPage, HomePage) make the process easier, but not complete. To create truly compelling online pages, someone needs to study and know the ins and outs of HTML, including advanced functions.

It is at the production phase that the online world differs from the traditional print production world. With a print project, like a brochure, you must create text, graphics and layout. These are usually created using text and graphics software applications and then placed into a pre-press software application (Adobe®PageMaker™ or Quark XPress™). At this point, they are ready for review and approval. Then they move on to a system that creates negatives, and then on to the actual press to be printed. With your intranet, as soon as your layout, text and graphics are placed in HTML format, they are ready to "make live" on your intranet. There are no intermediate steps. HTML can be proofed and made live immediately.

Understanding Nonlinear Information

Growing the Content Tree

Your intranet structure (tree) will always begin at the root — your home page. This is the first page your users will come to when they access your intranet. Each site has such a page, and depending on how the server is set, it will be named either "default" or "index." You may hear it referred to as the "top page," "front page," "default page" or "index page," but most often it is called the "home page". All major sections and areas of particular interest are listed as links on the home page.

```
Intranets and their other online cousins are built to be
viewed in any order. The user controls the experience not
the author. The content must be constructed so that every
user experience, in any order, is a logical and valuable
one. The work you do with your users as you begin your plan-
ning process will help you make decisions about your intra-
net structure.
```

You will, most likely, have some major content areas on the site. A typical intranet structure may look like this:

About Us
    Organizational structure
    1998 Organizational goals
    Organization charts
    Employee news
    Organizational mission
    1997 Financial information

News Room
    News clipping service
    Organizational calendar
    Weather
    Breaking news
    Employee newsletter online

Library
    Newsletters
    Speeches
    Brochures
    Organization annual report
    Q & A about the intranet
    Savings plan

Employee Section
    Classified ads
    Merchant discounts
    Employee spotlight
    Family events
    Job opportunities
    Promotions/job change
    Service anniversaries
    Retirements
    Volunteer opportunities
    Intramural sports news
    Customer mailbag
    In Remembrance

Information Exchange
    News groups
    Forums
    Chat rooms

Customer Area
    Product/service information
    Product/service pricing information
    On-line catalog
    Production schedule
    Current inventory
    Customer service

Vendor Area
    Billing information
    Partner program
    Production schedule
    Purchasing department online

Your intranet structure will, in many ways, mirror your organizational structure. Gathering user input and feedback will ensure that your site structure is logical and valuable from the user perspective.

Designing an Internal Linking Scheme

Readers turn pages to move around a book. The online equivalent to turning pages is the hypertext link: it's simpler, requires less effort, and you don't get ink on your fingers! Links can be text or graphics. Links can take you to another part of the document, another section in your intranet or another site halfway around the world.

On-line linking is similar to the encyclopedic style of referring the reader to another topic for more information. With links, however, the information is only a mouse click away — not in some other volume or section of the encyclopedia.

There are two kinds of links on your intranet site: navigation and internal.

Navigation links typically move users from one area to another — usually between one content menu page and another.

Internal links are useful within documents when you want to point your users to more information about the topic. For example, if you are posting a story that mentions the 1995 Annual Report, you may link the words "Annual Report" to the online annual report on your site. Internal links can add a valuable dimension to your intranet site by making related information easier to find. They can, however, be overused. Remember, when your user links off to another document somewhere else on your site, they must return to the original document to continue. Including several internal links in one document can be distracting to the user and can make it difficult to continue on with the original document with so many detours.

```
Rule of thumb — Use internal links within documents to add
clarity to the content. Limit internal links to one or two
per document.
```

Selecting Appropriate Content

If your organization has been around for a while, it has probably accumulated several metric tons of information. Just think of all the information you come into contact with during the course of a typical day — employee phone listings, financial statements, spreadsheets, schedules, product information, timesheets, benefits information, order forms, newsletters, bulletin board announcements, training videos, policies and procedures manuals, plant layouts, leases, inventory records, operating instructions, invoices, etc., etc., etc. Well, you get the point. There's a wealth of information out there that could be put on your intranet. But where do you start?

What Exists Now and In What Format?

The first step in the content selection phase is taking an inventory of what information exists now in your organization. Where are the databases? Brochures? Research reports? Order forecasts? You should make a complete list of these elements sorted by department, group or type. This is a good task in which to involve your Ad Hoc Committee.

As these elements are being recorded, it is important to note their current format. In other words, what is being generated electronically, and what is being generated manually. You will want to start with the electronic files first. These can be translated into HTML pages through the use of an HTML plug-in within the host application, or by the addition of HTML tags to the existing content. It's not a difficult task, but it is complex and requires a concerted effort to accomplish.

In dealing with manual information — that is information that does not reside on any computer in any form — another step is necessary: Digitizing. You may find a wealth of photography or manual illustrations that have never been digitized. These will require the use of a scanner and a graphics manipulation software package like Adobe® PhotoShop™. This can be a slow and tedious process since each image should be enhanced, color corrected and sized for online use. Text is a bit easier. Most clean text documents can be scanned using optical character reader software. In most cases, it scans fairly clean, although it may need a bit of touching up. This manual conversion process can be time-consuming and expensive to accomplish. You should have a game plan worked out before hand to determine who will pay for the work.

You will also need to determine the relative sensitivity of each element. Is the information appropriate for a limited audience, or can anyone in the organization make use of it? Can this information be shared with customers or vendors? Answers to these questions will determine how you will process the information.

What Is Appropriate For Online Use?

Everything and anything is appropriate for online use. As you collect and examine the wealth of information you have gathered for your intranet project, you may be overwhelmed by the shear volume. Remember that your intranet project is never complete. You don't have to include everything at first launch to provide a valuable service.

A good strategy for content development is to select the obvious high-interest content elements and include them in your initial launch. As you ask for and get feedback and

Planning Your Intranet

input from your users, they will begin to direct you toward additional content they think would be valuable to include. Add these items to your own roll-out list and you have a living, expanding guide for intranet development.

As you make your online content selections, make sure you add value to the content whenever possible. You can do this by adding internal links, graphics, sound, video or interactivity. A boring report placed online will still be boring. Obviously, you won't be able to enhance everything you touch — there won't be time or resources for that. But you may want to select a few, key content elements and add some interest to them.

How To Repurpose Existing Materials and Information

In most cases where the existing materials are already digital, you will be able to work within the host application (Microsoft® Word™, Microsoft® XL™, Adobe® PageMaker™, Quark® XPress™, etc.) to convert the documents to HTML pages. Almost every one of the applications in common use within your organization has added some form of HTML converter in the latest update or version. Your technical staff can be a great help to you as you take an inventory of existing content and the host applications. Chances are you have an approved list of software applications within your organization. Have your technical staff make sure your content team has the latest versions of the applications with built-in HTML converters.

If you find the content all over the place in lots of non-standard software applications, you can use one of a number of relatively good HTML editors on the market today.

Surveying Your Current Enterprise for Inclusion

Some content elements will be obvious. For example, you might want to include portions or all of the content from other communication media — your newsletter, management bulletins, press clippings, brochures, flyers, etc. All of these documents should be examined for online publication. Many organizations have been able to reduce printing and distribution costs for traditional media by moving content to the intranet. You may also want to begin the process of archiving these documents, thereby adding another valuable service to your online product.

Building an online reference library for marketing, sales and documentation purposes (proposals, brochures, product sheets, specification sheets, build and test documentation, product manuals, etc.) can save hours of searching through manual resources.

Building In Interactivity

The Two-Way Street

The online world is intensely personal. It's very much a one-to-one medium. It's much more tactile than other media. It requires the use of a keyboard and mouse. The user must turn on a computer, connect to a network, launch a browser and select a destination online.

The most successful online sites involve their users to enhance the user experience. This interaction can range from simple mouse clicks to complex online forms to interactive games. Generally speaking, the more interaction, the more memorable the user experience.

The Internet and the World Wide Web have been widely criticized as being flat, ugly, and unexciting. After all, we are used to instantaneous, broadband communication in our home. The fact that a user in Tampa, Florida, can access a text document from a Web site in Israel is pretty amazing — the first time. Even visiting the Louvre Museum online is exciting the first few times. (http://mistral.culture.fr/louvre/) After that, it's like watching television repeats. *Now show me something new.*

Encouraging Feedback

Your intranet is never finished. It is very much a work in progress that grows and improves through the active participation of your partners — the users. As you design your intranet you will want to make sure you build in lots of opportunities for your users to provide you with their good ideas and comments.

E-mail within the Site

It's a very good idea to place an e-mail form (mailto) on every page on the site, so your users can provide you with comments and ideas relevant to any content anywhere on the site. Your technical staff should be able to mark each e-mail with a reference to an individual page address otherwise known as the Uniform Resource Locator (URL).

As with all e-mail messages, make sure you respond to the sender within a day or two at the most. Even if you can't consider the comment or idea immediately, it's a good idea to send at least an acknowledgment that you received the message — and to thank the user for their time.

You can also create a system that will automatically send out e-mail messages to multiple users advising them of new content when it is posted.

Forums

Forums provide a platform for the exchange of ideas among you and your users. Forums can be either hosted or unhosted, and can be placed anywhere on the site that makes sense.

Hosted forums feature a leader (host) who guides the online conversation, selects topics, keeps the postings focused on the topic, edits postings when necessary.

Planning Your Intranet 99

> **online forum**
>
> **kinetoscope**
>
> **Welcome to the Florida Webmasters Forum.**
>
> This forum is for the webmaster who would like to communicate with other professionals in their field. Here you can find tons of information to questions you may have or you can leave your message here for others to see.
>
> This forum is hosted. That means that you will not see your postings as soon as you submit them. Postings are stored in an administrator's holding area until the Administrator reviews them. The Administrator reserves the right to refuse to post anything that is objectionable or off the topic. The Administrator also reserves the right to edit postings without changing meaning for the sake of brevity. At times, the Administrator may combine similar postings or choose one that represents others of a similar nature or theme.
>
> Choose a discussion group
>
> Webmaster Board
> Help!
> HTML Tips and Tricks
> Job Resource Center
> Legal Bits
> The Reading Lounge
> On-line-Tools-Comments & Critiques

You can find forum hosts all over the organization. The members of your Ad Hoc committee are good candidates. You will probably want to recruit individuals who have some online aptitude, a well-developed writing skill, and the time to dedicate to the care and feeding of forums. Make sure they understand the commitment they are making and are willing to spend some time every day to keep the forum fresh and interesting.

Ideas for forum topics will come from all parts of the organization. You may start with whatever your organizational hot topics are — reorganization, new benefits plan, executive compensation, etc. Give your hosts lots of freedom to go where the interest is. However, make sure you give your forum hosts well-developed guidelines to control online behavior among forum participants.

Surveys

Keep them short and simple, but keep them coming. Topical surveys are a powerful way to keep your users coming back to your intranet. Use checkboxes, radio buttons and pop-ups to make the user experience quicker and easier. Have your technical staff write a Common Gateway Interface (CGI) to flow the results into a database.

Sample Intranet User Survey (Post Launch)

1. Which area of the intranet has been the most useful in helping you do your job?
2. Which area of the intranet has been the least useful in helping you do your job?
3. What three areas of the intranet do you use most?
4. Do you have access to the Internet from your computer? If not, do you feel it would be useful for your job if you did?
5. Have you found the intranet to be a time saver in doing your work? If so, how? If not, why not?
6. Do you feel you have received enough training to efficiently and effectively use the intranet? If not, what areas do you feel you need training in?
7. Have you found the intranet to be a good resource for sharing ideas and information with other employees? If so, how? If not, why not?
8. Do you feel you are more informed about company happenings, policies, changes, etc. as a result of using the intranet. If so, how? If not, why not?
9. Do you feel the intranet helps make your job easier? If so, why? If not, why not?
10. Do you have any suggestions on what you'd like to see change or improve about the intranet?
11. How many times a day would you say you access information from the intranet?
12. Have you ever contacted the intranet webmaster for any questions about the intranet? If so, did you get a satisfactory response? If not, why not?
13. Do you feel the intranet has helped you to provide better customer service to our customers? Yes/No/Not applicable to my job
14. On a scale of 1 to 10, with 10 being the most useful, how would you rate the overall usefulness of using the intranet to do your job?
15. What else would you like to say about the intranet?
16. Publish the results of the last survey as you post the new one. You may also want to keep an archive of previous surveys going back a certain amount of time — say a few months. Plot charts and graphs from the results to dress up the online survey results.

Games

All kinds of users appreciate online games. They're not just for kids anymore. Games with an educational value (edutainment) are most effective and valuable in making a point with your users. If safety is a big organizational issue, create a safety game with cartoon figures, animation and sound. Challenge users to make an expert score on the game and post their names in the safety hall of fame.

Enlisting Management Support

Regardless of which part of the organization owns the intranet, all parts of the organization must buy into the project for it to be successful in the long run. The things you do early on to enlist management support will pay handsome dividends throughout your intranet development effort.

Strategic Planning Group

This is the group that sets the strategic direction and overall goals for the intranet project. Typically, its membership is made up of high-level executives from Marketing, Communications, Information Technology and other staff-level groups like the Legal or Finance Department.

Steering Committee

This is usually a standing committee made up of key components of your intranet effort. The project manager, Webmaster, technical lead, and representatives from the general content areas are usually members. This group deals with the day-to-day operational issues. You may want to rotate membership on this committee every year to keep producing fresh ideas.

Justifying the Resources

As with any new organizational endeavor, your intranet project must be given sufficient resources to operate successfully. These resources can be justified by the benefits you can expect to realize from the intranet project. You will be able to quantify the savings associated with the elimination of certain printed reports and other print products. If you make the monthly financial reports available online and eliminate a printing run of several thousand sheets, you can quantify those savings.

Overcoming Objections

> "We don't need an intranet, we already use Lotus Notes."
>
> "We can't afford the hardware and software costs"
>
> "Who is going to pay for all this?"

You may hear comments like this from your organization. Do your homework. Read the reports and case histories. Understand the online advantages. Be ready with factual information to overcome these and other objections.

Objection:

> "We don't need an intranet, we already use Lotus Notes."

Response:

Lotus Notes is an expensive, closed system that is difficult to maintain and grow. Converting our existing applications to HTML will allow us to build and grow an open and relatively inexpensive solution to our information-sharing needs within the organization.

Objection:

"We can't afford the hardware and software costs"

Response:

Almost any hardware platform can be used as an intranet server. We can start small with an inexpensive system and grow into something larger as the usage within the organization grows.

Objection:

"Who is going to pay for all this?"

Response:

"Talk about cost savings realized elsewhere, distribution, priority, same staff positions."

Defining Responsibilities

Resolving the issues of who does what early on in the process will go a long way toward avoiding conflicts and misunderstandings later.

Content Generation and Maintenance

One person should have the overall content responsibilities for the intranet. With a small staff, this can be the Webmaster. In a larger staff, you may create a content editor position. This person will work with your Ad Hoc committee members and all other content providers. It's also important to provide this person with a comprehensive content guide.

Page Construction and Maintenance

In some cases this responsibility will also fall to the Webmaster. Whereever possible, this function should fall to a graphic design person or group, much as it does in the print production world.

Most important here is having one person check all HTML pages for links, images and other potential problems before a page is placed on the active server.

Technical Support

Look to your IT or IS department for all your "back-end" issues. cgi and Perl scripting are usually beyond the skill level of the webmaster.

Protecting Your Intranet from Copyright and Libel Violations

As with any work created and distributed by your company, your corporate intranet must conform to copyright and libel laws. The policies and management structure your company has in place to protect itself from employees creating print and broadcast works that violate copyright and libel laws should also be implemented for the company's intranet. If your company does not have a specific review process in place that provides protection against copyright and libel infractions in every medium, then the creation of your intranet is a great reason to implement one.

In today's litigious society, the very nature of online publishing requires that your company have some sort of formal structure in place that protects it from its employees violating copyright and libel laws. The natural ease and accessibility of online publishing, its robust environment and its ability to create a rapid, ever-changing pace of multi-faceted communication and interaction make it even more vulnerable to copyright and libel infringements than other media.

Why? Intranets give all who work for your company a vast space in which to communicate and contribute, and in ways they've never been able to do so before. Over time, you'll notice that employee desire and motivation to contribute and have input into information posted on the intranet will be comparatively much greater than in your pre-intranet days. Why? There's only one reason: Because they can. The intranet's ease, accessibility, robustness and multi-functional nature make it a thriving Garden of Eden for communication growth, and thus naturally increases your company's chances of its employees being tempted — though most likely unknowingly — by the poisonous apple that is copyright and libel violations. It is, afterall, very easy for employees to leap out onto the Internet and grab bits and pieces from newsletters, comic strips, magazines, etc., and use them to build their departmental intranet site.

Indeed, virtually every employee who would ever come close to a copyright or libel violation does so unknowingly. People in general just aren't familiar with copyright and libel law unless they have had mass communication or legal training. But it is your company's responsibility to, at a minimum, make sure it gives them the information and resources they need to ask questions about posting copyrighted or libelous material on the intranet before it's published. Of course, you're always going to have "accidental violations" (like, for example, retransmitting postings on newsgroups verbatim). However, you can greatly reduce the company's risk for lawsuits by properly educating employees from your intranet's inception.

At a minimum, all those with the ability to access your company's intranet should be trained on and given a copy of the following:

1. Your company's policy on posting copyrighted or libelous material, which should include how to go about having material reviewed by company legal staff or consultants before it's posted
2. Definitions of what copyright and libel are and a summary of the laws

Everyone with access to your company's intranet should be thoroughly trained on these legal issues. You may even choose to have each person sign a training completion form affirming they understand the company's policies and procedures. However, from a legal standpoint, that piece of paper will not absolve the company itself of responsibility. According to copyright and libel laws, the publisher — your company — is generally held responsible for breaking the law as well as the person generating the violation.

Sidebar/Boxed Information

Copyright. The exclusive right to reproduce and distribute an original work is protected by the U.S. Constitution and international treaties. Nearly every original work privately created in the United States is copyrighted and protected whether or not the work bears a copyright notice. Copyright protects only an author's original expression. A work is copyrighted as soon as it is created. (For example, all the e-mail you write on your intranet is copyrighted.)

Not Copyrightable

- Ideas
- Facts
- Titles
- Names
- Short phrases
- Blank forms
- A system or factual information that is conveyed in a copyrighted work
- Pre-existing material that the author has incorporated into a work

Fair Use. The right to reproduce portions of a copyrighted work for news reporting, criticism and scholarship without obtaining permission or paying a license or royalty fee. Fair use passages should be kept short and to a minimum, and should always be attributed. Place copyright information on the bottom of every page of your intranet in the following format:

```
Copyright [first year of the publication]
[author/owner, which is your company]. All Rights Reserved.
```

Public Domain. A work in the public domain is one that can be used by anyone for any purpose.

Copyright Registration. To register a copyright, file the appropriate form with the U.S. Copyright Office, including the payment for registration costs ($20). For most types of work being published in the United States, two copies of the work being registered must be deposited with the Copyright Office for the use of the Library of Congress. The deposit of the work is not a requirement for copyright. However, failing to make the deposit at the time of publication can result in fines.

Getting Sued. In order for someone to sue your company for infringement (with some exceptions) their work must be registered with the Copyright Office. However, they may register after the infringement occurs, as long as it's before filing their lawsuit. If they're registered prior to infringement it allows them to collect statutory damages and attorney's fees if a case is ruled in their favor.

Copyright Information Websites

`http://lcweb.loc.gov/copyright`
`http://www.benedict.com`

Also, Abitec International has developed the first commercially available intranet training program on this topic called the "Copyright and Netiquette Primer™." It's an excellent tool to educate employees about how to avoid innocent mistakes as they develop their departmental intranet web pages. Visit Abitec at `http://www.abitec.com.`

Libel. Broadly printed, written or broadcast communication that defame, therefore exposing a person to hatred, ridicule, or contempt, and lowering him in the esteem of his fellows, causing him to be shunned, or injuring him in his business or calling.

8

Designing Your Intranet

Designing for a computer screen is very different from designing for the printed page. While an intranet opens the door to lots of compelling things, like video, audio and animation, it also carries some restraints that are being addressed by such current technologies as Java and ActiveX.

For those of you who have been producing print products, multimedia or video, this new world will look somewhat strange, and yet somewhat familiar. Most of the tools used to create compelling online graphics are the same ones that are used in other media. Photoshop, Illustrator, Painter and all the other typical graphics applications are right at home online.

Bandwidth and network speed are the real problems associated with creating for online delivery. Of course these problems are minimized within an organization, since the intranet usually piggybacks on the existing data network. Still, the people who administer the data network are going to be concerned with your files clogging up their pipes. So it's always a good idea to aim for the smallest possible files when designing your intranet. Network speed is increasing as a lot of companies are upgrading to faster networks.

Allison Kimery, the insurance administrator of the XYZ corporation has just had a visit from the human resources director — and with it some frightening instructions.

> "We're going to make the insurance area our initial content on the company intranet. Pull all your insurance information and forms together and let's get this ball rolling. I'd like the site up within 60 days."

Now what? Fortunately for her, the intranet committee at XYZ has made it very easy for her to make the transition from concept to online reality. Allison logs onto the company intranet and clicks on the "building your pages" section. Here she finds a series of HTML templates that all comply to the company online design standards. She picks a color, background, and other graphic elements from the template directory and she's in business. She copies and pastes her content into the template forms and checks the final product on her desktop browser. She next checks the online image library for some stock photos or illustrations to dress up her pages. These are all drag and drop graphics, pre-sized, and saved in the appropriate graphics format. Her design work done, she turns her efforts to the more complex task of translating her insurance claims forms from the printed page to online. She enters the "forms" area of the site and is presented with a number of forms templates. She picks one that most resembles the form she needs to translate and begins to answer a series of on-screen prompts. As she provides answers to all the questions, her online form is ready. She assembles all the HTML files she has just created and sends them to the intranet Webmaster for final review before her section is made live.

Elapsed time: a few weeks.

HTML/CGI knowledge required: none. (Assuming the Webmaster is going to write the CGI scripts for the form).

Outcome: a group of happy people who can now submit insurance claims online; a happy insurance administrator who has less paper shuffling to do; and a very happy human resources director who is getting accolades from other managers for her pioneering efforts on the intranet.

"Look-and-Feel" Issues

"Look-and-feel" in the online world is the equivalent of "overall appearance" in the print world. Since the online experience is user-controlled, and somewhat tactile (given the use of the mouse and keyboard to read it), it's more than just how the screen looks. Look and feel is a description of the overall appearance PLUS the layout, navigation and structure of your site.

Unlike the print world where page size and physical makeup is virtually unlimited, the online world is defined by the browser window and the resolution and size of the viewing monitor. It's a "light through" world (like looking at a backlit transparency at your local movie theater), not a "light on" world like the pages of a book. It's a low resolution world (72 dots per inch), not the typical high resolution world of brochures (600 dots per inch or higher).

Establishing a Unique Look For Your Intranet

Everyone is the same size online.

One of the great features of online publishing is that everyone has basically the same tools and workspace to make their statement. A quick look around the World Wide Web illustrates the egalitarian nature of the medium. A mom and pop enterprise stands on an equal footing with huge syndicates. In fact, many industry observers have noted that it is sometimes easier for a small, start-up operation to take advantage of a new medium than it is for an established power. For example, **amazon.com** is a very successful reseller of books on the World Wide Web because they were able to fashion an online bookstore that takes advantage of the interactivity of the Web. They feature over a million titles that can be found through an on-site search engine by subject, author or title. They invite publishers to add their books to the amazon site. They invite authors to review their own books. Visitors order books at substantial discounts over conventional bookstores using an online order form.

Welcome to Amazon.com Books!

Search one million titles.
Enjoy consistently low prices.

~ Win $1,000 worth of books ~
~ Browse our Editors' Favorites ~
~ Sell books from *your* Web site ~

SPOTLIGHT!
  Today: bibliomania, blue Mondays, commodification of culture, the "great books", madness and artistry; the sciences of risk and rebellion, Howard Hughes and chess--all **discounted 30%**.

THE BOOK OF THE DAY!
  A different title every day for the next 3,000 years.

WILL YOU BE MINE?
  From mushy love to pure lust, our Valentine's books are 100 percent doily-free. You can play the game of love--enter Amazon.com's contest to win books and bouquets for your sweetie!

NBCC ANNOUNCES AWARD NOMINEES
  The National Book Critics Circle has announced the nominees for their 1996 awards for best poetry, fiction, biography/autobiography, general nonfiction, and criticism. See if your faves made the cut!

FEATURED
  The Bankers: The Next Generation - *New!*
    Technology has Martin Mayer counting change in this update of his financial classic.
  William Greider's One World, Ready or Not: The Manic Logic of Global Capitalism
    Gently applying brakes may prevent a skid.
  Oliver Sacks's The Island of the Colorblind

Amazon has been successful because they were able to think in new terms — out of the box. They were not encumbered by the old ways of doing things. They saw the potential of the new business paradigm and fashioned a new business model to fit it.

One of the constant challenges facing any organizational communicator is to establish and maintain a consistent look to all organizational communication elements. Designing an intranet is certainly no different. In fact, in many ways it is more of a challenge due to the "real time" nature of the medium. Unlike the next issue of your organizational newsletter that works its way through several approval cycles, your intranet content should flow quickly and easily onto your intranet. Remember, timeliness is one of its principal advantages over print.

Your challenge as the intranet architect is to create a compelling, interesting and graphically pleasing environment in which your users will have a rewarding experience. Most organizations already have well-defined style standards established for traditional media. This is usually a good jumping-off place for your online style definition. You may find, however, that the style standards may have little to say about electronic or new media — simply because they are so new to the world of organizational communication. With a little imagination and some involvement by the standards group, you should be able to create an effective and pleasant framework for online standards production.

The Process

As with any definition of style, creating an online style guide will be an iterative process involving the various stakeholders in your intranet project.

Step One: Review existing organizational style guidelines

If you have comprehensive (and up-to-date) guidelines for print, video, signage, etc., you will be able to translate much of what already exists to your online style. For example, if specific PMS™ (Pantone Matching System — a widely recognized color matching system for print products) color for logos or trademarks, these can easily be carried into the online world.

```
Note about online color: For those of you who are used to
spending lots of time and effort getting those corporate
colors exactly right throughout the print production cycle,
your online experience will be quite different. On-line col-
or, for a variety of good reasons, is not an exact science.
It is affected by all kinds of factors from choice of color
palette to type of processor to quality of display screen.
Another factor why colors are going to look different on
different computer monitors is that not all monitors are
calibrated the same. What looks like dark blue on one mon-
itor may look like dark green on another.
```

Don't be alarmed if you spend a great deal of time creating beautiful graphics that look perfect on your monitor set to millions of colors, only to have it look absolutely horrible on a VGA monitor. The online world is the farthest thing from standardized, and color is one of the saddest victims.

You might also find it useful to review typography standard and layout for traditional media. You will be able to use any font on your intranet as long as you create it as a graphic file.

On-line type is usually preset within the browser. With Netscape's browser you get Times. Period. The user has some control over font selection in the later versions (3.0 and above), but fonts are still seriously limited online. New browser versions allow much more flexibility in font selection. Remember, however, that you are restricted by the browser(s) employed by your users. Some organizations select a browser and distribute it to all those with access to the intranet. In these cases you need to learn the capabilities of the browser. Each time a new browser is released or updated, a flurry of articles and books usually appears soon thereafter. Since Netscape and Microsoft now control almost the entire browser market, their sites are good places to seek and find the latest information and capabilities.

Adobe, Apple, and Netscape have a new font initiative underway and Microsoft is working on cascading style sheets. Their Websites will provide a wealth of continuing information about their progress.

For example, Netscape offers an online reviewer's guide for their new Navigator 3.0 browser. Check it out at the Netscape site at this URL:

http://home.netscape.com/comprod/products/navigator/version_3.0/review.html

On the Microsoft side, they offer a complete compendium of site building information in their Site Builder Workshop found at this URL:

http://www.microsoft.com/workshop/

Either of these sites will tell you what you need to know about the capabilities of the browser you are using and how to get the maximum performance and results from your site design efforts.

Layout is another story. You should be able to pull quite a lot of layout style from your existing print publications if you want your intranet to look like them. The use of color headers, graphic elements and graphic style can easily translate to the online world.

> One word of caution: On-line design is more challenging than
> print design. It is more restrictive in terms of real es-
> tate, color and construction.

In the print world, once you have created a print master, and seen a press proof, you can be relatively sure of what the final product will look like. Not so in the online world. For example, many designers work on multimedia systems designed for print production. They work with monitors capable of showing millions of colors. In most cases, their users are going to have 256 color (or less) monitors with 640 × 480 pixel resolution. So the lesson for the designer is to create in the world most common to the user. A lot of online designers work with two monitors — a large (17 to 20 inch) capable of displaying millions of colors to create the work, and another 640 by 480, 256 color monitor for a reality check.

A quirk of online layout involves the expandable browser window. Straight HTML pages (no tables or frames), will expand or contract to fill the browser window. This makes it particularly difficult for designers to know exactly what their final product will look like on a user screen set to different window dimensions. That's one of the reasons most good site designers will insist on using tables or frames to hold their page layouts.

Another word of caution. There are also differences in how each browser displays the same page — even in tables or frames. Layouts are also different between Macs, PCs, and UNIX clients. A page on a Mac running Microsoft Internet Explorer will appear slightly different from the same page on a Mac running Netscape Navigator. A PC running Netscape Navigator will display a page differently from a Mac running Netscape Navigator. There are good technical reasons for the differences. The result, however, is murder on the designer. The best advice that can be given here is to create the pages on the most popular system and browser being used by your organization. If that is a Windows 95 PC running Internet Explorer, then use that combination as your design default. You will also want to check your designs on other platforms and browsers to see how much deviation there is. Sometimes it's possible to move an element a pixel or two to make the page look good on all combinations of platforms and browsers. The key is to be aware that differences exist in the online world that make design an incredibly complex undertaking.

Step Two: Review other online style guides

The Web offers a wide variety of style guides that you can use as models for your site plans.

Since the online design world is so new and so browser-dependent, make sure you check the notes on each style guide. Try to determine if the guide is specific to a particular browser. For example, tables were not widely supported until the release of Netscape 2.0. If you are looking at a style guide written before 1996, you will miss out on a lot of new innovations and capabilities.

Web Style Manual
Patrick J. Lynch
YALE CENTER FOR ADVANCED INSTRUCTIONAL MEDIA

This manual describes the design principles used to create the pages within the Center for Advanced Instructional Media's (C/AIM) World Wide Web site. This is not an introduction to HTML authoring, as excellent resources already exist for those purposes. This manual is also available as in consolidated pages, for downloading and printing.

Manual Overview

INTRODUCTION

I. INTERFACE DESIGN IN WWW SYSTEMS
- Hypermedia and Conventional Document Design
- Navigation in Hyperspace
- WWW Site Structure
- WWW Page Design
- Efficient Use of the World Wide Web
  - System Responsiveness
  - Well-balanced Page and Menu Designs

II. WWW PAGE DESIGN
- Design Integrity in WWW Systems
- Essential Elements of WWW Pages
- Page Length
- Design Grids for HTML
- Sample Templates for an WWW Pages
- Local Links and Navigation Aids
- Page Headers
- Typography
- Page Footers: Verifying Origin and Authorship
- Official Seals or Marks of the Institution
- Contact Information
- Copyright
- Page Date
- Page URL

III. OPTIMIZING PERFORMANCE IN WWW PAGES
- Sizing Inlined Graphics
- Interlacing GIF Graphics
- Using Width and Height in Graphic Anchors
- Loading Low Res/High Res Graphics
- Trimming graphics by Limiting Bit Depth
- JPEG Graphics

This is the top page of the Yale Style Guide, one of the best examples of a comprehensive style guide available on the Web. The guide is found at ***http://info.med.yale.edu/caim/StyleManual_Top.HTML***

Many universities have produced extensive style guides to facilitate page production by their internal colleges, departments and faculty. The sample shown below was produced by the University of South Florida in Tampa.

It includes template pages for colleges, departments, and staff members.

This is the online template page for a USF College top page.

The use of these templates encourages a wide variety of potential information providers within the university community to post quick, easy and conforming online pages. By providing the graphic elements, the Webmaster ensures that the site's look and feel will be consistent and of the highest possible quality.

Designing Your Intranet 115

This is the template for a USF Department top page.

    The compelling point here is to learn from what others have experienced. You probably will not find an existing style guide that meets all your needs. You may find parts of many guides that appeal to you. You may end up sampling from a wide variety of existing guides and adding elements that make the site uniquely yours.

    Remember, nothing is hidden online. One of the most compelling features of browsers is their ability to display the actual HTML document that is used to create the online screen you are looking at. So when you find a site or a page that appeals to you, take a look at the document source to discover how it is done.

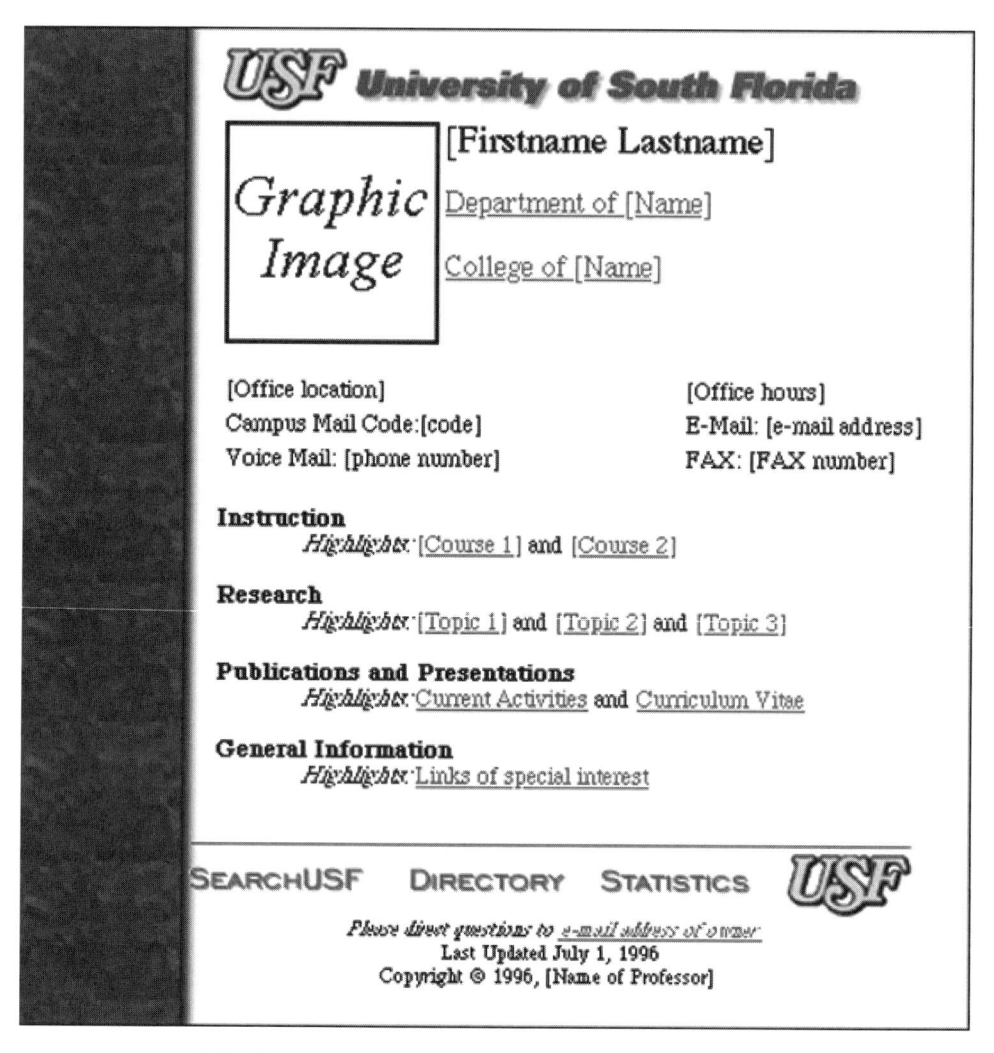

And finally, a template page for an individual USF staff member.

Following is the actual HTML document used to create the online page above:

```
<!DOCTYPE HTML PUBLIC "-//IETF//DTD HTML 2.0//EN">

<HTML>
<! -- FACULTY WEB PAGE TEMPLATE
This template is meant to assist the author in designing
Official World Wide Web pages for USF faculty and staff. The
generic information must be replaced with actual informa-
tion before it can be considered compliant with the USF WWW
Style Guide. This template can be modified as needed. The
actual page should contain pertinent information as described
in the USF WWW Style Guide.-->
```

Designing Your Intranet

```
<HEAD>
<LINK REV = "made" HREF = "mailto:e-mail address of owner">
<META NAME = "usf" CONTENT = "e-mail address of owner">
<TITLE>USF: Professor [Name]</TITLE>


</HEAD>
<BODY bgcolor = "#FFFBF0" background = "bg.gif" link =
"#238E23" alink = "#CC7F32" vlink = "#CC7F32">
<blockquote><blockquote><blockquote>
<a href = "http://www.usf.edu/"><img border = 0 width = 312
height = 33 src = "logo.gif" alt = "USF"></a>
<br clear = left><img align = left src = "imgsmall.gif"
width = "104" height = "104" alt = "Description">
<font size = "+2">[Firstname Lastname]</font>
<p>
<font size = "+1"><a href = "http://URL of Home Depart-
ment">Department of [Name]</a><p>
<a href = "http://URL of Home College">College of
[Name]</a>
</font>
<br clear = left>
<p>
<table cellpadding = 0 width = 75%>
<tr>
<td align = left>[Office location]
<td align = left>[Office hours]
<tr>
<td align = left>Campus Mail Code:[code]
<td align = left>E-Mail: [e-mail address]
<tr>
<td align = left>Voice Mail: [phone number]
<td align = left>FAX: [FAX number]
</table>
<dl>
<dt><b>Instruction</b>
<dd><i>Highlights:</i>
<a href = "http://URL of description document">[Course
1]</a> and
<a href = "http://URL of description document">[Course
2]</a>
<p>
<dt><b>Research</b>
```

```
<dd><i>Highlights:</i>
<a href = "http://URL of description document">[Topic
1]</a> and
<a href = "http://URL of description document">[Topic
2]</a> and
<a href = "http://URL of description document">[Topic
3]</a>
<p>
<dt><b>Publications and Presentations</b>
<dd><i>Highlights:</i>
<a href = "http://URL of description document">Current
Activities</a> and
<a href = "http://URL of description document">Curriculum
Vitae</a>
<p>
<dt><b>General Information</b>
<dd><i>Highlights:</i>
<a href = "http://URL of description document">Links of
special interest</a>
</dl>
</blockquote></blockquote></blockquote>
<center><a href = "/cgi-bin/imagemap/barusf"><img width =
"419" height = "47" src = "barusf.gif" ISMAP border = 0
alt = "USF Bar"></a><br>
<font size = "-1">
<i>Please direct questions to <a href = "mailto:e-mail ad-
dress of owner">e-mail address of owner</a></i><br>
Last Updated July 1, 1996<br>

Copyright & copy; 1996, [Name of Professor]
</font></center>
</BODY></HTML>
```

Notice that the author of this page placed certain notes within the HTML tagging to provide additional information to the person using this template to create their own page. Those comments are set off from the standard HTML by the use of <! — at the beginning and — > at the end.

Step Three: talk to your intranet committee

The decisions you make about your site's look and feel are among the most important you will make as you put together your intranet project. But before you get into any substantive conversations with your steering committee about the actual site style issues, you should answer this question: How restrictive do we want to be with our style guide? There are several factors to consider as you try to come up with an answer that fits your organization.

Do we want guidelines or rules?
How restrictive are your other communication guidelines? Are there extremely creative people throughout the organization who are capable of producing well-designed and attractive pages? If someone really likes green and red together, is that okay? There is a fine line between dictating a very narrow style to maintain the appearance of the site and inhibiting creativity — and enthusiasm among your information providers. Be very careful where you draw your line.

What is the approval process?
You will probably want to establish two separate and distinct approval process cycles — one for content and one for style. The content cycle will normally track through the individual department or group posting the information. It is more about appropriateness and security than it is about style of writing. Once this content review is complete, the information can be massaged into the site style in any number of ways.

Who monitors continuing inputs?
As your site grows and expands to new information providers, how will you ensure that the initial energy to produce a stylistically coherent site carries over to new content and content areas? Many organizations have formed committees that exist to provide the tactical review necessary. These committees should be made up of representatives from departments with content areas on the site. Subgroups can be established to review the writing and graphics. This takes a great burden off the Webmaster who must usually be occupied with daily site administrative duties.

When do we consider changing the existing look and feel?
Just as with printed materials that represent your company, your intranet should be examined periodically. Changes — even cosmetic — can do much to ensure that users will visit the site more often. Smart Webmasters with limited resources find ways to change their sites a little at a time. As new content areas are added, their style and appearance may be different enough to be distinctive but similar enough to belong to the style family. Changing one area at a time by adding new navigation elements or other graphics is a good way to keep your site fresh and new looking. The rule of thumb is this: change something on the site every day, preferably something prominent on the home page; add new content or refit an existing section every month; make significant look and feel changes twice a year.

The Three-Phase Approach to Site Style

As your intranet project unfolds and begins to involve a wider and wider circle of information providers, you will likely find that your contributors fall into three fairly well-defined groups according to their knowledge of and concern for HTML publishing.

Beginners (or *"Here's my stuff, you do it"*) Group

You will probably find that this is the largest of the three groups. These are the people who have either been assigned the task of posting information to the intranet by someone else, or who are much too busy to bother with the issues of converting traditional content to the intranet. In other words, they don't know and don't care to know how the process works. For this group you need to consider a process into which they can toss their content, walk away, and see a finished product some time in the future. The don't necessarily want to attend any HTML authoring classes offered by the organization. They don't care that most text applications now have HTML converters built in. They don't want to hear how easy it is to create compelling online pages. Simply, they want you to do it.

To meet the needs of this group you must identify resources (internal or external) who can provide one-stop, full-service support. In many ways, this is the easiest group to work with because you will probably eliminate some of the style issue debates that are unavoidable with more knowledgeable groups. You will find that their key motivation is to complete a task within the guidelines you have created for the project. They are most likely to have the least "hands-on" contact with the project after they hand it off to you or your creative resources.

```
Bottom line: be ready with a process and identified resources
capable of handling the potential onslaught of intranet pro-
duction requests.
```

Intermediate (or *"I can learn to do this with some help"*) Group

Proceed cautiously. This group is the most dangerous group you will encounter in your intranet project. You never know where they will appear, or from what department or professional discipline. But one thing is sure — they know just enough about the online world to be dangerous. They know that GIF is not a brand of peanut butter and JPEG is not a place to hang tools in the garage. They're pretty sure they could become very proficient with this online publishing game with enough practice. The problem is they want to practice with your system.

There is a lot to online publishing that isn't readily apparent to the casual observer. Issues such as graphics file size and type; server issues with file naming; site back end structure issues; and network issues can cause a host of problems if not properly managed. Simple things like whether the server limits file names to eight characters or is case sensitive, can cause links to break or prevent files from being served.

For this group you want to provide lots of coaching and support documents. Many intranets publish their style standards online as part of the intranet so all information providers have ready access to them. Many organizations sponsor seminars and workshops about online publishing issues. To be most effective the content of these sessions should be specific to the organization's intranet. General sessions that cover a wide gamut of HTML issues tend to be less effective because of the sheer volume of information they must cover. Provide detailed instructions about the specific requirements associated with your intranet. If these hardy souls want to cover the HTML waterfront, they can do that through a variety of publications and Websites. Like most "just in time" training you will get the maximum benefit by offering the specific tools your information providers will need to create pages for your intranet tomorrow. Making these tools readily available online as part of your intranet will help these "dangerous minds" become productive contributors to your intranet project.

You may also discover that certain members from this group go on to become HTML gurus within your organization and help you spread the word about the intranet.

Advanced (or *"Just Show Me the Roadmap"*) Group

Every organization has some. These are the people who are running their own personal Website from their PC in the garage. They may be more fluent with online publishing than any member of your staff. Your challenge is to channel their knowledge and energy into productive work. This group will need little handholding. For them, a simple set of style requirements will suffice. They will probably create their own compelling graphics — properly formatted for online delivery. For this group you may want to post a special, high-tech area on your site that explains your back-end architecture, naming convention, file format preferences, table or frames preferences, etc.

They will be able to figure the rest of it out without a lot of effort on your part.

One word of warning. This group may want to have direct access to the live server to post their own pages. Resist that. Typically, only one person — usually the Webmaster — is authorized to "make live" portions of the site. A lot of things can happen when multiple users are allowed into the live site back-end — and most of them are bad. Many file names within the site are the same or similar. Existing files can be inadvertently overwritten by new files. Most intranets have a separate server set up as a testbed, or sandbox server. All files are posted here before they are moved to the live server. All server architecture and software is identical to the live server. Seeing their completed work on the sandbox server is usually enough for these power users. When they are satisfied with their sections, the Webmaster makes a final check and moves the files to the live server.

The Limitations of Hypertext Markup Language (HTML)

Style

HTML is not a very robust publishing language. Its strength is in its ability to "link" elements to other HTML elements, making navigation simple and intuitive. HTML was created to make "cross platform" (similar displays on PCs, Macs, and UNIX computers) publishing a possibility. And as with most things that try to be versatile, they must sacrifice some capabilities to do it. So it is with HTML.

Print vs. Online

Print designers will find HTML stifling. Visions of full-page (or screen) graphics are wiped out by file-size limitations. Elements cannot overlap. Text size and font choices are limited, although getting better with newer browser versions.

Other online authoring languages (Sun's Java) and tools (Macromedia's Shockwave) are adding new design possibilities to intranet creation, but basic HTML — and its design limitations — will be the standard for online publishing for the immediate future. So rather than curse the HTML darkness there are ways to light a few candles.

Networks

In many cases, intranets are going to ride over networks (Local Area Networks or LANs) created for other purposes. These LANs, like pipes, can handle a limited volume (bandwidth) of information flow. Your intranet operates as a client-server system. Simply, that means that your users (clients) request information in the form of files from the system server where these files are stored. When the client request is received, the server locates the requested files (as indicated on the host HTML document.

Download Time

As you think about the limitations of HTML, one of your overriding concerns needs to be download time. People today, including your users, are used to instant gratification. When they turn their television on at home, they get an instant picture and sound. They can watch an athletic event taking place live thousands of miles away, and yet they see and hear everything just as though they were in the stands. That's because your television system at home has much more speed and capacity than your LAN at work. They are two different species.

One of the important things to keep in mind when designing your intranet is how long it will take your users to download the graphics, text and other media types. The amount of time that it takes to download images or text from your HTTP/web server is determined by the size of the file you are downloading, the bandwidth of the network, the speed of your web server. Keep this in mind when you are designing the use of graphic images in your content. Smaller files load much faster and will therefore allow your users to view your content faster.

```
Nothing will turn off a user faster than waiting minutes for
a file to download on their computer screen — especially if
the file does not add significantly to the impact of the
experience.
```

Sure, we all love pretty graphics and catchy animation and video. But we must also remember that this intranet is intended as an informational medium. That's not to say that pretty graphics and things that move have no place. It's simply a matter of allocation of scarce resources. You, as the intranet creator, need to recognize your network bandwidth as a scarce and absolutely critical resource that must be guarded at all costs. A short chat with your network administrator will point out the potential problems with an overloaded network. Have you ever heard the phrase, "The network is down"?

Text files are tiny. Moving even large quantities of text over your LAN will rarely clog up the pipes or slow down the flow.

Graphics File Sizes

It's the graphics that cause problems. When creative people get involved in technology, things start to happen. They don't readily accept artistic limitations. They want to know why they can't send pictures and illustrations over the intranet. Actually, in the larger world of the Internet, the desire to send and receive graphics led to the development of the World Wide Web (WWW). From humble beginnings in the 1990s, the Web has evolved into a media-rich environment, full of video and virtual reality, and sound and games…if you don't mind the wait. This maddening, frustrating time delay has caused many to rename the World Wide Web, the World Wide Wait!

As file sizes continue to increase, the situation will only get worse until a wideband solution — like cable modems using coaxial or fiber optic cable with much higher bandwidth — comes along.

Until there is a technological cure for clogged pipes, you will have to find other ways to create compelling content within small files. This is not as difficult as it sounds. This topic is covered in some detail later in the book, but here are some basic ground rules that will allow you to pack as much information as possible into the smallest possible package.

1. Use the correct graphic compression format. (GIF) created by CompuServe in 1987
    The Graphic Inline Format is an efficient and universally supported file format for online use.
    Joint Photographic Experts Group (JPEG) is the preferred compression algorithm for continuous tone images — photos and tone illustrations. JPEGs (or JPGs) provide maximum image quality with minimum file sizes.
2. Size the graphics appropriately.
    If the finished size for the on-screen graphic is 350 pixels wide by 60 pixels high, the GIF or JPG file should be created and saved to that exact dimension. This creates the smallest file size possible and eliminates the need for the user's browser to fit a larger graphic into a smaller screen size.

Site Attitude

It has been described in various terms, but the personality of an Internet or intranet site can best be described by the word attitude. In most cases, the personality of the site closely parallels the personality of the organization it represents. HotWired **(www.hotwired.com)** looks a lot like its magazine parent, *Wired,* while **(www.wsj.com)** looks a lot like its newspaper parent, the *Wall Street Journal.* This is the intentional act of online designers who have spent a lot of time and effort thinking through the "personality" issues involved with creating a digital publishing identity for their parent owners.

So it is with your intranet. Assigning it an online identity is every bit as involved a process as creating a new corporate identity for the larger organization.

What is the first impression you want your user to have when they log onto your intranet home page? Should it be friendly and welcoming? Or maybe formal? Does it take itself seriously or have fun with itself?

This site uses a "funhouse" metaphor to create a very informal, fun attitude for the site. This is the home page for an advertising agency (FKQ in Clearwater, FL), so a display of maximum creativity was a must for the site designer.

Attitude is one of the first design issues you need to resolve. It affects all of the design decisions that come later. As with most issues related to your intranet project, it is a good idea to involve a group of people who each have a vested interest in the success of the project.

Designing Your Intranet

This funhouse theme is carried on throughout the site as demonstrated by this menu screen.

And, as with all effective communication, it's a very good idea to establish your intranet attitude based on your users. What kind of site will encourage them to visit and come back often? What kind of an attitude will make your users most comfortable? Will the site personality make sense to them and to the company at large? Of course the worse thing that can happen is to come up with a great personality for the site — and no one outside the creative group "gets it".

```
Another heads up. Humor is very difficult online. Many peo-
ple misinterpret is as irreverence, or worse. Approach humor
with caution. Test it out with a number of potential users
to get their reactions before incorporating it into the site
personality.
```

One large company decided to convene a committee of current and potential content providers to review a number of proposed metaphors and personalities. Each member of the group was able to comment on each proposal. Members were also able to combine components of each proposal to create hybrids. By keeping the number of options to just a few (no more than 3) and encouraging maximum interaction among committee members, the group was able to reach consensus in just two meetings. They decided on a combination of elements from the various proposals and decided that different areas within the site could reflect different personalities while keeping within the overall site attitude. This could be done by adhering to a rather irreverent writing style throughout the site while changing the graphical metaphor for each area.

Company XYZ decided on an office metaphor, naming the various site sections "Bulletin Board" (company announcements), "Water Cooler" (people news), and "Locker Room" (company sports news). The committee felt this gave employees a comfortable and familiar environment for this new media adventure.

Another company chose its business — aerospace — to emulate on its intranet site. "Countdown" is their weekly news events, "Booster" is their community activities section, and "Launching Pad" is where new jobs are posted.

Content Drives Style

Within the framework of what you have established as your site attitude, you will find lots of room to create variations on that theme for your major site areas. For example, Human Resources areas are likely to be much different from Finance and Accounting areas in content, style, and users. As with all good communication, try out your ideas with potential intranet users. Are your major sections named appropriately? Will people understand what they can find in a section called, "About Us"?

Make sure you spend adequate time on the selection and placement of content within the site. The Internet, in its brief life, has spawned a sort of *de facto* structure for online content. Certain online jargon and naming conventions have carried over into intranet development. And that's not all bad, since many of your primary intranet users will be well-versed in how the Internet is structured. To see how some of these elements fit into a typical intranet site, see Chapter 12.

Writing for Online Delivery

Good writing is good writing online. It is coherent, concise and interesting. But there are real differences in online writing that deserve mention here.

Information Date Stamping

It is always a good idea to attach a date to each content component within your site. It's good for two reasons. First, it lets your user know when that information was posted — sort of a freshness date on your milk carton. Second, it lets you know when something needs to be updated, replaced, or deleted. Many good Webmasters have used this date-stamping method to keep their sites constantly fresh so their users will want to stop by often so they don't miss anything new.

Online Linking

One great advantage of HyperText Markup Language (HTML) is in its ability to link words and other objects within the network — whether that network extends to your company walls or beyond to the wider Internet world. As you develop your intranet site you will discover a tendency to overuse linking within documents. Intranet newbies (beginners) are so taken with the notion that a hypertext link can connect to another document, a photo, an illustration, a movie or a sound, that they find reasons to have multiple links within all their documents. This can be confusing to the user because as they follow these links they are leaving the flow of your story or document to go somewhere else. Continuity suffers.

```
As content providers mature, they discover a delicate bal-
ance between too many and too few links. The general rule
of thumb is this: use links as you would use sidebars in a
newspaper or magazine article. Make sure the link adds sig-
nificantly to the content.
```

Keep It Short and Simple

In the online world, everything is connected to everything else, or so it seems. The trick to having compelling content is to treat your user with respect. As a publisher you must think about packaging content as well as generating it. A few short articles, each dealing with a major content point, are usually more effective than one longer article that tries to cover everything. Think of the browser window as a single text page. Make an attempt to keep each page's content within the confines of the window without the need for scrolling. Of course there will be times when important and connected content will not fit on a single page. Here you have two options. First, you can simply run the text (as long as it is) down the page and force the user to scroll down to read the whole thing. Or you can include a "next" navigation button at the bottom of the single-screen page linking it to another HTML document. Both are accepted. Both have advantages and disadvantages. Keeping all the text in one, long document can be simpler for the user since all they have to do is scroll down the page. Lots of scrolling, however, can become tiresome for the user.

Breaking up the text into smaller, screen-sized pages requires more navigation, but it eliminates the need for constant scrolling. The user gets the full view of all the page content within the default window.

The One-Voice Edit

Someone connected with the intranet project should have overall responsibility for the editing of all content placed on the site. This person should ensure that all site content adheres to the online writing style guide mentioned above. In large organizations it is not realistic to assume that everyone who has something to say on your intranet site will take the time to read and understand the style guide before submitting it for publication.

Intranet Content Providers

Let's talk again about the three, very distinct types of content providers you might encounter as you build and maintain your intranet: beginners, intermediate, and advanced.

Beginners

You can usually pick these people out by the glazed look in their eyes as they talk about their new intranet duties as a content provider. Their goal is to collect some things that already exist, write some new things, and hand off the whole package to someone else to make the conversion to HTML.

Intermediate

These folks are at least familiar with some of the nuances of online publishing. They may, in reality, think they know more than they actually know. Their desire is to use some tools you provide to them and try to create their own HTML pages.

Advanced

This group knows HTML. They will probably add some advanced technology touches you haven't even heard of yet. What they want is for you to set up the guardrails describing what they can and cannot do stylistically, and they are off.

How Restrictive Do You Want to Be?

Style is always a touchy question. It's touchy because many people think they have a flair for design and can create compelling works of art with little or no direction from you. If your intranet project follows true to form, you will begin to get "style challenges" right from the start. You will begin to field questions about horrid background and text colors, illegal usages of the corporate logo, huge files that cripple your network, and the like.

When these questions and challenges come (and they will come), make sure you have consensus among your intranet committee about style issues.

You might take a clue from your corporate identity guidelines (if you have a set). In some companies, these documents are several hundred pages thick and address such trivial issues as how letters must be folded and inserted into envelopes. Other companies manage to survive nicely with a few rules and regulations dealing with such broad issues as treatment of the corporate logo and trademarks.

Creating HTML templates for your site can be an involved proposition, depending on how "automatic" you want the templates to be — and who will be using them. Your beginners probably won't pay much attention to your templates one way or the other. Remember, they want to hand off their content to someone else. Most newbies will not get very involved in the design process. Some, however, will want some creative input, and they should be encouraged to give it. Your content providers form the backbone of what makes your intranet interesting and valuable to your users. If, by giving them some amount of artistic control over their work, you can motivate them to become key contributors, that makes a good deal for everyone. The key is to create a set of standards that are firm enough to provide recognizable consistency in the site design while remaining flexible enough to encourage experimentation and innovation.

Your intermediate-level content providers will probably welcome the use of any automated system you can provide for them. They will learn to create compelling intranet pages with just a bit of hand-holding and direction from you and the intranet committee.

Your advanced content providers will probably only need you to point them in the right direction, tell them how far out they can go, stand back and let them go. They will probably push the technology window as well, trying Java or Shockwave or other online innovations long before they are commonplace.

```
One word of advice: you don't want to restrict these power
users without good cause. You and your committee should have
thought through some of the content and technical issues be-
fore allowing content providers to post new information on
the intranet.
```

For example, will your site encourage or allow the use of frames, or Java? Rest assured that as each new technology innovation hits the World Wide Web, your more advanced content providers will want to add them to their intranet sections. When that happens you should be ready with an answer about whether or not your system can handle it.

If you live in the online world, all of your operating instructions should be kept online. This is more than a philosophical decision. Make no mistake about it, you and your intranet project will substantially affect the ways in which your organization operates in the future. Changes of this magnitude do not happen easily. You, as intranet guru, must embrace the new technology fully and completely, never looking back to the way things were. This may seem extreme, but when you are trying to get people to make fundamental changes in the way they communicate, you must force-feed them the new technology. The bottom line — don't publish your intranet design and development documents in printed form. Your content providers must begin to learn the nuances of Internet-based technology to become effective contributors to your intranet site. Forcing them the use the intranet site in this way will do much toward convincing them that online publishing is a powerful way to communicate information.

Establishing an Online Style Guide

Your style guide will most likely be the result of a consensus-building process over several months. Style is one of those issues that almost everyone has strong feelings (or at least opinions) about. Just as with print publications, online style ranges from plain gray backgrounds with HTML text only to elaborate online pages with compelling graphics, animations, sound, and more.

In the process of defining your intranet style, you might begin with some thumbnail sketches of possible page layouts to circulate among your staff, content providers and committees. You can begin the process with fairly rough pencil sketches just to collect reactions. As the process moves along, you will be able to refine the design and eventually find a style that fits the project.

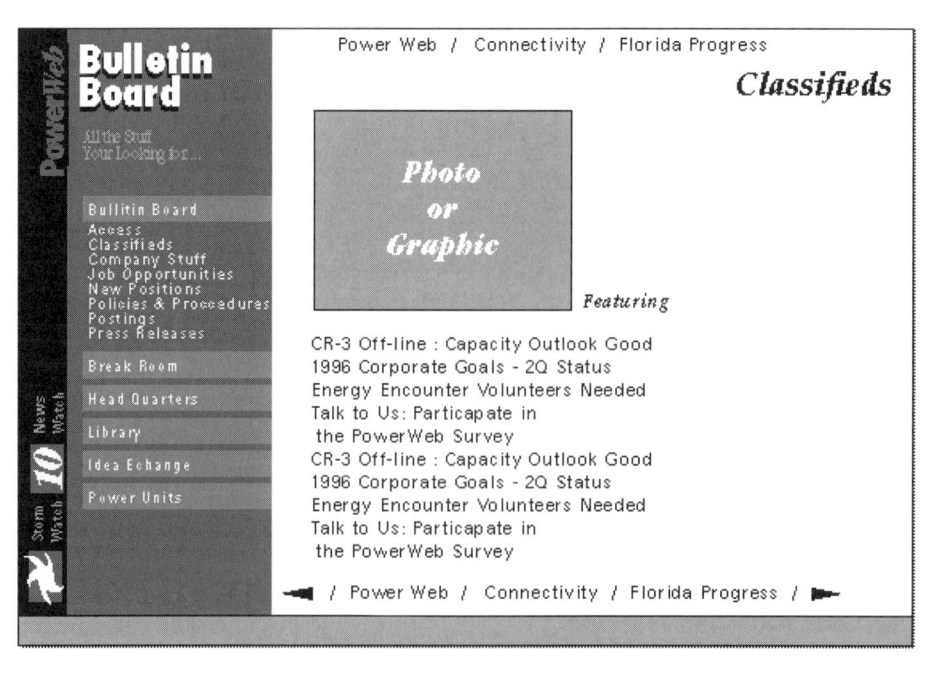

These are examples of rough sketches used to convey different styles based on the same key elements. These sketches were used by a design review committee at Florida Power Corporation to select an overall design for their intranet site. The final design was actually a combination of elements from several of these original sketches.

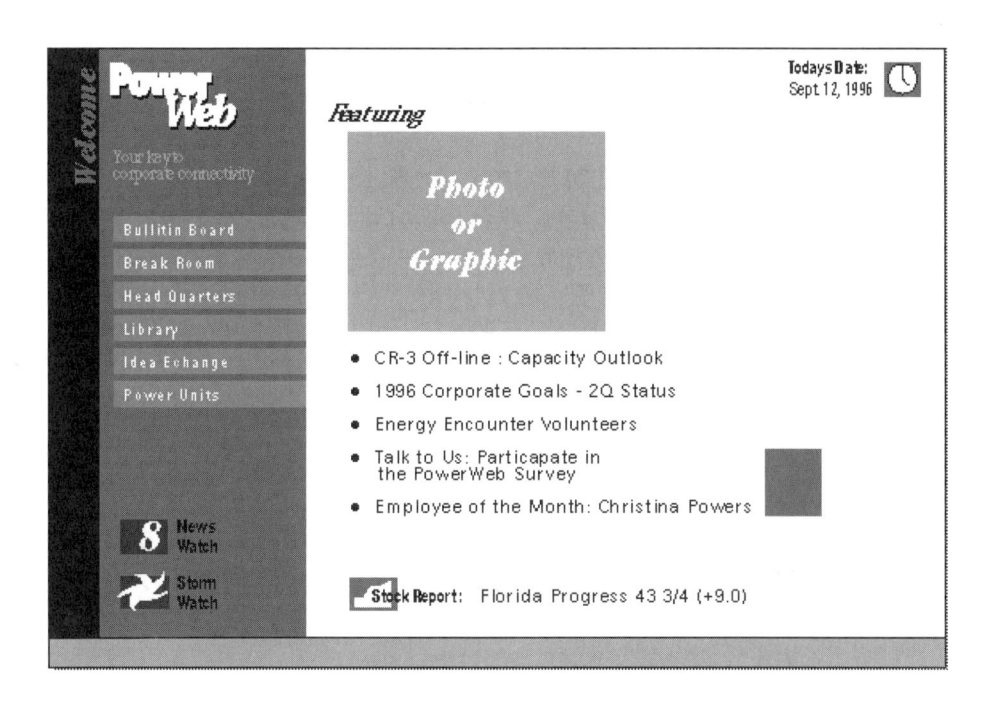

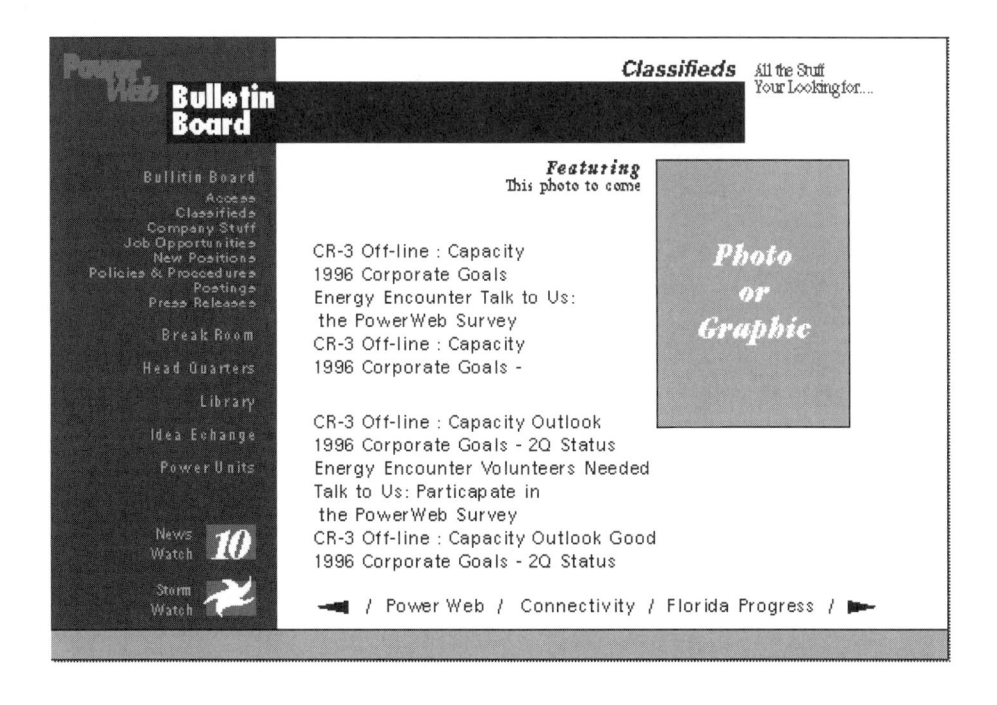

Designing Your Intranet 131

PowerWeb

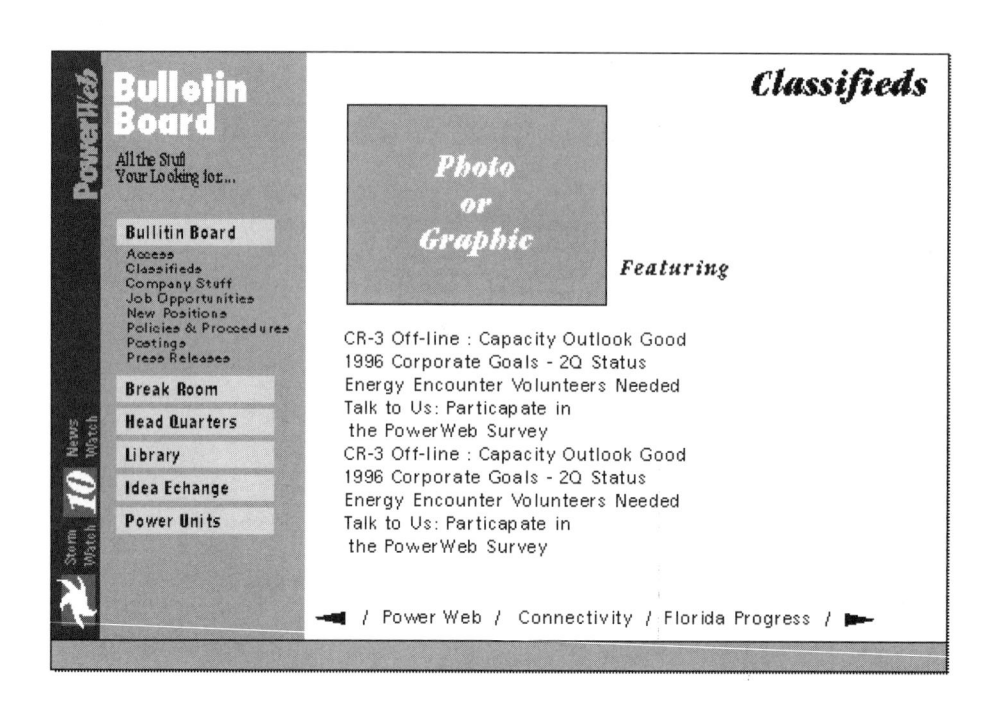

Bulletin Board
All the Stuff You're Looking for...

Bullitin Board
 Access
 Classifieds
 Company Stuff
 Job Opportunities
 New Positions
 Policies & Proceedures
 Postings
 Press Releases

Break Room

Head Quarters

Library

Idea Echange

Power Units

News Watch 10 Storm Watch

Photo or Graphic

Classifieds

Featuring

CR-3 Off-line : Capacity Outlook Good
1996 Corporate Goals - 2Q Status
Energy Encounter Volunteers Needed
Talk to Us: Particapate in
 the PowerWeb Survey
CR-3 Off-line : Capacity Outlook Good
1996 Corporate Goals - 2Q Status
Energy Encounter Volunteers Needed
Talk to Us: Particapate in
 the PowerWeb Survey

◀ / Power Web / Connectivity / Florida Progress / ▶

9

Building Your Intranet

This is where the rubber meets the road — where you get down to the nitty-gritty job of building something from nothing. For the most part, you are on your own, since there are few visible intranets to emulate. We have included a typical intranet in Chapter 12 and have detailed the Site Dynamics intranet in Chapter 13. These two examples will give you much information about what goes into a working intranet.

The other problem is that there are really no typical intranets anymore than there are typical companies that sponsor them. Intranets will typically reflect the nature and style of its host organization. And that is as it should be. Your intranet will be a unique creation of a long and complex process that can take anywhere from 90 days to a full year to go online.

This chapter deals with the next to last last phase of that development cycle — the actual production of your intranet site. It truly is a grand undertaking, involving every element of the company — from Human Resources to Accounting to Information Systems.

Building a Production Team

One of your greatest challenges will be assembling a group of people with the necessary technical and people skills to pull it off. The eternal staffing decision — staff from within the company or go outside — plays a big role in how your plan rolls out. You may find people within the company who have the required skills and background to create an intranet, but the odds are better you will have to look outside the company for at least one key position. Let's take a look at a typical basic intranet staff structure.

Intranet Manager
    Content Manager
        Writer
        Editor
        Designer
        Illustrator
    Technical Manager
        Webmaster
        Programmer
        System Administrator

Intranet Manager

This person assumes overall project responsibility for the intranet. Typical duties would include:

- Interface with organizational management
- Helping set strategic project direction
- Overall budget responsibility
- Staff supervision

Content Manager

On smaller staffs, this position can be eliminated in favor of the writer or editor. The content manager's duties would include:

- Overall responsibility for site look and feel and content
- Overall management of content team

Technical Manager

On smaller staffs this position can be eliminated in favor of the Webmaster or system administrator. Typical duties would include the following:

- Overall responsibility for the operation of the intranet
- Management of the technical team
- Technology selection and implementaation

Writer

On smaller staffs this position can be combined with the editor. The writer creates original content for the intranet site and rewrites existing content from other sources. Responsibilities normally include:

- heading up the editorial function
- interfacing with other content providers elsewhere in the company

Editor

This person ensures that content placed on the site is well written and appropriate for the medium.

Designer

On smaller staffs this position can be combined with the illustrator. This person has overall responsibility for the look and feel of the site. They must stary current with evolving online graphics technology and design issues.

Illustrator

This person creates the graphics that appear on the site. A thorough knowledge of digital graphics techniques and systems is a necessity.

Webmaster

This is the person most responsible for the successful operation of the intranet. On smaller staffs the Webmaster will also assume system administrator responsibilities. They may also be expected to know Common Gateway Interface (CGI) and PERL programming to add functionality to the intranet site. Responsibilites include continual maintenance of the site; adding new content and features.

Systems Administrator

Creating a working intranet involves an extensive knowledge of telecommunication, computers, networks and software issues. Intranets typically ride on existing Local Area Networks (LANs) or Wide Area Networks (WANs) so this person must understand the functionality of the underlying networks. They will also participate in system configuration decisions.

Programmer

This person will create all the custom programming necessary to add functionality to your intranet site. This includes writing software that connects HTML forms with databases.

Where Do You Look for Staff?

Larger companies have internal communication and MIS functions that may be home to people with the kinds of skills you need for your staff. People who are skilled at creating newsletter copy and graphics are usually good candidates for the content staff positions. The software tools they must use for the intranet are the same tools they are probably already using in their current assignments. Technical people with the necessary online skills might be found in any of a number of places within the organization. You might be surprised at how many people have an intense interest in the online world. They may already be hosting a Web site from their home. They may also be operating a guerrilla intranet within the company (with or without management's blessing). These people will probably seek you out when they find out the company is developing an intranet. Chances are they may volunteer to help whether or not they are recruited to join the official intranet staff.

On the other hand, you may end up going outside the company to find staff. Local advertising agencies, graphics production houses, prepress shops and the like are good hunting grounds for content talent. Don't overlook people operating existing Web sites or Internet Service or Presence Providers. This whole industry is very much in its infancy and finding good people may require a lot of time and effort on your part. Unless you are located in a small, rural area set apart from any major population center, you should be able to find qualified local people to fill out your staff.

Creative and Technical People *Can* Work Together

If tasks and responsibilities are well-defined, clearly understood and compatible, your staff should be able to build your intranet in perfect harmony. If, however, people are confused about roles and relationships, you are in trouble. At the *St. Petersburg Times*, the creative staff had an expression for the technical staff, "We won't write code if you don't write copy".

Such a clear delineation of responsibilites is absolutely vital to a successful project. It also creates a comfort zone for each staff member to offer criticism and comments to other staff members. For example, the entire staff should be called together when any substantive decisions are made — on either the content or technical side. That way, everyone is on the same page when the decisions are rolled out. No one is surprised by new decisions and everyone feels a sense of overall project ownership.

Obviously, the technical decisions will be made by the technical staff, but they should be made with the input and buy in from the creative staff. Since technology and creativity are so intertwined in an intranet project, no decision in either area is without impact on the other area. For example, the creative staff must clearly understand the limitations of the network before they decide on the use of large audio or video files on the intranet. The technical staff must understand the creative process so they can properly support the creative staff with test servers and the like.

There are certain issues, like the choice of server hardware and software on the technical side and the choice of graphics software on the creative side, that belong entirely on one side or the other. Even these issues, however, should be discussed, explained and shared with the entire group.

Building Your Intranet

> Your staff will become your primary evangelists within the company, spreading the word about this new intranet project and helping to recruit content providers, volunteer technologists, and users. You want to make sure that each staff member is aware of as much of the total project as is possible within the limits of time and resources.

If you can meld this group of diverse people into a dedicated, motivated production team, your job of creating a successful intranet is off to a great start.

Typical Relationship Issues

Creative people resist limits as a general matter. The process of creativity requires walking the path less travelled, thinking outside the box and breaking the boundaries of existing paradigms. Now you are going to take those freewheeling souls and put severe restrictions on what they can create online. They are probably not going to like that very much.

Your technical staff likes things orderly and predictable. Asking them to find new ways to do things to accommodate someone's creative urges will probably not sit well with them. They would just as soon operate a very stable, uninteresting site than take a chance on pushing the limits of technology with new graphics or multimedia plug-ins, like Macromedia's ShockWave and the like.

So there you sit, in the middle of a tug-of-war. One side is fighting to break out and the other fighting to hold them in. It can get to be a management challenge. Smart intranet project managers will understand the divergent natures at work on their staff and do all they can to find a comfortable middle ground that both sides can live with.

The Content Function

The content team is responsible for everything that appears on the intranet site, including what's in it and how it looks. It generates clear and concise text, appropriate and compelling graphics and multimedia content, and pleasing page layouts.

Successful intranet content people share these characteristics:

- *Creativity.* Above all else, your intranet must be an interesting place to visit — the first time and every time thereafter. It's a living project that demands high levels of creativity to withstand the test of time.
- *Discipline.* Creative people are wonderful, but your creative people need the self control necessary to live within the confines of existing technology. This discipline will help your creative staff find new ways to be creative.

- *Deadline driven.* Even more than traditional publications, your intranet is expected to be current. Your users will demand new content and frequent updates online. On-line time is measured in minutes and hours, not days and weeks.
- *Multi-tasking capable.* These highly creative people must keep multiple projects and tasks moving forward simultaneously. The online world does not permit the luxury of working on one project at a time through to completion.
- *Flexible.* The online world moves in fits and starts. New technology arrives on the scene almost daily. New possibilities render yesterday's ideas obsolete. The staff must learn to embrace change as a primary motivator and use it to move forward.

What Is Effective Online Content?

There is no single answer to this question because every online situation is different. A successful intranet project is the result of an orderly process that begins with a clear definition of project goals. Your intranet goals will help shape your intranet content.

Types of Information

Information can be defined as a collection of facts and data. In the online world, we would add one more element to that definition — context. On-line information, to be most effective, must be molded and shaped into a usable form by your content staff. One of the most frequent criticisms of the World Wide Web is that there is a ton of information out there but users cannot find it. One reason for that is the nature of the Web itself. It is made up of hundreds if not thousands of small groups who share one or more special interests. It is a diverse community of information seekers who have little in common except their browsers.

```
Your intranet should be much different from the larger on-
line world. First, all your users have one very important
characteristic in common — they all work for, or with, your
company or organization. They may be as varied in interests
as the wider online community, but their affiliation with
your company or organization represents a powerful unifying
element that can help you define your intranet content.
```

Information can be divided up into two categories — current and archival.

Current Information

Current information is anything that has a measurable shelf-life and represents the most recent facts and data available on a certain topic. As soon as newer information is available, current information becomes archival information.

Archival Information

Your ability to store huge amounts of archival information is one of the most valuable characteristics of your intranet project. Digital storage space is relatively inexpensive and text files are very small to begin with. A well designed intranet provides its users with a virtually limitless storehouse of valuable information. And why not? Information used in last year's proposal still has value to this year's proposal writers. Historical trends take on new life when the original documents are available at the click of a mouse.

General Information

Virtually everyone in the organization needs certain types of information, like vacation policy, benefits information and company goals. Much of this information has a relatively long shelf-life and will come from the traditional human resources function. Other functional areas within the organization also have information of interest to all users. Monthly status reports, program progress reports, quality and safety information are examples of these. Anything that would normally find its way onto a general employee newsletter is usually good general content for your intranet.

Special Interest Information

Certain users need information in the conduct of their specific jobs. This could include everything from assembly plans to hazardous materials handling guidelines. Special interest information is usually placed in the open, unsecure areas of the intranet unless there is something sensitive or proprietary about the content. This way, those with only a passing interest in the information can find it easily. And frequent users are not bothered with the requirement to enter a password or user ID each time they visit. Much of this information will come from your group of content providers, each representing a major segment of your user population.

Individual Information

You can also design your intranet to contain information pertaining to one individual user. For example, you can design a forms page that will allow individuals to check on their retirement savings account balance or the number of unused vacation days left in the year. Obviously, this information must be kept highly secure due to its sensitive and personal nature. You may also allow individual users to create their own intranet pages on your site. This practice can get unwieldy, as many of your users will want to take advantage of the offer, and many will have little or no skills required to produce a compelling online page. They may also have some pretty wild ideas about design and content that may run counter to your guidelines. The rewards, however, of having a host of individuals contributing information to your intranet will probably outweigh any potential problems along the way.

Where Do You Find Intranet Content?

As you begin your intranet production phase, you will find that much of the information you want to include falls into two major categories — electronic files and everything else. Let's begin with the easy one first.

Electronic files. If your organization has been computer literate for some time, you may find that much of the information it generates is stored in electronic format. It is either stored in a central storage archive, on individual work stations, or on storage media like floppy disks, Zip drives, optical drives, or CD-ROMs. Finding the information you want in electronic form dramatically reduces the amount of work required to place that content on your intranet.

Manual sources. Much of what you want will not be available electronically. Graphics and photos, especially, because of their large file sizes, may only be available in their original format. These manual sources must be converted to electronic files to ride on your intranet.

Translation Process

Text

Text can be scanned using any of a number of commercially available text scanning applications generally referred to as Optical Character Scanners (OCS). The quality of the original document (type font, size, physical condition), determines the quality of the OCS scan. Small type in non-standard fonts do not translate well. Most OCS software will substitute a "best guess" for characters they do not recognize, leading to some very interesting reading in many cases. You may also decide to re-enter the text from existing manual documents into word processing software applications. Even the most skilled keyboard wizards are prone to some errors, especially if they are translating difficult or alien terminology (often the case with specialized content). Both these techniques are likely to introduce errors. Both are realtively slow and very labor intensive.

Graphics and Photos

In most cases, these elements are only going to be available in hard copy. In fact, you may find it difficult to find the original copies and be forced to use copies printed for another purpose — newsletters, brochures, etc. Converting graphics for online use is much more daunting than working with text.

Printed graphics are usually produced in very high resolution (fine line screen) to preserve as much of the original quality as possible. The higher the resolution, the finer the line screen, the better the final product looks on paper. Your computer CRT screen is another matter. It operates at a fixed resolution of 72 dots per inch (DPI). That's it. No more is possible.

For that reason, on-screen graphics should be saved as 72 DPI files in either Graphic Inline Format (GIF) or Joint Photographic Experts Guild (JPEG) formats. Both these formats use compression to reduce the file size.

GIF compression is better suited to line graphics with few if any continuous tones. Logos and icons are good examples of line graphics. JPEG compression is better suited to photos or tone illustrations using lots of blended colors.

> ```
> Converting manual content into electronic form can repre-
> sent a significant investment in time and resources for your
> intranet project. Make sure you plan enough time in the de-
> velopment cycle to accommodate it.
> ```

Typical Development Work Flow

Whether you decide to build your own intranet or have someone else build it for you, it is a good idea to understand the process by which content becomes online content. We will look at each function independently.

Surveying

What is out there? What do we want to include in our intranet site? Where does the information exist? Who can help us find it? All these questions must be answered in order to build a content pursuit plan for your project.

Mining

Also called "filling the shoebox." Once you have identified target topics for your intranet, your content team must survey the organization to determine what is out there and in what form. This requires a lot of leg work, phone calls, and personal conversations. The person who does the surveying should have some overall understanding of existing organizational communication structures. Many times, the job involved going through stacks of old documents, shelves of policy manuals, and file cabinets of maps and layouts.

Translating

Here's where the real manual labor comes into your project, with lots of scanning, keyboarding and manipulating. Glossy 8 × 10 inch photos must be scanned, color corrected, and converted to small, JPEG images. Printed logos must be scanned, reduced, and saved as small GIF files. This process requires very sophisticated computer systems (hardware and software) and operators who are familiar with graphics software applications.

Converting

After all the electronic files have been created, they must be converted into appropriate Hypertext Markup Language (HTML) documents for use on your intranet. Here, the job gets a little bit easier. Many of the most recent versions of today's popular software packages (including Microsoft Office, Adobe Pagemaker, Quark XPress) include automatic HTML translators that are about 90% effective. This is a real help because people who are already familiar with these traditional software packages can now migrate into the online world through the use of plug-ins and translators built into the software. They don't need to learn any of the new HTML authoring applications currently flooding the marketplace. If, however, you want to create HTML documents from scratch, these HTML authoring applications make the task fairly routine.

Testing

When the HTML pages are complete, they must be tested in an HTTP (Hypertext Transfer Protocol) environment. In other words, they must be loaded onto a server with the appropriate server software and operating system. Normally there are two ways to handle this. New content can be loaded onto a "hidden" area of the live server. Since no one knows the location of the content on the site, no one but those testing it can access it. This system is effective in that it utilizes existing server systems for testing. It is perilous, though, because many things can happen (and most of them are bad) when the live server is used for any purpose other than supporting the live intranet site. The other way is to provide a test server that is identical in all ways to the live server. This method adds cost to your project, but it also preserves the integrity of your live server.

Posting

When the new content has been thoroughly tested — all the links work, all the graphics appear, all the text is proofed — it's show time. Posting new content to the intranet site is a very precise activity. For that reason, only the Webmaster, and a backup person, should have access to the live server.

The Technical Function

Chapter 5 provides a concise technical overview of an intranet site. This section deals with the people involved in the day-to-day operation of the intranet site.

Working with technical people, as in your IS shop, is quite different than working with Human Resources or Sales. By and large, technical people are problem/process oriented. You give them a problem to solve technically and they will do their best to solve it. When you need a database problem solved, this is a good type of person to have around. But if you make the assumption that an intranet is a communication tool, the problem solving can get in the way. An example is a form layout for data entry. If you let a programmer or technical person determine the layout it will be functional, simple, loaded with acronyms and nearly useless for normal people. Take that same layout and turn it over to a graphics artist and the end-users, the result will be a pleasing, easy to understand, useful tool. The difference is that technical people think in process and solutions, normal people think about outcomes. They leap over process and worry about will it work kind of issues. Rarely will you find a technical person that communicates well and can translate your ideas into tech talk for the problem/process people. Making the assumption that you don't have one of these people on your team we will turn our attention to working with ordinary technical folks.

What kind of person from the technical department do I need on my team for the intranet project? If you haven't asked that question yet you better think about it right now. Choosing a good technical person and working, communicating well with him or her is a critical success factor. Choose a super techie and while your site may run fast, it may never have the flexibility and ability to dynamically grow.

In general you really need two technical staff. One is the administrator and the other an analyst. While much of the talents overlap between the two positions the focus of each is quite different.

System Administrator

The administrator spends his or her time in maintenance of the site. This becomes essential right away and even more important as the site grows and becomes more dynamic. The administrator will become the key contact between the content developers, the analyst, and the users. He will also become the expert in HTML tagging. The role is part of the following communication model.

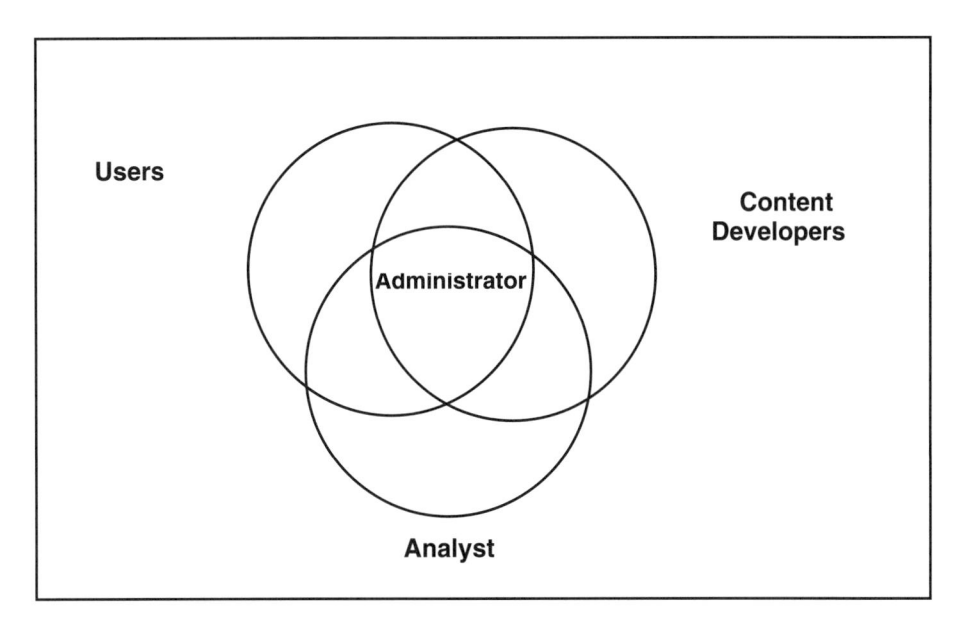

It will be the administrator's job to keep the intranet site updated, working, and most of all simple to maintain. It will be the administrator's task to develop the content/system plan in close coordination with the content developers. This plan should address site structure, file naming and other technical issues.

A firm built its intranet without a content/system plan. All components to the over two hundred pages were placed in a single directory. At last count there were nearly one thousand files in that directory. The administrator's ability to update and manage the site is hampered by the lack of file naming conventions as well as the basic limits on eight dot three file names. It is estimated that to break the sections into separate directories or to move them to another server would require each page to be manually updated.

The administrator also is the key contact for the users when questions arise on how to use the intranet site. The key talents for the administrator are good communication skills, (not too technical a speaker) an attention to details and a willingness to learn. This is a great entry level position and the type of people that fill it well are new college graduates from Computer Science departments.

Programmer

The second person of the technical team is the programmer. Their talents are crucial for developing automated services and integrating real-time information. This person will focus on connecting to company systems for real-time information and developing database systems for information automation.

A company that produced mounded plastics pieces judged their productivity by how many pieces were produced each day. Automated sensors made the count but the rest of the company never would hear of the count until the totals were posted the next day. A small application that took the totals each hour, posted them on the intranet site and graphed the historical results tied the entire company into the core business information. Now the administration and sales departments could share in the performance of the production department.

The analyst/integrator position is a senior one. It needs a person with both development and systems integration skills. Key experience in SQL database development, scripting or C programming makes the needed integrations easier. With a little luck you will find this talent in-house. Depending on how much integration you may plan for your intranet you may be able to use contract talent.

How do you communicate with technology people? If you haven't had the pleasure of working with your computer technology department, be prepared for some extra work. Remember that computer technology people are solution and process oriented. This means that as you talk about what you want to achieve with your intranet, the administrator and programmer are way out ahead of you coming up with solutions and processes for your site. Sounds good, but if you don't make your statements clear, the solutions very likely won't be the right ones. The key is to communicate with your administrator and analyst through example and prototype. Spend some time surfing the Web for examples of how you site should look and function. Capture the pages and URLs for the technology staff. Take your pencil and paper, or computer drawing program, and draw out the pages, flow, and overall look and feel of your site. Last, make up prototype pages to illustrate the functionality you are trying to achieve.

A local publishing firm wanted some circulation reports placed on its intranet. The reports were handed to the analyst and after a very hard effort the multi-column reports were squeezed onto very tightly packed pages. After viewing the pages, the management pointed out that they only wanted some summary information from the reports gathered on one single simple page.

From the example you can see that a prototype of the desired page would have saved everyone a lot of effort. Spend the time up front in the development phase to create the communication material for the technical staff.

Last, when technical staff tells you that something you ask for can't be done, what they are most likely saying is that what you are asking for can't be done they way you are asking. Take a moment to ask them for a solution and then be quiet. Given the opportunity to deliver a solution, your technical staff will often surprise you. Remember, they are the experts at process and solutions. Let them excel at their chosen field.

10

Marketing Your Intranet

Earlier in this book we indicated that intranets are not about technology, they are about people. Now, let's take that one step farther. Successful intranets are not about projects, they are about processes. Launching an intranet is a daunting task, filled with complex organizational issues. This chapter examines a critical process step in rolling out a successful intranet project — marketing the new product to your potential users.

If you build it, they may NOT come. That sounds ridiculous, doesn't it? After all the time, effort and resources required to develop this new communication medium, many Webmasters believe that everyone will flock to it and embrace it. That may not be the case.

Not Just Another Newsletter

One reason they may not embrace your new intranet is something called technophobia. This is not just another newsletter you are rolling out. This is a completely new way for people to share information. It represents a quantum leap in communication and requires a leap of faith to assume that its adoption will be easy. A large part of your planning process should be an education/promotion campaign designed to ease your company and its employees into this radical new era.

Within your organization you are likely to find very different levels of technical expertise among the various employees. Younger employees will be more likely to embrace new technology. Older employees may be another story. Knowledge workers will typically lead the charge to new technologies. Executives may get others to perform the more technical aspects of their jobs.

The publisher of a major business magazine does not own a computer. She doesn't have one on her desk at work or anywhere in her home. She has managed to survive and even thrive in this electronic age without being wired, connected or even digitized. Now she wants a Website for her magazine and she is being forced into the computer age in one giant leap.

At a major utility company, many of the senior management team are not computer literate. They simply do not have enough time in their professional lives to learn new ways of operating — and that includes the extensive use of personal computers. To some, the machines represent the new order of business, a clear threat to the old management styles. Many believe they can finish their careers before they are forced to learn the new technologies.

Whatever your unique organizational makeup is, you can be certain that your intranet project will not become successful without a major promotional effort — one that includes a healthy portion of education as well as hype.

Educating and Evangelizing

You may find that your entire organization is very well aware of the state of the Internet, of Hypertext Markup Language and the like. On the other hand, you may find a few people in your company that have not surfed the Web, gone online or even sent or received an e-mail. The first step in any educational project is to determine the knowledge level of the potential audience, and develop materials suited to that level.

You will most likely find a wide variety of online knowledge levels among your potential users. In fact, you may find certain pockets within your company that are very technologically backward. How many people in your company have PCs on their desks? How many use them in their everyday jobs? How many of those PCs are connected to a network? How many have access to the Internet?

These are all questions you should be able to answer before you begin to develop an educational program for your intranet project. As you survey your potential users about their knowledge levels, you may find that your users are divided into three distinct groups: Newbies, Surfers, and Power Users.

Newbies

The beginners could be your largest group, depending on how well your company has embraced new computer technologies. These are people who probably do not have a PC on their desk. Their jobs, up to this point, have not required their use. They may have a PC at home, but it is probably not online. They may know the basics of computer operation. They may use such general business applications as word processors and spreadsheets. They are totally dependent on their MIS support group for all their computing needs and problem solving. They probably know very little if anything about how a computer operates, and they frankly don't care.

An Approach

This group will be pivotal in the success of your intranet project. You must find a way to reach out to them and bring them gently into the digital world. It's been said that people don't know what they don't know. Your challenge here is to make them aware of what they don't know and give them a reason to want to learn it.

This would be an excellent group to invite to focus groups or brown-bag luncheons in which you present the latest online technologies. You might even show them a prototype of your intranet if it is sufficiently ready to show. A tour of WWW sites of particular interest to your company is another good educational tool. The most important thing to accomplish with the newbies is to open their eyes to what they have been missing.

You should remember, however, that this group may not have sufficient background knowledge to appreciate what you are showing them. If they are not familiar with computers at all, you may decide to begin their education with some basic computer operation instructions. Your MIS department professionals should be able to help you with this.

You should also be careful about creating unrealistic expectations among the newbies. There is usually a very good reason these people don't have computers sitting on their desks. In some cases, that is because someone has determined that they do not need a computer for their job. After all, a computer is a major expense for a company, and there are very few companies that provide PCs for every employee. Some of your newbies will never have a PC at their personal use. They may have to use one in their work group, or they may even have to go to the computer center or library. In any case, creating the need for these newbies to use your intranet as part of their daily work lives is a good first step. They will find a PC to use if their need is great enough.

You may also want to create a "User Guide" area on your intranet right from the launch. This area should contain a basic, step-by-step, assume the user knows nothing approach to understanding the online world. It should cover the basics of Hypertext Transfer Protocol (HTTP) and Hypertext Markup Language (HTML). There are a number of Websites that do a great job explaining these technologies. Having this user guide on your intranet site tells these Newbies that there is a place for them to go if they have questions about operating in the online world. It also tells them that they can find the help they need easily and quickly right on your intranet site. last, it tells them that you want them to be able to use this new technology and you have cared enough about them to make their experiences positive ones.

Surfers

These folks use computers routinely. Most will have a PC on their desk and another one at home. They may also have access to a portable system. They are familiar with computer operation, and may even feel comfortable loading a new operating system on their PC. They know how to use their CD-ROM drive and their modem. They probably have an America Online (AOL) account at home for e-mail and chat sessions. They may even venture onto the Internet with their browser software. They understand the concept of being "wired" and are comfortable with the online world. They probably own several CD-ROM titles, maybe even a CD-ROM encyclopedia their kids use at home for homework research. They have been to the White House Web site, know how to use Yahoo and AltaVista search sites, have downloaded the newest version of Netscape Communicator, Microsoft Internet Explorer, ShockWave and RealAudio plug-ins, read Wired Magazine, and have done an online search for their surname.

An Approach

Surfers are already way-cool dudes and dudettes. They will most likely welcome your intranet with a resounding, "What took you so long?" They will embrace this new medium and probably become its primary user group. For them, it will be enough to provide them with a good roadmap of your site content and great site navigation. Education with this group will be a two-way street right from the start. They will be able to offer you much in the way of suggestions about the site and its content. Make it easy for these people to give you their input. Placing automatic e-mail forms throughout the site will help. Remember to acknowledge feedback within 24 hours. You may also want to establish a forum or newsgroup on your site expressly to share ideas about the intranet project and making it better.

Power Users

Power users are also known as hackers, propeller-heads, techno-geeks. These are all appropriate terms for this small, but elite band of computer wizards. Most have multiple PCs, some of which they built from parts. They are familiar with computer operation to the point that they can reverse-engineer virtually any software to find out how it works. They keep up with the latest programming languages. They know Java has nothing to do with Colombian coffee. They read several hardware and software magazines regularly. They subscribe to dozens of online discussion groups and news groups. They may even be beta testers for new software applications. They long ago embraced the online world, and probably were close to charter members of CompuServe® (Sears and IBM's technology-savvy online service). They may have started their own Websites at home or they may be maintaining a guerrilla intranet operation at their desk for a closed circle of other power users. They know more about the online world than you or any member of your committee does.

An Approach

Hang onto your hat with these folks. They will probably push you from the start to include the most advanced technologies available — probably before you are ready to do that. Education with this group will probably revolve around why you can't do some of the things the Power Users want you to do. You may need to make them aware of network limitations that will prohibit you from including very large files (like QuickTime video or ShockWave) in your site. It is important to the success of your intranet project to include Power Users in every step of the process. They can act as advocates for this new technology throughout the company if they are involved. They can also act as inhibitors to your success if you exclude them. Your greatest challenge with Power Users is to reign in their enthusiasm for innovation.

Promotion

Quite separate from your need to educate the various groups of potential users is your need to spread the word about your intranet project to everyone. Many times, the project group gets so tied up with the actual development of the intranet site that they do not spend much time thinking about spreading the word.

It is always dangerous to assume that if you put a good product out on the streets that everyone will somehow know about it through some strange process of osmosis. Word of mouth will only carry your project so far. You should treat the launch of your intranet project as a major event in the company's history and give it the promotion due something of that magnitude.

Florida Power Corporation, which is headquartered in St. Petersburg, Florida, launched their intranet in mid-1996 amid considerable fanfare. Their internal communication department understood the value of a concerted promotional campaign and decided to introduce the "PowerWeb" in a big way.

They published a four-color, 8 page brochure and circulated it to all their employees. The brochure presents an overview of the entire PowerWeb project, operating instructions and an overview of site content.

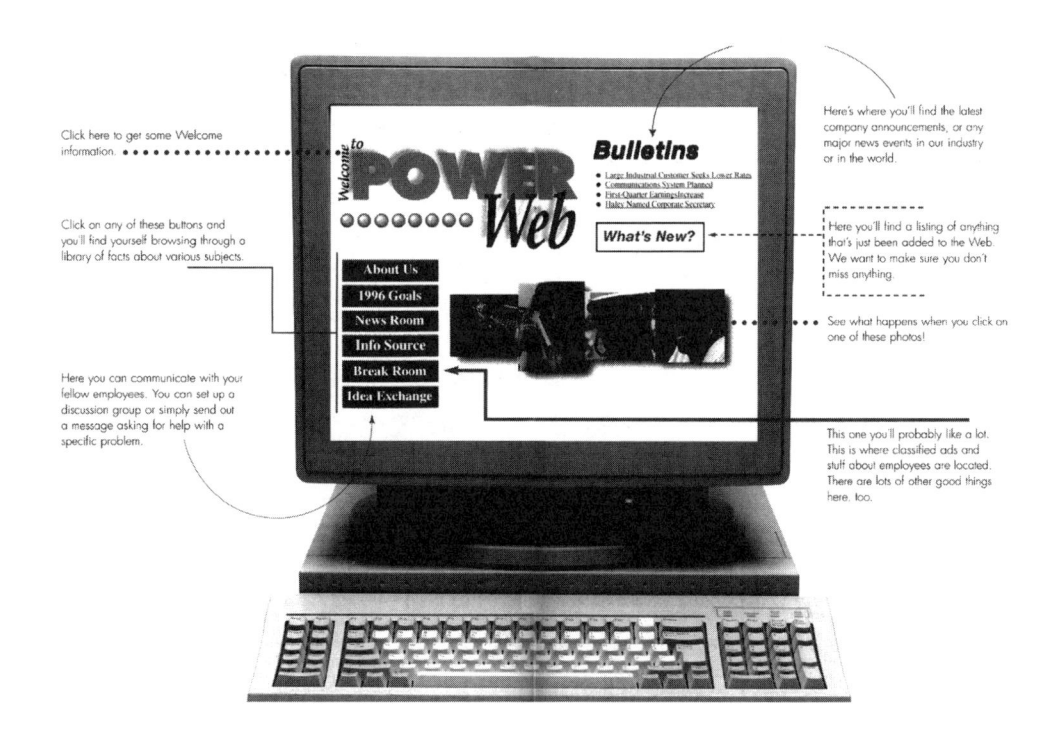

Creating a promotional brochure accomplishes several things. First, it presents the new medium in a form that is familiar and non-threatening to the potential Newbie user. Next, it demystifies the process by showing screen shots in the brochure. This gives the user a frame of reference when first venturing out onto the intranet site. Last, it demonstrates a high level of commitment to the project. Users will understand the time and resources that went into the development of the brochure and conclude that the intranet project is important to the overall company.

Florida Power also commissioned a video to be shown at staff meetings prior to the PowerWeb launch. The video features a cartoon character who walks users through the entire site while pointing out the major content areas and benefits to the user.

In addition to these two new communication pieces created especially for the introduction of the PowerWeb, Florida Power used its existing communication media to spread the PowerWeb word. They made extensive use of their employee newsletter, PowerLines, and their in-house, closed-circuit video network as the launch date approached.

The result of all this activity was an extremely successful launch. In fact, the launch was so successful that the Webmaster and his committees were beseiged with requests from several Florida Power departments to create their own content areas on the site. To date, four departments have added their content to the site and several more are in various stages of content preparation. Will Rodgers, Florida Power's Webmaster reports that the site gets an average of 700 users each day (out of a potential of 3,000 employees). These results were far beyond their expectations when the project began.

```
The bottom line is this — the initial success and acceptance
of your intranet will, in no small part, be due to the ad-
vance promotional efforts. Part of a successful intranet
launch is creating a sense of urgency and excitement among
the workforce in anticipation of this new medium.
```

11

Maintaining Your Intranet

Many Webmasters have much in common with first-time parents. There is a period of time when the idea of an intranet grows into a project plan and finally a project. All during this time, the Webmaster and the development group experience a wide range of emotions, from the sheer terror of creating something brand new from scratch, to the exhilaration of seeing ideas take shape on screen. All this preparation and planning lead up to the moment of birth — the official launch of the intranet. So, after all that time, the site is up and the Webmaster can light up a cigar and declare it a job well done.

That euphoria lasts about 10 seconds, though, as the Webmaster and the development committee realize that, like the new parents, their job is just beginning. Yes, bringing this creation to life was difficult. But in hindsight, that period will be remembered as the prelude to the real work of raising and rearing this new creation.

In other words, the real work has just begun.

Involving the Entire Organization

Other eyes in the company will now see your work. Many will feel compelled to tell you what you did wrong, or what you might change to improve it. Others will complain about transfer rates and traffic on the network. Your MIS people will face the reality of another system that needs constant vigilance. All those involved with the creation of the intranet must now assume a different role — growing and maintaining the site.

Every hand involved in the launch of the intranet should have a role in its evolution.

Management Information Systems (MIS)

The MIS group has just inherited another system that requires monitoring and maintenance. The planning group should decide the maintenance requirements for the site early on in the project planning cycle.

What happens if the server (the computer that is home to the intranet content) goes down?

If you begin to deliver mission-critical information over your intranet (and nowhere else) you may find any service interruption unacceptable. If, however, there are alternate sources for getting the same information out (e-mail, pages, faxes) you might be able to tolerate system outages for several hours.

Should someone constantly monitor the site for just such an eventuality?

Some companies have installed automatic monitoring systems that constantly check the server's status. If the server goes down, a technician is paged or the backup server is automatically engaged.

Should the system be monitored 24 hours per day and 7 days per week (commonly called 24/7 maintenance)?

If your intranet serves users across several shifts, you may want to consider 24.7 monitoring, especially if mission-critical information is hosted on the site. If, however, your company operates on a one-shift, five days per week schedule, 24/7 monitoring may be too much. Remember that any constant monitoring activity requires hardware and personnel, and those costs can add up quickly.

Will you need a separate "development server" for content providers to use as a staging area for their content?

Granting access to the "backend" of your live server to anyone other than the Webmaster and a small technical staff can be dangerous. If you have several people or groups who are building future content for your site it is a good idea to give them a developmental server to test their content before moving it to the live server. It's a good idea to limit access to the live server to the Webmaster and a small group of technical staff.

Strategy Committee

Whatever its name and makeup, the committee that sets the strategic direction for the intranet project must continue to be involved in the project after launch. Its on-going role should include creating a master plan for future site development. It is almost impossible for anyone to understand all the dynamics involved with moving an organization into the electronic publishing age. This committee is the sounding board for organizational feedback about the intranet project. As the intranet matures, this group should constantly reevaluate goals and direction.

One of their primary responsibilities is to meld this new communication medium into the existing organizational communication structure and methodology. The new intranet should not be created in a vacuum, as a separate entity from the other communication media. It should be fully integrated into a master communication plan so the role and scope of the intranet are known and understood within the larger context of organizational communication. This integration activity is not a one-shot project. For the intranet to assume its place in the organizational communication scheme of things, its role must be evaluated and adjusted. Just as the early founders of television could not possibly have seen the total impact this new medium would have on the world of communication, today's intranet pioneers cannot see how this new medium will affect their organizations. For that reason they must remain nimble and open to new directions and new horizons.

Ad Hoc Content Committee

These folks will play a critical role in the evolution of your project. Many organizations have adopted the traditional publishing model for membership on this committee. As departments or functional groups prepare to create a content area on the intranet, one individual is appointed as the "publisher" for that group and has overall responsibility for identifying, collecting and translating content into online form. These publishers should meet occasionally — once a week or twice a month to begin — to discuss their progress and projects.

A typical agenda for these ongoing meetings would include the following:

Introductions of all members
- New members joining the group get a snapshot of the group and the various parts of the organization represented there.

Updates on content projects
- Each member talks about their overall project, paying special attention to the project structure, budget and schedule.

Problems or roadblocks
- A reality check for everyone as common threads and similar issues begin to appear in a wide variety of projects. Special attention should be paid to how the project team intends to overcome the problems.

Technology issues
- Sharing new discoveries helps broaden the entire group's understanding.

Opening a "Tips and Tricks" area on the intranet for these technology issues will give the committee a real-time, all the time resource.

Improvement ideas
- This discussion should focus on general site improvement ideas based on feedback from users. These ideas and suggestions should be evaluated and prioritized so they become the basis for your future development plans.

Users

Your users will always be the best source of new ideas and content to keep your site fresh and alive. Give your users a variety of ways to provide you with feedback about the site.

E-mail

At a minimum you can place automated e-mail form links (called mailtos in Netscape) on each page within the site. These e-mails can be coded according to the page of origin so you (or whoever will review such input) will know the exact page the user was on when the message was sent. This will enable you to make a direct connection between the message and the content it refers to. It also makes it easier for the user to provide timely and precise feedback about selected content.

Online Discussions

These can take a variety of forms, ranging from threaded newsgroups to hosted chat sessions. The interactive nature of your intranet allows you to create places where your users can gather and talk about topics of interest to them. These discussions are usually ranked among the most popular features of Web sites and intranet sites. These discussions can provide you with invaluable information about your project, especially if they are set up to do just that.

```
Your users will appreciate a forum or threaded discussion
group focused on improvements to the intranet. In the be-
ginning, members of the development team can serve as forum
hosts or discussion leaders.
```

Automation

Even on small sites the maintenance task can become a real time hog. The Webmaster's day can become consumed easily with routine maintenance tasks. This can create a problem, especially on sites that are supported by very small staffs. The site must be kept fresh, and it also must grow and evolve. Minimizing the amount of time necessary for routine maintenance will allow for more time to be spent on the more productive tasks of growing and improving the site.

The first step in maintenance automation is to determine the shelf-life of all the content on the site. If, for example, you are posting weekly program updates, these need to be changed every week. Other content may not be so clear-cut. It is a good rule of thumb to date everything that goes up on the site. This is helpful for two reasons. First, it gives the user a sense of how useful information is by its age. Some information (like annual company goals) have a long shelf life and are still valuable 11 months after their initial posting. Other information (like stock prices) has an extremely limited usable life. Next, it gives you, the site maintenance crew, a heads-up when content becomes old and stale. Date stamps are a constant reminder that intranets should be alive and constantly evolving. If you look through your site and everything on it is months old, you have a very static site. If your users continue to visit your site and find nothing new on it, they will begin to wonder about the value of this new medium.

As you construct a site maintanance plan, make sure you understand all the content on the site and how often it should be updated. As you make these determinations, you will want to have your technical staff help coordinate an automation process. Simple Common Gateway Interface (CGI) scripts can be written to allow periodic updates for all kinds of site information. In many cases, this automation process is also helpful to the person or group that generates the information in the first place.

> Debra Wigle works in the contracts department of a major defense contractor. Her job is to collect program status reports for the government customer each month. Various functional groups within the contractor produce their own status reports. The Finance and Accounting report concentrates on the state of the program budget. The Engineering report focuses on the program's technical progress. In all, seven departments create independent reports that differ widely in content and format. Debra's job is to gather these reports in their various forms (some are in word processing documents, others in spreadsheets) and combine them into a unified, company-wide report back to the government customer. Recently Debra just made her job a lot easier. The contractor had just put up an intranet, and Debra realized its potential for making her job much easier. She worked with the Webmaster and her technical staff to create online forms to be used by all seven departments in submitting their monthly status reports. The forms include pop-up menus, check-boxes and radio buttons to make submission quicker, easier and more uniform. All responses are fed into a database where a new summary report is generated. The new process shaves days off the total time needed to generate the report. Since the input is stored in a program database, it can be used for other reports as well. Bottom line - the online process is quicker, easier and much more useful than its manual predecessor.

A few days spent analyzing the process of collecting and translating information can yield a system that streamlines and improves the entire process.

In 1993, the *St. Petersburg Times* decided to create an online version of its daily newspaper on the World Wide Web. It was one of the first newspapers to embrace full publishing on the Web. The prospect of posting the entire contents of the daily newspaper, including Saturdays and Sundays, became a serious challenge for the small staff (one illustrator, one editor and one Webmaster). They quickly discovered that they could not manually convert the content. From the start, their goal was to automate as much of the site content as was possible. Taking a cue from Access Atlanta, the *Atlanta Journal and Constitution's* online presence, the staff adopted the operating philosophy, "Don't touch content unless absolutely necessary."

John Buchenhorst, *The Times* Webmaster, who had come from the internal publishing group, was aware of the entire publishing process and was able to write CGI translators to automate fully the online conversion. Every morning, after the newspaper was on the press, the online department server received a complete electronic file of the newspaper. Within 15 minutes the entire file was converted into the online format and was ready for the Web.

Automating this daily process left the staff with full time and attention to devote to creating the special features of the site — like an area guide, local history, restaurant guide, The Florida Aquarium, and the St. Petersburg International Museum.

The payoff to the *Times* staff was substantial. They were able to accomplish a great deal with a very small staff. By automating the majority of the repetitive publishing function, they were able to create compelling, original online content unique to the Web site.

For you, automation can have the same effect. Handling routine documents takes time. As your site develops and matures, the use of routine documents will increase. Departments will find the need to post weekly progress reports, monthly quality reports, quarterly goals, daily status reports, etc.

An effective way to manage the problem is to go to the source and try to automate the entire process. If reports are being created manually, push to get them created in electronic form. If possible, automate the process by which you receive the document. In other words, if the document is being sent to an e-mail list, make sure you are on that list. Your technical staff should be able to create translation programs that automatically generate HTML pages from these routine documents, regardless of their format.

Your goal should be to automate as much routine content as possible, leaving you and your staff free to concentrate on other value-added site elements.

Provide Online Templates for Content Providers

Your automation process will be most productive if your technical staff is able to work directly with the content providers to produce online templates for their content.

At Kinetoscope, even though the staff is small, it was difficult for everyone to keep up with everyone else's goals and accomplishments. Early efforts to gather input and publish it on the company's intranet proved futile. There was simply too much to do in the days and weeks to squeeze in time to write a weekly goals summary. The intranet Webmaster, too, was very busy with expanding and updating the site. Enter the database team. They proposed creating a simple HTML form for updating goals that would streamline the process, and take the Webmaster out of the loop. It worked. Every Monday, the staff spends a few minutes updating their goals and reviewing the others' goals.

Maintaining Your Intranet

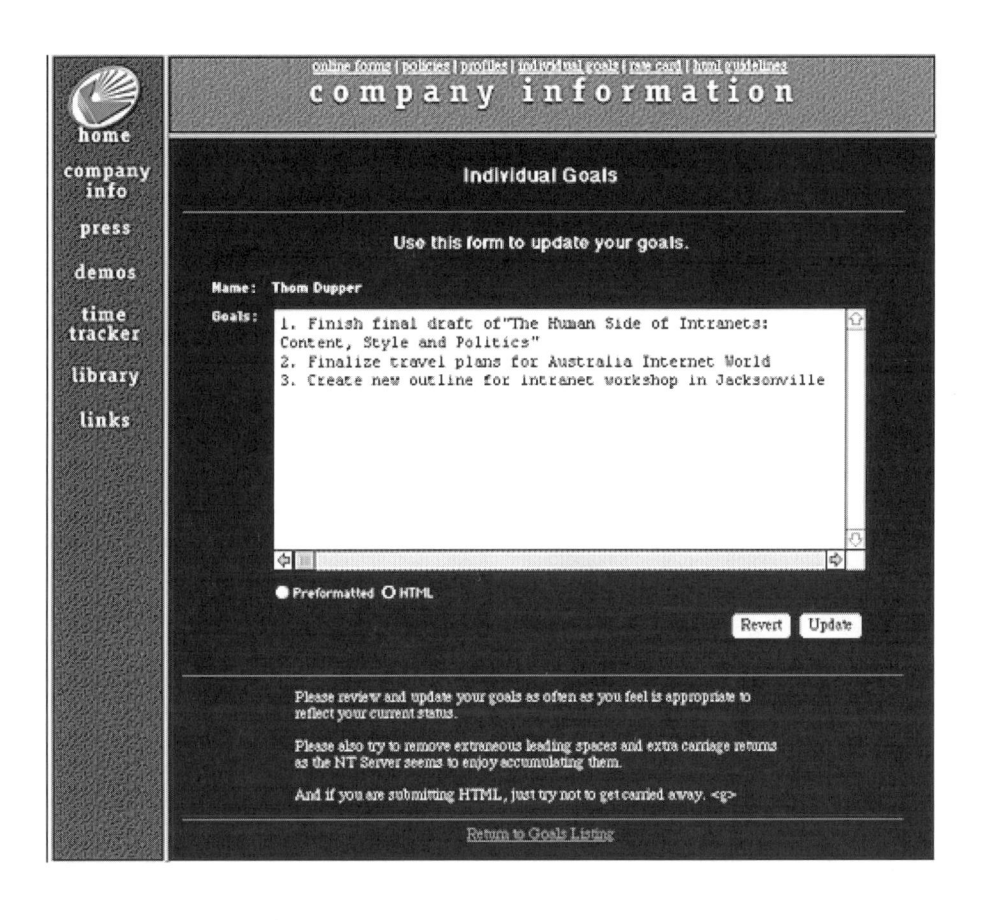

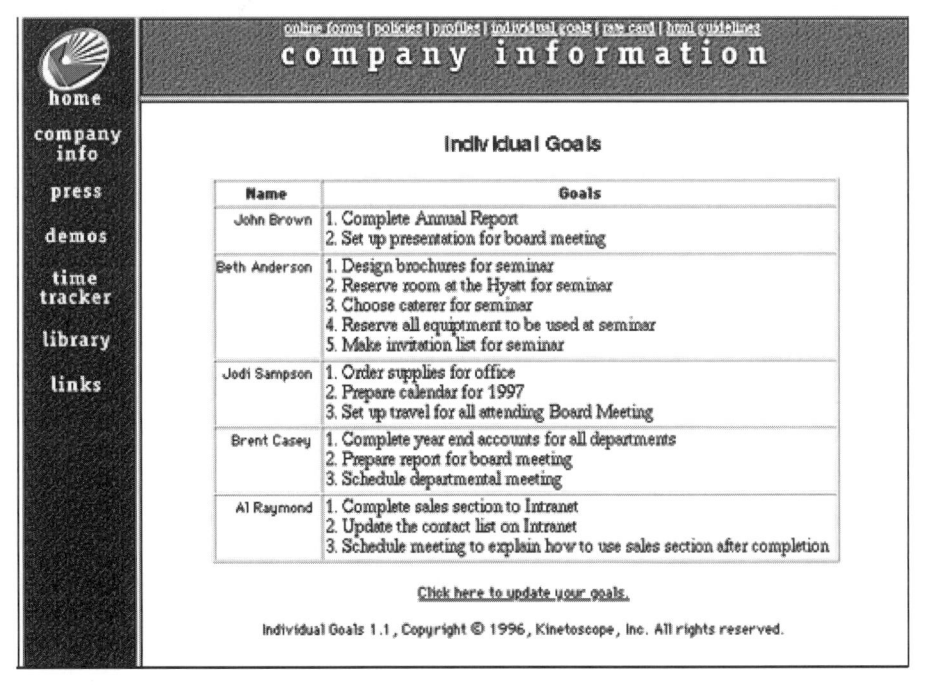

Repurpose Content From Other Online Sources

Many intranets are not connected to the larger Internet due to security concerns. This can be a problem because some users may be used to hopping all over the globe within their browsers. Restricting access to internal information in an intranet can be a little like handcuffing users and forcing them to stay within the company walls.

Many of your users may be used to checking real-time weather on the Web, or getting recent stock quotes, or making airline reservations online, or any of a number of other activities.

All, however, is not lost. Many intranets that are cut off from the larger world by security firewalls have found ways to bring outside information into their intranets.

Many of the general information sites (news, weather, sports, business news) allow intranets to take information from their Web sites and repost it on internal nets. As you pursue other external resources for content, remember that you have a captive audience within your company that most site hosts would be happy to reach with their information. Some corporate intranets have reached agreements with local television station or newspaper Web sites to mirror their content internally. This only makes sense because most sites on the WWW give their content away free anyway. Many have adopted the traditional media advertising model to raise revenue online. Adding more users through your intranet helps them claim more traffic and charge more for advertising on their sites.

This is a relatively simple process that can be accomplished easily by your technical staff.

Adding local news, weather, traffic reports and other information of interest to your users will give them added reasons to use your intranet. Just make sure you have written approval from the target site to mirror their content.

Keeping It Fresh

One of the early criticisms of the Web was that it was a mile wide and an inch deep. Another was that it was extremely static and boring.

The days of launching an online site and walking away from it are long gone. That has become the equivalent of showing a test pattern in the early days of television. Today's online users are sophisticated consumers of interactive information. They expect more than static pages of static information over long periods of time. They expect to see new content frequently — even daily. Pioneering sites like the *Wall Street Journal* (www.wsj.com) and the *San Jose Mercury News* (www.sjmercury.com) provide updated information continually throughout the day.

Intranet users are no different. They will quickly tire of a site that presents them with the same look, the same graphics and the same content each time they log on. Fortunately for you, many technology companies heard and acted upon those early Web criticisms.

They have created new software applications that provide automated updating of online sites by rotating graphics or generating customized pages from databases rather than using static HTML pages. Some of these applications make it possible for users to request certain kinds of information on personalized home pages based on their interest profile. It should be noted here that these applications are in their infancy and should be tested very carefully before you commit big dollars to their purchase.

Just over the horizon is the era of active notification systems. Advanced technology companies like Kinetoscope are developing new tools that will transform the online world into an active, responsive place. Software "notification agents" will seek out and report back information they find anywhere on the Web.

Fresh — Quick and Easy

There are a variety of things you can do to give your site that fresh and new look on a regular basis. They range from rotating home pages to providing the curent date and time. Since your home page is the front door to your site, you should spend much of your updating time on it.

Date and Time. This can be a simple task for your technical team. The information can be taken directly from the server's internal clock.

Weather. There are lots of public domain weather sites out there on the WWW.

News Headlines. Make a deal with a local newspaper or television station Web site to mirror their content on your site.

Photos. Create an archive of interesting, company-related photos to be used on your home page and create an automated script to rotate them frequently.

Internal Advertising. This is a philosophical decision you and your management need to make. Some intranet sites are accepting paid advertising and installing ad rotation software.

Seasonal Promotions. Dig into your clip art library and pull together some interesting seasonal graphics. With a little bit of effort you can create some compelling, simple animations, too.

Special Events. Your company probably sponsors activities within the company and beyond in the larger community. These are great sources for fresh, current content.

Responding to User Feedback

Where do other ideas for site maintenance come from? Your users, of course. Remember, your intranet site allows for real-time interaction with your audience, unlike other, traditional media. Smart Webmasters will seize this opportunity to find new ways to involve users in site development activities.

You may decide to enlist a group of users who can serve as "beta testers" for new content or site elements. This is especially useful if you have facilities where several of these users can sit down together at PCs in the same location. It's even better if you can be there with them to record their observations. You should consider at least audio recording the session so nothing is lost. Video taping the test is a good idea in that it allows you to see facial expressions and non-verbal behavior of the group. It can, however, be inhibiting to the free-flow of feedback and reaction. Its use, therefore, should be carefully evaluated by the group beforehand.

If you cannot use beta testers in a focus group, you can still recruit users to evaluate new content individually. It is a good idea to provide them with an HTML form to use for feedback and response. If you are testing new software on the site, it is also a good idea to include a problem report form on the site to gather specific information about problems uncovered during testing.

This dialog with your users will provide you with valuable information about how your site is being used and what you can do to make it better. In addition to providing you with this valuable feedback, it also engenders a sense of ownership among your users. Ownership is one of the most powerful motivators around for encouraging users to continue their use of the site and their input about the site. This is clearly your best source for gathering ideas about how to maintain and grow your intranet.

Recruiting and Training Content Providers

Expanding and growing your site means finding new people to participate. Intranets grow best in a climate of collaboration. If your site is to reflect your entire organization, you should seek to recruit a point person from each major functional area within the organization. These people are your eyes and ears within the organization. You must rely on them to make decisions about what content should be placed on your intranet. You must also rely on them to do most of the work to create that content.

For those reasons, you should select someone with a good, broad view of their particular organization. Some organizations already have "stringers" appointed to feed their information into traditional company media like newsletters. These people can be tapped to provide similar information to the intranet. With a little training in HTML authoring and some authoring tools, these people can become key contributors to the success of the intranet project. Content providers are the backbone of any intranet. Certainly the Webmaster plays a critical role in the success of the site, but alone, the Webmaster cannot maintain and grow a successful intranet. It takes the combined efforts of many content providers to ensure that the site is well stocked with content and information, and that it reflects the overall organization.

```
The Webmaster should invest considerable time and resources
in cultivating and encouraging content providers.
```

Recruiting and Training Online Discussion Hosts

Another excellent way to expand the reach of the intranet is to enlist "content experts" to act as online discussion hosts. These may or may not be members of any of the committees or groups that participated in the intranet project. Hosts serve the function of keeping the discussion focused on a particular topic. They also make sure that the participation in the forum or discussion is in keeping with established corporate communication policies.

Your hosts will allow you to expand the value and variety of discussions you offer on your site. Hosts can also do a good job of recruiting others to join in the discussions, especially if the topics are of interest to all your users or to smaller segments of special interest groups.

12

A Model Online Site

There are no typical online sites. Every site is a unique creation, in constant evolution, reflecting the style and structure of the host organization. Having said that, there are certain elements that are common to most online projects. This chapter provides a "parts list" of those elements.

Structure

The online world is nonlinear in structure. By its very nature, your online site is user controlled. Your users decide what they want to see and in what order. They also decide how much time to spend in each area. Keeping this in mind, it is very important that the user be provided with a comprehensive site-navigation plan, since they are determining the course of their trip through your site.

Home Page (`default.htm`)

This is the page your users see first. It is also referred to as the default or index page. Its primary function is to set the style, tone, and structure of the entire site. As a general rule this page should contain links to the major content sections within the site.

- *Text.* A general welcome message is appropriate. You may also want to provide some indication of the site content. Many sites include an invitation here to provide feedback and suggestions about improving the site.
- *Layout.* Should set the standard for the rest of the site, although it may be somewhat different.
- *Graphics.* They should be attractive and compelling without being overpowering. Remember this is still a medium very much controlled by the speed of the network

over which it travels. Download times on large graphics can be patience-killers for your users during peak times. Try to limit your graphics file size to 30K or less. At normal dial-up download speeds (9600/14,400 bps) it would require about 30 seconds to download. Of course, faster connections mean quicker downloads and the potential for larger files. The rule of thumb, however, is to design for the slowest user connection. Graphics should contribute to the overall message of the page, rather than just being window dressing.
- *Navigation.*   Include links to every major content section within the site. You might also provide an e-mail link to capture feedback and suggestions. Your users will probably also appreciate a link to the site map page.

Top Page   /section/default.htm

Each primary content section within the site has a top (or menu) page. It provides an overview of what is contained within that section.

- *Text.*   A content-specific welcome message is appropriate. You might also include some narrative about the section and its content.
- *Layout.*   These pages should be variations on the home page but different enough to be recognized as section top pages. Some online sites have developed different "personalities" for each section based on the particular content of the section.
- *Graphics.*   Content-specific and small.
- *Navigation.*   Links to the major subsections within the sections.

Submenu Page   /section/section/default.htm

A primary content section may contain enough information that it needs to be sorted into major sub-areas, each with its own top page (typically called a submenu page). Submenu pages should only be included when they add a sense of clarity and order to the larger section. Your users will appreciate your efforts to make site navigation easier. They will also tire quickly of clicking through a number of menu pages to get to their desired destination.

Remember it's always a good idea to create and maintain a site map page so your users can get to any page on the entire site in one click of the mouse.

Content Page   /section/content.htm

These pages contain the site's information. They can range from text documents to online forms, to audio and video files, to multimedia presentations and games.

- *Text.*   If the page is primarily text, it is a good idea to use frames or tables to display the text in a narrow (usually 4 to 5.5 inch wide) column resembling a page in a typical paperback novel. Content text is most easily read if it resembles a printed page, that is, black text on a white (or very light colored) background. Text should also be limited

A Model Online Site

to two screens in length. Users typically do not like to scroll through excessively long documents. Long text documents should be broken up into shorter documents with series navigation (previous and next navigation buttons) on each page. As an alternate, very long pages can use anchor links to move the user to any subsection on the page in one click.

- *Layout.*   Content page layout should be more functional than decorative. Many sites have established a narrow (about 2 inch) column down the left-hand side of content screens to be used as a buffer for the text. This area can also be used for small graphics relating to the text and callouts or sidebars.
- *Graphics.*   Content specific and small.
- *Navigation.*   Each content page should have links back up to the section top page and back to the home page. If the content page is part of a content series, it should also contain series navigation (forward and back, previous and next).

This is a content page from the Florida Trend Magazine *site. Notice the lateral navigation in the left-hand column. This is a long article so anchor links are included right after the title. The left-hand column is also used to display the graphics that were part of the original print article.*

Typical Intranet Elements

Animation

On-line sites have been criticized for being flat and not very exciting. Animations are a simple way to move some pixels around on a page and create some added interest.

Just as in the cartoon world of movies and TV, there are very sophisticated animations (Toy Story from Pixar) and very simple animations (old Rocky and Bullwinkle cartoons).

For your online, you had better stick with simple, two-dimensional animations. They are small file sizes and easy to create.

Animations are not difficult to produce. The first step is to conceive the animation in your mind and then translate that image to a simple storyboard. The next step is to create a series of animation cells (just like in those animated, flip-through books you used to get in Cracker Jack boxes). Remember to keep the graphics simple so the parts will be easier to animate.

This is an example of a very simple, six-step animation. The entire file is only 13Kbytes in size.

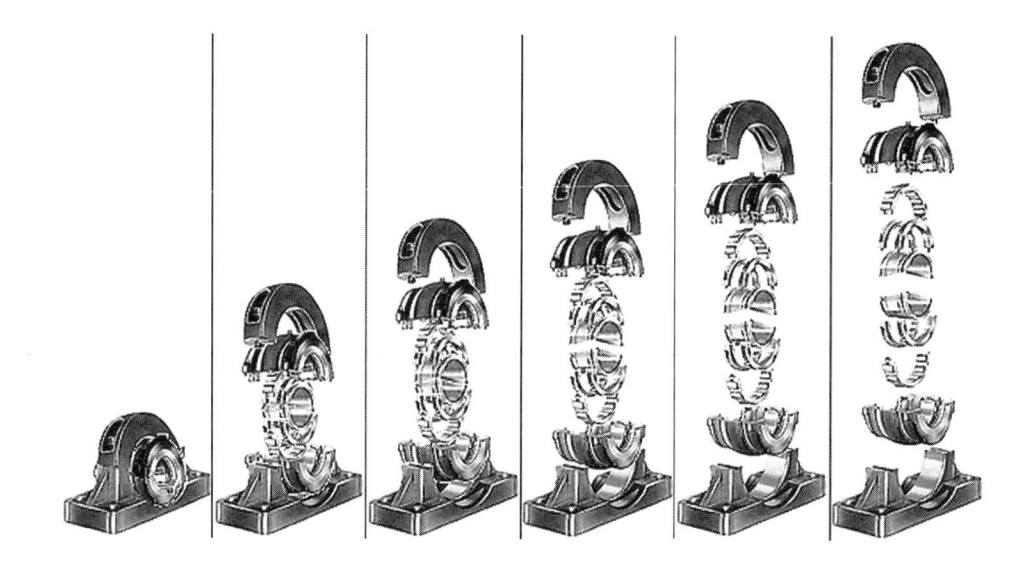

Each frame was created separately and then assembled in a application called GIF Animator where the mechanics of the animation can be selected. This particular sequence is continuously looped (moves through all five frames and then repeats indefinitely) and each step is on-screen for 1/4 second, making the entire animation last just over one full second.

Audio

Audio files are fairly large in general. Several different audio file formats have been gaining acceptance on the World Wide Web. If you choose to use audio on your online site, you should select one audio file format and make it your standard.

Regardless of which standard you choose, there are a few things you should know about audio. Your users will need audio-compatible systems (that means sound cards and speakers) to hear the files. Of course, Macintoshes are audio-capable with no additional hardware. Audio files tend to be much larger than other types of files on your online. Consequently, download times might become a problem. Your network administrator may also have some reservations about such large files clogging up the system.

Streaming audio (RealAudio **http://www.realaudio.com/** and others) is a more efficient way to handle audio on your site, but it requires additional software to create and to replay the files.

Backgrounds

On-line backgrounds can be solid colors or patterns. Solid color backgrounds are formed in the <BODY> tag line by selecting the hexadecimal code equivalent to the desired color.

A white background is formed using the following tag line:

<BODY BGCOLOR = "#FFFFFF"> Here's the translation — make the body (BODY) background color (BGCOLOR) equal to the hexadecimal number FFFFFF. (These six numbers equate to numerical settings for each of the Red, Green, and Blue color settings on a 256 color monitor, with 00 being 0 and FF being 255 for each color. A setting of FFFFFF means red, green and blue are fully on creating white. A setting of 000000 means red, green, and blue are fully off creating black.

Some really useful tools are available today to help determine the hexadecimal code of various colors.

Patterned backgrounds are created using small (usually 50 pixels square) GIF graphics and placing a different tag in the <BODY> tag line:

<BODY BACKGROUND = "graphics/background.gif"> Here's the translation — create the body (BODY) background (BACKGROUND) by taking a GIF file located in the graphics folder and named background.gif and tiling it across the entire browser window. '

Using a graphic background creates a mosaic of that graphic filling the browser window. For that reason, you must make certain that the graphic image will tile well.

Copyright

In most cases, it's a good idea to include a copyright notice on each page within your site. This is the first step in claiming ownership to the content on your site. It does not establish ownership, but it does put users on notice that you are claiming ownership. For that reason, it is imperative that everything on your site is owned by your organization or appears with the permission of the owner. This might be a good time to review your corporate policies about who owns the work produced by employees.

In any case, the following is generally accepted as a complete and legal copyright claim:

```
Copyright © 1997, Site Dynamics. All rights reserved.
```

E-mail

It's a good idea to include a link to an automated e-mail form on each page in your site. Both Netscape Navigator 2.0 (and later) and Microsoft Internet Explorer 3.0 (and later) support the "mailto" HTML tag:

<AHREF = "mailto:thom@kinetoscope.com">

When this link is activated, a window like the one above appears outside the browser window. As you can see, the e-mail form is pre-addressed and ready for the user to enter a subject, the message and add any necessary attachments.

File Names

To avoid confusion and potential problems with different server hardware/software, your online file names should follow the 8.3 DOS naming convention. 8.3 means eight alphanumeric characters followed by a period followed by a three character file type. The first eight characters should describe the contents of the file.

Following are some typical online file names:

> default.htm (the first page users see on a given site)
> index.htm (another name for default)
> logosm.gif (logo small in GIF format)
> doughead.jpg (Doug headshot in JPEG format)

Your filenames should reflect the file's contents as much as possible within an 8 character limitation. It is useful to check out file names on other WWW sites to see how they name their files. As your site and online experience evolve you will settle on a particular naming process that makes sense for your site.

```
          On-line file names are always in all lower case.
```

Footers

Page footers can be used to add navigational consistency and copyright information throughout your site. Many onlines also include e-mail forms within the footer to gather user feedback and comments specific to each page's content.

A typical online footer might look like this:

```
      Site Index | Home
      Send us your comments and suggestions about this page
      Copyright 1997, Site Dynamics. All Rights Reserved.
```

A Model Online Site 171

The top line provides a link directly back to the Index and to the Kinetoscope Home Page.

The middle line is a link to an automated e-mail form (called a mailto in Netscape).

Forums (Online Discussions)

These areas allow your users to participate in the interactive nature of online publishing. Whether you decide on traditional newsgroups (threaded discussions, difficult to use but very functional) or more user-friendly forums (hosted or unhosted), the important thing is to give your users a place to interact with you and with each other.

Newsgroups

Newsgroups provide many people with access to others who share the same interests. Some newsgroups are controlled by individuals or small groups, others allow freeform discussions without editing or censorship. Many newsgroups have their own operating procedures — sometimes referred to as Netiquette. People who violate the rules are usually dealt with harshly, sometimes referred to as "flaming". Newsgroups within organizations can be tightly focused on communities of interest, and can be powerful tools in sharing topical information across the organization.

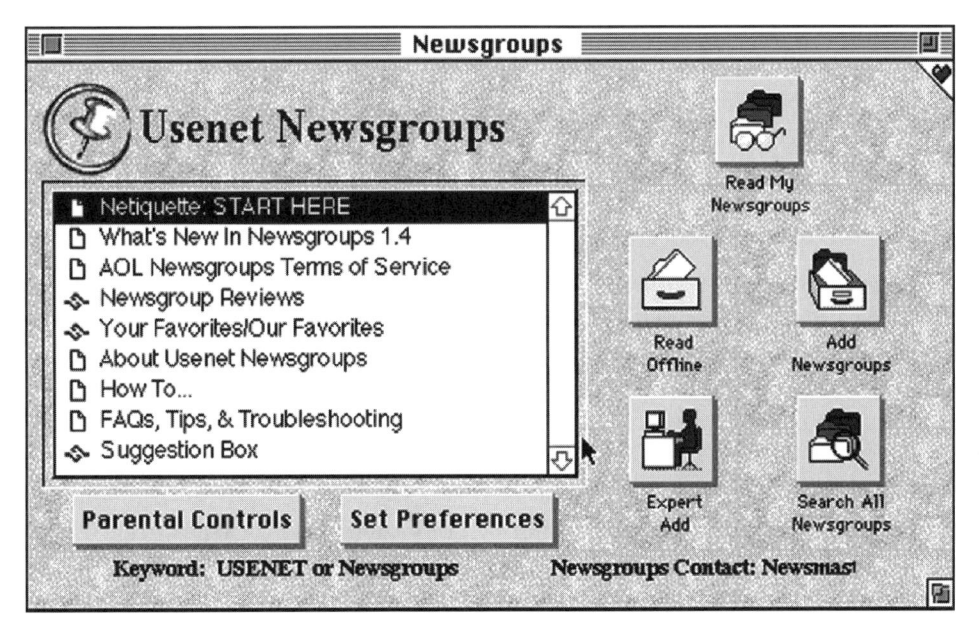

This America Online© newsgroup entry screen provides the user with a variety of navigational options.

Unhosted Forum

Very similar to the newsgroup, the unhosted forum adds the advantage of a simple HTML input screen, so the user doesn't have to learn a new form. Unhosted forums usually provide a topic or range of topics for the discussion, and ask that contributors stay on topic with their postings. The danger of unhosted forums is the same danger that exists with any open forum — online behavior. There is the distinct possibility that a user or users may get involved in a personal exchange of unpleasantries or downright vulgar, or inappropriate language. The upside is there is no maintenance required, and the postings are made live as soon as they are submitted to the server. You may decide to limit the number of recent postings the user sees when entering the forum, or you may decide to show them all. Be aware that these forums can get quite lengthy. It's also a good idea to change topics or create new forums periodically to keep the idea exchange fresh and new.

Hosted Forum

The only difference between the hosted and unhosted forum is the administrative function of the host. The host creates the original forum topic and may even include some initial seed comments to get the conversation started. In many cases the host will become a very visible and controlling influence on the conduct of the forum. Some forum hosts include their photos and biographical information for the user's benefit. These serve to add a personal touch to the forum and establish the host's credibility in dealing with the topic at hand.

Hosted forums eliminate the possibility of inappropriate postings since the forum host must review each posting before it becomes live. Depending on how the program is written, the host may have the opportunity to edit postings, delete them, hold them or make them live. The upside is a well-maintained, topical forum that contains no offensive comments. The downside is that some people might find the practice of "censorship" objectionable.

You may find forums particularly useful as an information gathering place for geographically diverse employees performing similar functions. Using forums, everyone associated with a certain topic can participate in a dialog that builds upon earlier information.

Chat

Chat began as a feature of commercial online services (like America Online) and soon became one of the most popular areas within the site. Chat is real time keyboard conversations among users, and they are popular because they are usually focused on a particular interest group or geographic area. Chat groups exist all over the world across an incredibly wide range of topics and interests.

Because of bandwidth restrictions,. most online chats are offered only during certain time periods (usually during off-peak network hours) and around certain topics. Chat is the riskiest form of discussion because everything is happening in real-time and there is little or no mechanism for monitoring. On the upside, chat groups can be an extremely popular area within your online and provide a compelling reason for your users to visit your site often.

Graphics

The Graphic Inline Format (GIF) is an efficient and universally supported file format for online use. GIFs offer good compression and do a good job of preserving the quality of normal graphics like the one shown here.

kinetoscope INTRANET

Graphic Sizes

It is a good idea to establish a standard for graphics on your online site. Graphics 160 pixels wide by 120 pixels high — like the one shown above — are large enough to have impact and yet small enough in file size to download and display quickly.

In those cases where larger graphics are desirable, especially on top or menu pages, the maximum screen size should be 320 pixels wide by 240 pixels high.

In any case, the maximum file size should be 30K or less.

Thumbnails. In those cases where a larger graphic is needed for clarity (or other reasons), you should create a thumbnail of the larger graphic along with the file size of the larger graphic. This thumbnail image is then linked to the larger image.

This allows the user to decide whether to spend the time (usually 1 second per 1K file size) waiting for the larger image to download.

Headers

Page headers tell users where they are. The use of uniform headers throughout your online sections provides users with a standard format that can be customized with graphics, color and style selections.

Energy Supply

Generating Plants

Layouts

Just as in any of your print publications, it is important that your online site have a uniform layout so you convey a sense of uniformity. You may already have corporate standards established for print publications that can be modified for online publishing.

Layout design is very subjective. On-line sites will most usually reflect the character and personality of the host organization. Much has been written earlier in Chapter 7 about page design.

Layout here refers to how the page looks when the user sees it on an individual monitor using a specific browser. In the early days of online publishing, all the backgrounds were gray, all the text was one size and color, and the browser window and all its contents were expandable. That means that the size of the browser window was controlled by the user, and the content of the page would expand or contract with the size of the window. Graphics would move around. Text would expand as wide as the window opening. In other words, all screen elements were relatively fluid within the confines of the user's browser. That made page layout very difficult to control from user to user.

Modern browsers support layout elements called tables and frames. These were introduced to allow the publisher to control the look of the page regardless of user browser settings. Tables creates a grid of columns and rows, the sizes of which can be controlled through HTML tags. Specifying table cell sizes ensures that those cells will maintain the same size across all browsers. Frames takes tables one step farther by creating more than one window within the user's browser. Frames allow you to set up and maintain a constant navigation panel, for example, in an area that never changes throughout site navigation.

Navigation

Your users will appreciate a standardized site navigation area throughout your online. Many sites have established a navigation area along the left side of the screen that remains consistent throughout the site. Consistent navigation is one of the most valuable elements you can put in your site. It provides your users with a continuing sense of where they are in the site (remember, your site is nonlinear, unlike a book) no matter where they go.

You may decide to use a graphic navigation bar like the one above. Using frames on the site allows you to keep this macro menu constant throughout the site. A simpler form of navigation is the use of a text navigation line at the top or bottom of the page.

Text Navigation

```
home | company information | press | demos |
time tracker | library | links
```

A Model Online Site 175

> home
> company info
> press
> demos
> time tracker
> library
> links

Whether you use a graphic navigation panel or not, it is a good idea to include this text-only navigation because it will load instantly with the rest of the screen text. It will also appear if your user has graphics turned off within their browser.

In addition to this "macro site" navigation (links to each major section on the site), you need to consider navigation within the section. It is always a good idea to place links on the top of each content page back to the menu and submenu pages above it. For example, within the "Press" section of the site, you might have "Press Releases," "Articles" and "Links to other Publications" as major subsections. Within "Press Releases" you might list a dozen releases from the previous six months. Clicking on an individual press release title on the submenu page takes the user directly to that release. On the top of that press release page you might place links back to the Press Releases menu page and the Press section.

Press | Press Releases

This allows your user to quickly return to the menu or submenu within one particular section while maintaining a consistent macro site navigation.

Photos

Joint Photographic Experts Group (JPEG) (pronounced jay′-peg) is the preferred compression algorithm for continuous tone images — photos and tone illustrations. JPEGs (or JPGs) provide maximum image quality with minimum file sizes. Photos (or any continuous tone images) can be saved as a JPEG file from Photoshop, a standard photo manipulation software package from Adobe.

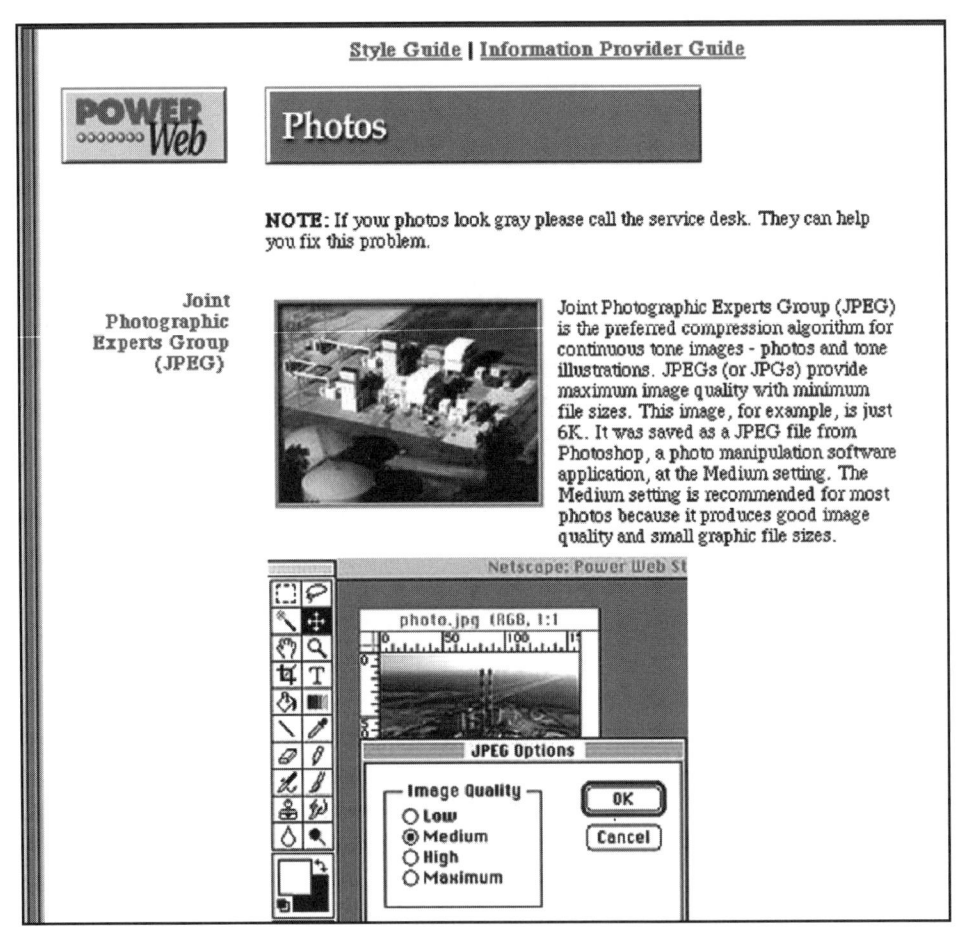

This is an example of a photo montage using JPEG compression. Although the screen size is relatively large, the file size is still only 23K.

Site Structure

Your online site can be assembled in any of a number of ways. Different people prefer different structures, and no one way can be declared, "the right way." However, having said that, there are certain considerations that suggest there is a better way to structure your site.

   Your entire site will reside within a directory on the server at what the techies call the "root level." This is the base level of your site. Everything on the site,(HTML files, graphics, audio, video, animation) will reside within the root directory. Depending on the size of your site, you may find that it is useful to create subdirectories within the root directory. A good way to do this is to identify the major sections of the site and assign each of them a subdirectory. Our example site would be structures like this:

Root Level
- Company Info
- Press
- Demos
- Time Tracker
- Library
- Links

Within each subdirectory there is an HTML document named default.htm. This is the first page that is served when that particular subdirectory is accessed.

It is also useful to keep site graphics in their appropriate location. Those graphics that are used throughout the site and its sections should be kept in a graphics directory at the root level. Graphics used only in one section should be kept in a graphics directory within that section. The same is true for audio and video files. So your completed site structure would look like this:

Text

Always remember that text carries the content of your site. Yes, graphics are nice additions and yes, one picture is worth a thousand words. But text will usually carry the content.

In the early browser days, you could choose only one font (Times) and one of only four possible sizes. New browsers are allowing much more flexibility when it comes to text sizes, fonts and color options.

On-screen text is usually easier to read when it is presented in a very dark color (preferably black or dark gray) against a light colored background. This simulates the normal print environment of black text on white paper. It's what your users are used to seeing and are most comfortable with.

Video

Video files tend to be huge. Using standard QuickTime compression, a typical video file will be 9 Megabytes per minute of video. Assuming even a very fast transfer rate on your system, a short video segment (say 20 seconds or 3Mb) can take several minutes to download. You must weigh the advantages gained by showing the video against the problems associated with such long download times and large files tracking across the network.

In any case, your users will need QuickTime plug-ins for their browsers, and you will need QuickTime authoring software to create the video files. Adobe Premier and other packages are commercially available for that purpose.

13

The Site Dynamics Intranet: A Case Study

Site Dynamics is a full-service, interactive communication company based in Clearwater, Florida. They specialize in delivering turnkey solutions to organizations seeking an online presence — whether that presence is a website, an intranet, an extranet or a combination.

Site Dynamics is a company fully immersed in the online world. It is made up of a consulting group, a creative group, a production group and a technical group.

"Eat Your Own Dogfood"

It's an old Microsoft expression that has become legendary in the software industry. It means that if you are selling software, you had better be using it yourself. In the case of Site Dynamics, developing a showcase intranet was key to the company's success. On the one hand the intranet would demonstrate its commitment to online publishing as a way of doing business. On the other hand, using an intranet would allow the company to make all its employees feel "connected" online. The Site Dynamics intranet project was begun soon after the company was formed. Today, the Site Dynamics intranet is fully integrated into the fabric of the company. Even so, its use and acceptance was neither simple nor immediate.

The Need

As with most valuable tools, the Site Dynamics intranet grew out of a real business need — keeping track of leads and clients across vastly different computer operating systems and across vast distances and time zones. The company needed a simple and easy-to-use system that would allow a variety of users, each working independently, to be able to access real-time information about clients and leads. The production manager requested a system that would allow her to keep track of all Site Dynamics employees and their labor charges to various projects. Some staff asked for a shared office calendar so everyone could keep up with all the meetings and appointments.

The Process

Ideas about what was needed came from everyone. In the beginning there was no mechanism for developing the intranet. Ideas were thrown out at weekly staff meetings. Everyone sat around the conference table and nodded their approvals. But the reality is that until someone owned the overall responsibility for the intranet project, it really didn't progress very far at all. About the third meeting, the group decided that Angie, the Webmaster, should become the Site Dynamics intranet Webmaster as well. That's when things really started to happen.

Angie began to send out e-mails to the staff asking for their input about which projects were the most important. Angie met with the graphics design team and came up with some look and feel options. She spent a few days reviewing existing corporate information and designed a site structure to accommodate it. She presented the ideas to the group and got quick closure on a direction.

Then the fun really started. Site Dynamics is a very technical company filled with technically proficient people. They were very comfortable with technology and quick to embrace all the latest technology tools. Everyone in the company would be considered a "power user" (expert in computer operation). In short, Site Dynamics was ideally structured to embrace an intranet. Even an organization like Site Dynamics had some problems converting to this new communications medium. It's not the technology, it's the people. Even in a small, technologically advanced organization like Site Dynamics, problems arose.

Following is an overview of the existing Site Dynamics intranet with an explanation of each major component and its benefits to the company.

Home Page Features

All Site Dynamics browsers are set to this screen as their "home." So each time a Site Dynamics employee launches their browser, they are brought to this screen and get a snapshot of what's new at the company. Important meetings and other significant events are entered and updated daily to keep a fresh face on the site. The Webmaster also adds human touches like seasonal messages and a quote of the day.

The Site Dynamics Intranet: A Case Study

Advantages

Every Site Dynamics employee is aware of every significant event taking place in the current week.

Major Content Areas

The site has evolved to this current list of major sections:

- Company
- Staff
- Clients
- Demos
- Guides
- Resources
- Links
- Tools

Company Info

This area is a repository for a wide variety of information and resources necessary to the day-to-day operation of the company. Major sub-areas include the following:

Company

Staff Addresses and Bios
To learn more about a certain employee click on their name.

    Thom Dupper
    Angela Lahti
    Doug Circle
    Jay Donaldson
    Dan Mackay
    John Buckenhorst

Rate Card
Current fees and rates as of March 21, 1997.

Press Releases
Archives of company press releases and releases mentioning Site Dynamics.

Office Phone Extension List
Updated FKQ/Site Dynamics telephone extension list as of April 11, 1997.

Local Competition Sites
Listing of S-D local competition.

Policies and Procedures
Anything that pertains to the company is in this section.

    Employee Handbook
        Table Of Contents
        Section 1: The Way We Work
        Section 2: Your Pay And Progress
        Section 3: Time Away From Work And Other Benefits
        Section 4: On The Job
        Section 5: Safety In The Workplace

- **Staff addresses and bios** contains all pertinent information about each Site Dynamics employee. This is particularly useful when they are out of the office — especially away on travel. Each employee lists several ways (usually including a pager number and cellphone) to keep in touch with them at all times.
- **The Site Dynamics rate card** provides detailed information about the various job functions and hourly labor rates within the company. This section makes the proposal process much smoother.
- **Press releases** is the official company press archive. Where appropriate, resulting news stories based on each release are included in electronic form.
- **The office phone extension list** is an easily maintained and updated resource for all three companies sharing the FKQ Advertising building in Clearwater. Prior to the intranet, each of the 60+ employees kept paper lists which were usually out of date

as soon as they were distributed. Now, the office administrator updates the list electronically using an administrative form that enters the information into a SQL database. Once done, the intranet is automatically updated and each employee has a correct list immediately online.

- **Competitive Sites** is an area used to track the direct and indirect competitors of Site Dynamics. The company initially identified over a hundred such companies and subsequently created a page of links to their sites. Each month at a minimum, the Site Dynamics marketing group visits key competitive sites to track competitive trends. Site Dynamics is committed to maintaining its position as an industry leader. This monthly review ensures that they do not fall behind any of their competitors. This online competitive analysis is one of the most powerful uses of intranets.
- **Online forms** include a non-disclosure agreement, suggestion form, supply order form, bug finder form (to report problems with Site Dynamics projects) and a customer registration form.
- **Policies and procedures** is a complete, online version of the printed employee manual. Site employees use this instant resource because it is up-to-date and always easy to access.

Staff

This section allows each Site Dynamics employee to construct a personal page on the site. There are no guidelines - except good taste. Everyone is encouraged to use this area to display their creative side and experiment with new technologies. This "sandbox" area provides a powerful tool for all employees to grow and learn from each other.

Clients

All of the past and present Site Dynamics clients are listed in this area. The staff uses this area as an information resource for lessons learned. Each client and each project is detailed in terms of the challenge, technical tools utilized, problems overcome and results. This section has become the official library of performance data so that valuable information is not lost from team to team and from project to project.

Guides

Fast-growing companies, like Site Dynamics, move so fast that information gets trampled in the rush. Many times, new staff members do not get the formal training required to perform the complex functions associated with website design and production. Site Dynamics has established an area on the intranet to provide an online resource for all company standards and guidelines.

HTML Guidelines gives a comprehensive overview of Hypertext Markup Language. This area contains helpful hints about common problems. This section is extremely useful to Site Dynamics staff and key customers who are just learning Hypertext Markup Language.

One of the most useful sections within the style guide is this graphics library. Stock and client photography and illustrations have been optimized for online usage (color pallette, file size, compression) and are available in three sizes. They are displayed on the top page as thumbnails. Clicking on a thumbnail takes the user to a screen displaying that particular item in its three sizes. The appropriate file name is displayed below each image so the user can find the actual electronic file easily and place it into their own HTML pages.

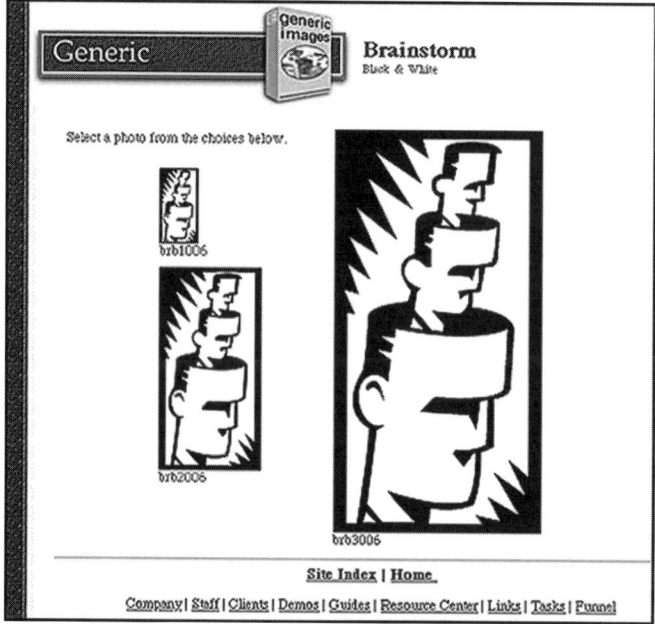

The Style Guide details the Site Dynamics style elements to be followed when adding content to the existing Site Dynamics site. The following style elements are covered in detail as part of the style guide:

The Site Dynamics Intranet: A Case Study

- Backgrounds
- File Names
- Footers
- Graphics

- Headers
- Live Area
- Navigation Area
- Page Layouts

- Photos
- Site Structure
- Style Summary
- Tabling Pages
- Writing Guide

[Screenshot of Power Web Style Guide page with sidebar links: Backgrounds, File Names, Footers, Graphics, Headers, Live Area, Navigation Area, Page Layouts, Photos, Site Structure, Style Summary, Tabling Pages, Writing Guide, Index, Talk back to us. Main content: "This style guide provides a comprehensive overview of the elements that make up a typical Power Web HTML document. It is intended to be used in conjunction with the HTML guide. It does not cover such topics as audio, video or animation, because of resource constraints. As with any living document, it will grow and evolve as the Power Web matures. You may want to start with our style summary document for a quick overview of Power Web style." Footer: Site Index | Power Web Home. Copyright 1996, Florida Power Corporation. All Rights Reserved.]

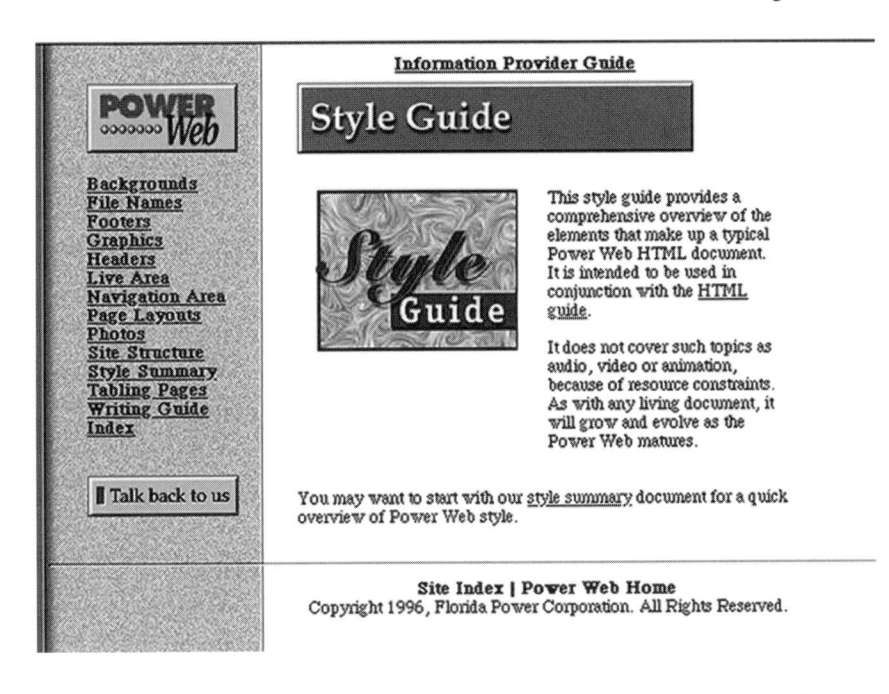

This is the "Information Provider Guide" page from the Site Dynamics intranet. From here, users can branch off into "Site Planning," "Site Building" and other helpful topic areas.

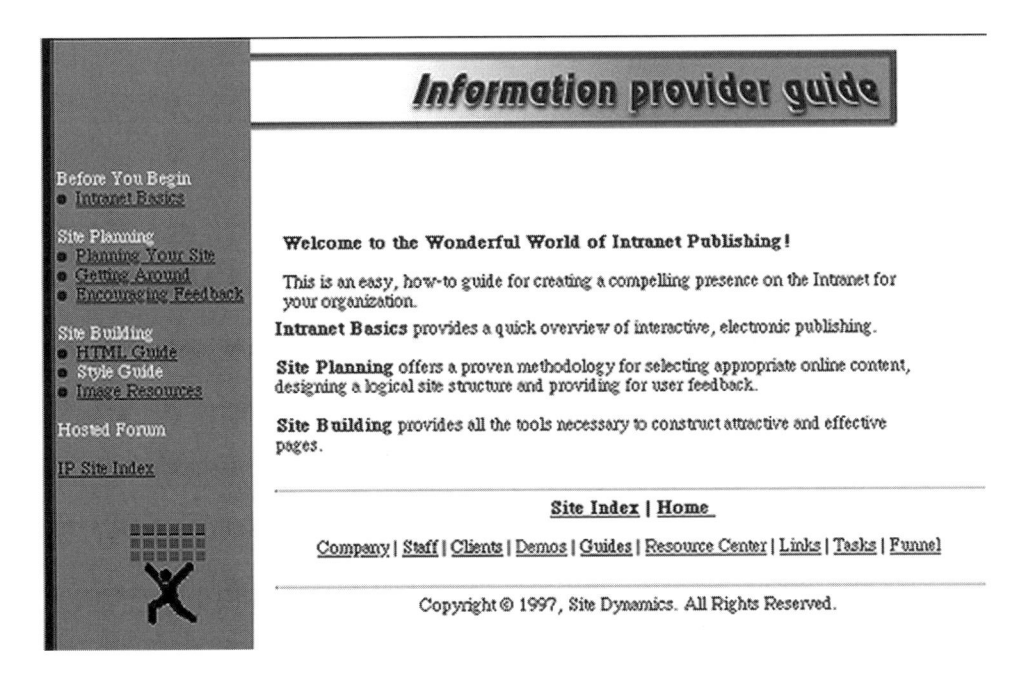

[Screenshot of Information provider guide page. Sidebar: Before You Begin – Intranet Basics; Site Planning – Planning Your Site, Getting Around, Encouraging Feedback; Site Building – HTML Guide, Style Guide, Image Resources; Hosted Forum; IP Site Index. Main content: "Welcome to the Wonderful World of Intranet Publishing! This is an easy, how-to guide for creating a compelling presence on the Intranet for your organization. **Intranet Basics** provides a quick overview of interactive, electronic publishing. **Site Planning** offers a proven methodology for selecting appropriate online content, designing a logical site structure and providing for user feedback. **Site Building** provides all the tools necessary to construct attractive and effective pages." Footer: Site Index | Home. Company | Staff | Clients | Demos | Guides | Resource Center | Links | Tasks | Funnel. Copyright © 1997, Site Dynamics. All Rights Reserved.]

Resources

This is one of the most popular sections of the Site Dynamics intranet. Since Internet technology and applications change and expand almost daily, the Site team decided to create an up-to-date online resource. Each staff member nominated their favorite five trade periodicals for inclusion in the resource list. A master list was created - a blend of technical and marketing magazines (printed and online) that would provide a broad overview of the entire online horizon. Staff members then chose the publications they would volunteer to scan each week for new and interesting articles and other information. Links to these articles are included on the intranet each week. Previous links are archived by date and subject area.

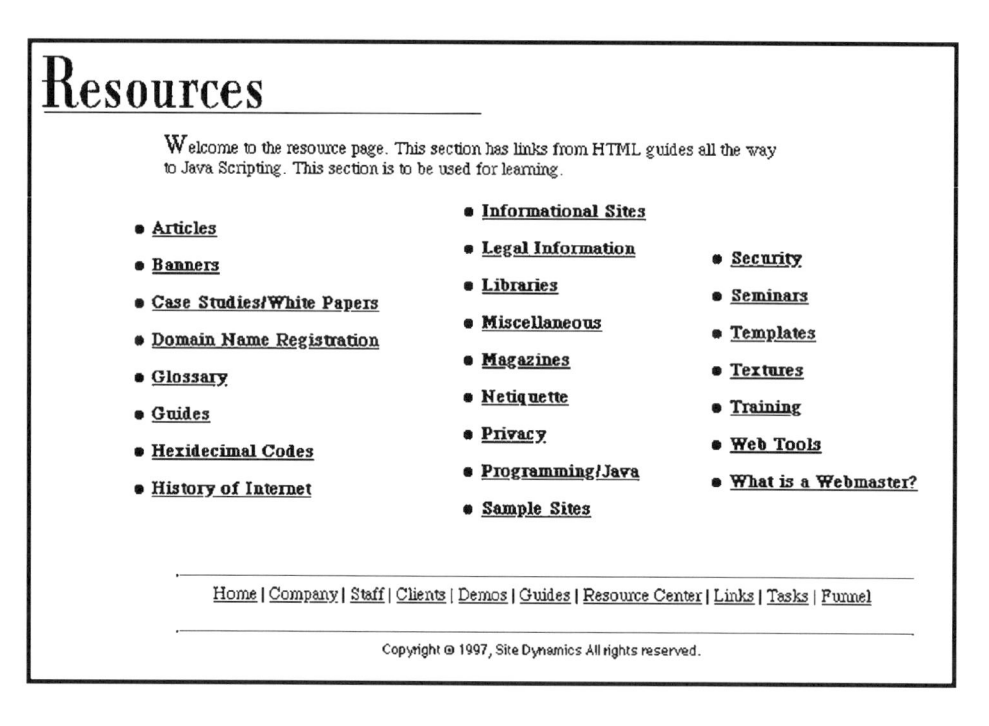

Resources

Welcome to the resource page. This section has links from HTML guides all the way to Java Scripting. This section is to be used for learning.

- Articles
- Banners
- Case Studies/White Papers
- Domain Name Registration
- Glossary
- Guides
- Hexidecimal Codes
- History of Internet
- Informational Sites
- Legal Information
- Libraries
- Miscellaneous
- Magazines
- Netiquette
- Privacy
- Programming/Java
- Sample Sites
- Security
- Seminars
- Templates
- Textures
- Training
- Web Tools
- What is a Webmaster?

Home | Company | Staff | Clients | Demos | Guides | Resource Center | Links | Tasks | Funnel

Copyright © 1997, Site Dynamics All rights reserved.

Links

The Links section provides a comprehensive list of online resources, ranging from local attractions and museums to software download sites. This section grows daily as each staff member adds links of interest as they are discovered. The intranet Webmaster is charged with the responsibility of checking and updating all the links periodically.

Tasks

This is the online action register used by Site Dynamics to keep everyone on task and on schedule. The staff originally thought that this idea was unnecessary. Each staff member had their own way of keeping track of assignments and tasks. More importantly, they were not sure whether they wanted everyone in the company to know the status of their tasks. Those concerns quickly faded when each staff member, in their own time and way, discovered how useful the task list really was to them personally. Each day, as they log onto the intranet, their daily tasks are right there in front of them. It has become a welcome planning tool for each staff member to organize their day's activities and coordinate with other staff members on various projects.

Tools

Time Tracker

The Time Tracker is used to record and display timesheet information for each Site Dynamics employee. As employees log onto the site, they are required to enter a UserID and Password. This information is used to provide default settings on the tracker screen.

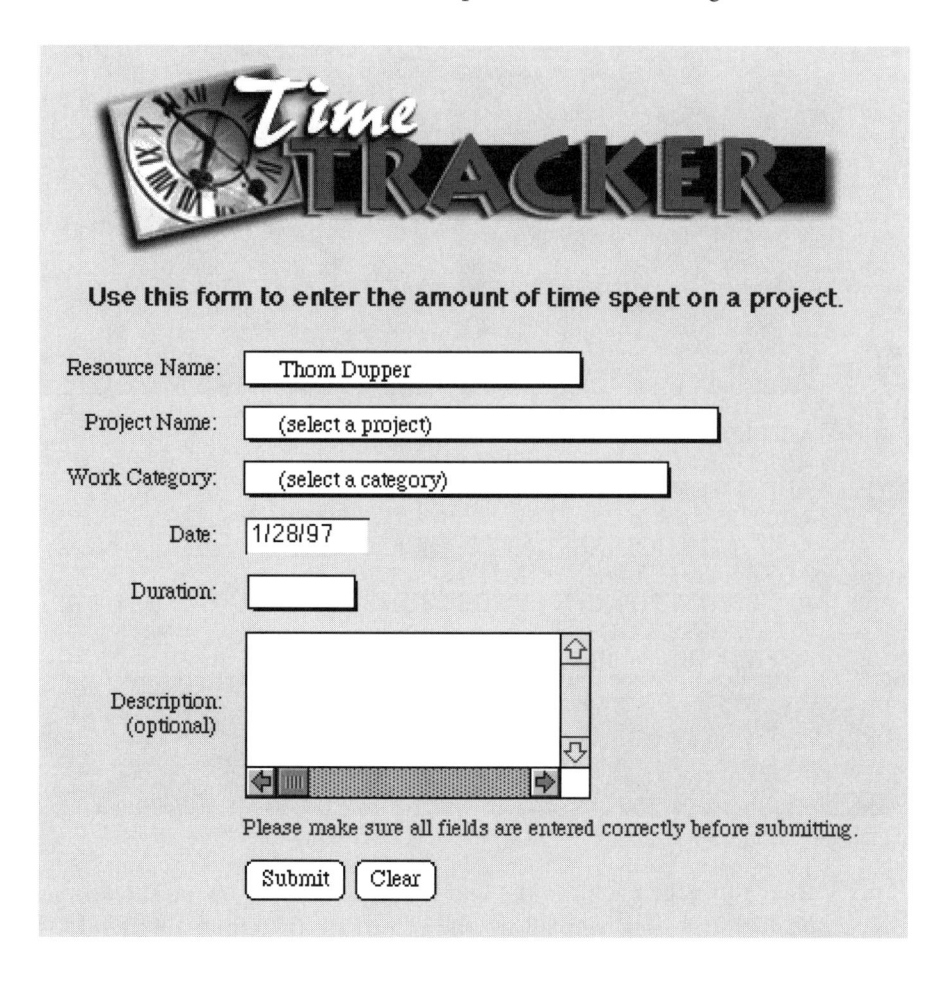

The UserID appears as the "Resource Name" and today's date appear as default settings. Each, of course, can be changed if necessary. The form uses pop up menus to reduce the time required to complete the form.

Site Dynamics provides consulting and online development services for a variety of clients. Employees and subcontractors in remote locations contribute labor to most projects. The Time Tracker provides an automated, quick and easy-to-use form. It replaces paper forms that required manual processing by the employee and the administrator. The new system allows for input and modification by the employee and automated reporting from the database to the administrator. Clients can be given permission to enter Time Tracker to get real-time information about changes to their projects.

Lead Tracker

This custom application was deployed so that Site Dynamics could track its contact with various potential clients — and would be accessible to everyone within the company. So regardless of who was making contact, from the receptionist to the engineers, their notes could be added to the database very easily using a standard HTML interface.

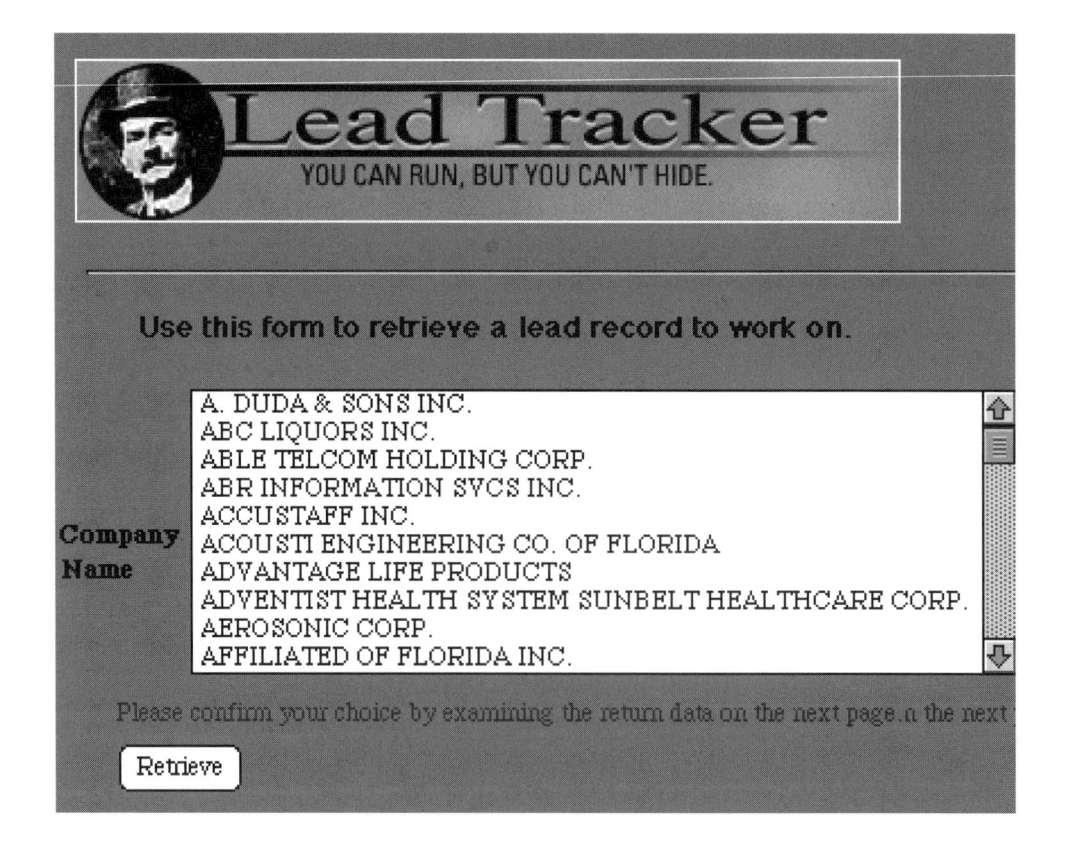

The Lead Tracker top page provides the user with a complete list of all companies on the active pursuit list. Any user can call up the record of any company by selecting the name and clicking on the "retrieve" button. All pertinent company information is contained on this input screen. Users can perform several activities from this page including updating the file.

The Site Dynamics Intranet: A Case Study   189

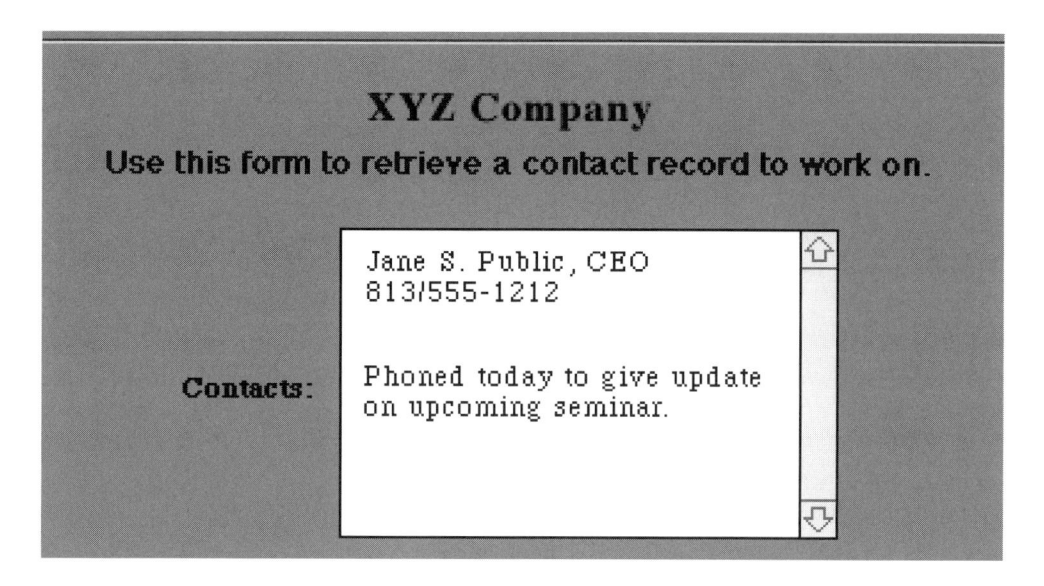

[XYZ Company contact form screenshot showing:
"Use this form to retrieve a contact record to work on."
Contacts:
Jane S. Public, CEO
813/555-1212

Phoned today to give update on upcoming seminar.]

This simple update screen is easy to use and provides access to the main database record for each company.

Calendar

This application gives the entire Site Dynamics office and remote locations a dynamic, real-time calendar for all office events. Each person can keep their own individual schedules that are rolled up into a master calendar for the entire organization. Individual paper calendars and wall schedules are eliminated. In one location, all interested parties can get a snapshot of individual and collective schedules, meetings and events.

[Calendar screenshot: "This is a demonstration of Site Dynamics' Calendar java component." Controls: Today, January, 1997, Previous, Next, Select a date in the calendar.

Sunday	Monday	Tuesday	Wednesday	Thursday	Friday	Saturday
			1	2	3	4
5	6	7	8	9	10	11
12	13	14	15	16	17	18
19	20	21	22	23	24	25
26	27	28	29	30	31	

Copyright © 1996, Site Dynamics, Inc. All rights reserved.]

Bottom Line

Bringing a functional, valuable intranet to Site Dynamics has been a daunting task. Even in a highly technical organization, habits are deeply entrenched and difficult to change. This is another verification that technology is the easy part of intranets. People present the real challenge. Today, the Site Dynamics intranet is an integral part of the company's daily culture. That transformation has happened because each Site Dynamics staff member has found significant value there.

Bringing information closer to those who need it; closing communications gaps in traditional organizations; opening up dialog channels; sharing corporate success stories; making it easier to sell a 1985 pop-up camper — these are all mentioned when discussing successful intranet projects. What will your staff mention about your intranet? What features or content will make them consider it a valuable part of their daily worklives? How will you collect and respond to your users' feedback about making your intranet better?

Ultimately, your success in building a successful intranet project will be measured in human terms — the human side of intranets.

14

Ten Common Intranet Mistakes

This chapter provides intranet project managers a short overview of what can go wrong when building a corporate intranet. It is based on Kinetoscope and Site Dynamics' experience as well as input from clients and industry leaders. We believe that it is highly useful for managers at any point in the game, from initial planning to upgrading a finished product.

There are as many good reasons for intranets as there are organizations building them. The technology is rock solid and well documented. The rewards can be extraordinary: improved inter-office communication, streamlined information publishing and increased employee productivity. But things can easily go wrong. Building an intranet is not like publishing a quarterly report or even creating a Web site. The reason for this is that enterprise-wide organizational dynamics and politics typically play a critical role in the development of any intranet.

1. Failing to Build Initial Support

Intranet development requires support from management, marketing and communication personnel, technical staff members, artists, "information providers" and, ultimately, all of the end users. Gathering support from key decision makers in each of these areas is crucial for the success of the finished product. The most important ally is an executive who is familiar with the Internet and who can allocate the resources needed to begin the project. In order to get the ball rolling, you will need to prove to this person that he or she will receive a positive return on their investment.

"The preliminary results from IDC's return on investment study of Netscape intranets found the typical ROI well over 1000% — far higher than usually found with any technology investment. The sooner an intranet becomes a core component of the corporate technology infrastructure, the sooner the company can reap the benefits."

"The intranet: Slashing the Cost of Business"
Ian Campbell, Director, Collaborative and intranet Computing,
International Data Corporation

Once you have secured this support, find project "drivers," or supporters from areas that are critical to the success of the project, like the information systems area. Brainstorm with them about defining the project's goals and how the project should be organized. These alliances will help you gain their buy-in and they will help you evangelize the project across the enterprise.

This table shows the price paid when you fail to build initial support or get support from the right people:

Problem With Support	Damage to the Project
No executive buy-in.	Little or no resource allocation, lack of respect or support from other departments
Your executive supporter has a limited budget	Partial completion of project, compromise of original concept, underdeveloped final product — no resources for site maintenance and expansion beyond launch
Drivers do not have support from executive-level management	Intranet fails to gain acceptance across departments, resources dry up; there is no enterprise-wide follow-through to maintain thefinished product
Driver is excited by the technology and not realistic about goals	Too many bells and whistles weigh the project down; it is viewed as a technical pilot or a "toy" and fails to gain respect from executives and end-users
Driver is indecisive or unwilling to act quickly	Project slows, executive support dissolves,interest fades, users find alternative solutions

2. Weak Plan of Action

An intranet requires serious consideration at the outset. Failing to create a workable action plan means that whatever you build is resting on a weak foundation. Because of this, it could topple at any point during the project or, worse yet, after the project has been deployed.

Give yourself ample time to plan everything out. Think through all of the potential pitfalls and unwanted outcomes. Specifically: what are your objectives with regard to communication? Who is/are your audience? What content are you going to publish? Who will be your organizational content providers? What is the overall structure of the intranet? How will results be measured?

Work with your drivers to find answers to these questions. They will be able to provide you with valuable information about proper resource allocation, what technologies to use and ones to avoid, and how their departments will make the best use of the intranet.

Problem With Plan	Damage to the Project
Fails to consider all needs or is too broad.	Budget is incorrect, project runs beyond its planned completion date, sub-projects are abandoned mid-stream.
Extends outside the project leader's area of expertise.	Resources are allocated improperly, sub-projects mushroom out of control or die from neglect.
Does not consider needs of drivers.	Drivers begin to cool to the original idea and support wanes or drops in quality.
Incorporates unproven technologies.	Time is wasted working around bugs or training personnel, other important areas of the project are underdeveloped.
No test period for finished product.	Bugs continually pop up while in real-world use, project loses credibility in the eyes of users, interest fades, users find alternative solutions.
Gives too much power to drivers.	Pet projects receive undue attention; focus is lost, support shifts from enterprise-wide buy-in to departmental factionalization.

3. Setting Unrealistic Goals

It is a cardinal rule of technology that if you promise unreasonable outcomes you will fail to deliver them. Simply put: overpromising means underdelivering. This cannot be overstated.

Talk to executives and your drivers about why past projects have failed. You may not get buy-in from some departments simply because of wrongs or perceived wrongs wrought long ago in one area or another. Information systems executives are frequently very conservative because of the number of over-hyped efforts they've seen over the years that ultimately failed to meet their expectations. Anticipating objections and being realistic at the outset will do more for your ultimate success than blue-sky projections and supposedly cure-all solutions.

4. Not Focusing on Users

Marketing and Communications personnel know that the value of an intranet will come from how it is seen by end users and not by what technologies are used. This understanding makes them extremely well-equipped to lead intranet projects.

Typically, technologists will see new projects from the opposite perspective: as a chance to deploy the latest or largest systems. Keeping the focus on workable solutions that meet the needs of end-users is more important than building a complex technological marvel that overwhelms its users.

Without a solid understanding of user needs and current information technology, the intranet will be more of a burden for everyone involved. You may find that a large number of your potential users don't even know what an intranet is, let alone how it will benefit them. Finally, without initial user input from focus groups, surveys or other means, there will be no buzz about the project. This could result in users seeing the intranet as another burden thrust upon them by management rather than a personal productivity enhancement.

5. Not Knowing the Technology

A Marketing and Communications background may be of primary importance, but technical literacy is also key. The marketing and communication side of the intranet will inevitably need to be developed in parallel with the technology. Don't forget — you may not cause technology-related problems, but they're going to be your responsibility.

Without knowing what technologies can be used for your project and why they are important, you will lose credibility with your information technology drivers. More importantly, you will need to report to information technology executives about project-related goals and sub-projects. Your management will expect you to cultivate a broad knowledge base of intranet-related technologies. Having a solid base of knowledge about technology at your fingertips will give you greater confidence when faced with these situations.

This technical literacy will increase your importance and credibility as the project leader. You can use your communication knowledge in concert with an awareness of available tools to build robust, compelling, valuable, and user-oriented solutions. The eventual outcome will be that your intranet is more successful and future opportunities for its growth are clearer.

This table describes the problems that may arise when you have limited technical knowledge:

Ten Common Intranet Mistakes

Intranet Element	Possible Outcomes
On-line graphics production	Large files that clog the system, download slowly and cause user frustration.
Server-side hardware and software	Slow systems, lack of scalability, upgrade problems.
Internet-based applications	Less interactivity, static pages, limited database access.
Browser or client software and enhancements	Limited user experience, interoperability problems, maintenance headaches, enterprise-widedeployment slowdowns.
Technical terminology and acronyms	Being closed out of information technology discussions, missing valuable information in magazines and other media.
Client-side hardware	Client and system slowdown, incompatibilities between software applications, servers and otherclient computers.
Your company's current information infrastructure	All of the above.

6. Failing to Encourage Interaction

The ultimate goal of any intranet is to improve enterprise communication and productivity. Interactivity promotes user involvement and produces a much more rewarding user experience. Without interaction not only will these goals not be met, but the intranet project could be ignored altogether.

Intranets are intensely personal systems. The network reaches one user at a time with an experience that is totally user controlled. The best intranets find ways to reach out and include the user in the experience. Some obvious examples of user interaction are online forms, newsgroups, forums, surveys, and questionnaires.

More advanced interactivity can take place with Internet-based applications like Java.

Placing these valuable tools on the site makes for a better user experience and gives your users more reason to return frequently to the site.

- Don't forget to keep the site fresh with new content and graphical updates.
- Change the face of your intranet frequently.
- Use a set style but make it flexible.
- Most users are highly visually literate: They expect things to change frequently while also maintaining a familiar look and feel.

7. Information Overload

The flow of information onto your intranet needs to be carefully controlled. Without some rules and style requirements, a well-planned intranet can become a jungle of competing information.

On one side of the equation, some individuals will want to publish everything they know. They toss out jokes, post family pictures and spend hours designing personal home pages. On the other side are users who feel like they can't keep up with the sheer volume of information available online.

Ultimately the result of this scenario is that valuable information will become lost in the shuffle and the system itself will slow down dramatically. Users will become frustrated, usage will wane, excitement will subside and the project itself could be in jeopardy.

This table shows how information overload can harm a project:

Type of Information	Possible Damage to the Project
Long reports, in-depth statistical analyses.	Burdens intranet servers, obscures important points and buries relevant information.
Lewd, obscene or offensive postings.	Infighting, anger and potential lawsuits.
Intensely personal content.	Irrelevant to organizational communication, distracts users from work, requires long-term maintenance.
Postings from outside sources.	Copyright infringements; pulls focus from enterprise-related information.

8. Stalling

Inertia is the leading killer of intranets.

All too often, well-intentioned projects get shelved simply because they ran out of steam. As with other information technology efforts, stalling could also mean that similar projects won't get off the ground for fear they will end badly.

The rush of inspiration that kick-starts an intranet effort often evaporates a couple of months into the project. The seemingly limitless enthusiasm that everyone began with turns into a typical cycle of working to meet deadlines, only to get more work assignments. Worse yet, combined with poor planning, deadlines don't get met and things fall further and further behind. Eventually the momentum is gone completely and the project stalls.

Stalling is a threat at any point in the project, from initial organization to maintenance of the final system. Once a project has stalled it is often much more difficult to re-initiate than it was to begin in the first place. As a result, both the project and its management lose credibility in the eyes of management and users.

This table lists ways in which intranets can stall and the consequences:

Reason for Stalling	Long-term Result
Driver or project staff enthusiasm diminishes.	Features are under-developed; the project goes beyond deadline or doesn't get deployed at all.
Executive enthusiasm diminishes.	Money and other resources dry up; there is littlesupport for the necessary follow-through once the intranet is deployed.
No publicity.	People don't know about the intranet and don't use it.
Lack of solid training.	Valuable features aren't utilized, the project is seen as shallow, updates are less useful than they could be.
Lack of maintenance or software updating.	Information, appearance and features grow stale.
No interaction capabilities.	The intranet is seen as nothing more than a glorified bulletin board or computer publishing system
No documentation.	The project leader and help staff are swamped withsupport calls; features are ignored, long-termtraining costs increase.

9. Project Leader Doesn't Keep Up with the Technology

Internet-related technologies and methodologies move at an incredibly fast pace. Because the industry moves so quickly, you may find that things that weren't possible when the project started can now be done quickly with off-the-shelf software.

Methodologies also change continually. A roadblock you encountered may be solved in an article by someone working on a similar project. If you are in the planning stages, there are new process white papers and how-to articles every month. The Netscape site (www.netscape.com) and Microsoft site (www.microsoft.com) are valuable resources for intranet case studies and other support material.

The pitfalls of falling behind with industry information are obvious. While keeping up to date may seem difficult and time-consuming, it is easier than spending valuable time and effort during the project only to read that there are better ways to do something. The only thing worse than finding out about a solution you should have been aware of is having someone else find out first.

10. Failing to Keep a Fresh Face

As with all other media, your corporate intranet is going to need an occasional facelift in order to maintain an inviting place in the day-to-day lives of its users. Overhauling is a necessary part of re-invigorating enterprise-wide support and gaining new support.

Without overhauling, your intranet's available information, feature sets and primary resources don't seem as vital as they once did. Users may feel they have "seen it all" and miss out on new and valuable content. The intranet experience can become like watching old television reruns all the time.

Make sure your intranet grows, either through your input or organically from user support. Keep searching for features and sub-projects that will introduce new information or add value to existing information. Apply new technologies like Java applications or Shockwave multimedia tools that enhance the user experience. Finally, create a long-term plan that charts a path for growth for future versions and beyond.

15

Intranet Best Practices

As with any communication project, intranet development begins with the basic set of questions:

- What are the communication objectives?
- Who is the audience?
- What is the content?
- What is the structure?
- How do we measure results?

With real-time information updating and interactive media, other issues need to be addressed:

- How will we encourage user interaction?
- How will we encourage and respond to user feedback?
- How will we keep the site fresh and timely?

Building something new within the existing organizational structure requires some additional considerations:

- What resources are necessary? People? Capital?
- What are the roles and responsibilities? Content? Technical?
- Will user training be necessary?
- How will we promote use of the site?

Finally, since many intranet users will also be content providers, these issues should be included:

- Who controls access to the intranet?
- Who can post information on the intranet?
- What is the posting process?
- What about copyright? Other legal issues?

The following information is based on involvement with various organizations during their intranet-building process. Because of this, all of the recommendations in this publication are based on real-world situations. There are, however, no pat answers, no cookie-cutter approach to such a complex undertaking. Your experiences, organization and personalities may be quite different from what you see here.

In the final analysis, finding what works for you and your project is the only way to truly measure your success.

Communications Objectives

Challenge:
How do you, as the project leader, set goals and manage expectations about this very public, much anticipated new communication medium?

Recommendations:
Fight the inclination to believe everything you hear or read about the success of online projects. On-line publishing will probably not eliminate paperwork around the office. It probably won't eliminate the need to produce an employee newsletter. It probably won't evolve the business overnight into a totally automated data retrieval system.

Establish your own reason(s) for implementing an intranet.
The first step in developing an intranet is establishing the need for an intranet. The promise of electronic publishing within an organization is tremendous. Technology is evolving every day making it easier to publish and share information online. But intranets are not a panacea. They require real planning and effort to succeed.

Some companies decide that the primary objective of their intranet is to provide a forum for its employees to exchange technical information. Other companies want to open up the flow of management information. Some opt for high-end solutions like secure video teleconferencing capabilities for their customers and vendors all over the world. There are different needs, different structures, different costs. But they all have one common objective: an intranet that fits their purpose, their budget and their organization.

Resist the "Ready, Fire, Aim" approach to launching your intranet.
Launching an intranet without a clear understanding of anticipated outcomes is usually dangerous. Organizational management wants to see a return on investment from the project. Beginning with a clear, concise goal statement can go a long way toward a smooth project roll-out.

Many organizations shy away from placing real dollar value on intranets. That may make sense in the short term to get a project rolling, but long term, your intranet needs to "pay its own way". As with all other forms of organizational communication, paying its own way may be measured in non-fiscal terms.

You should choose to measure success in speed of information access, improved employee participation or increased employee morale. Setting realistic goals and reporting on results are very important dimensions of successful intranet projects.

Who Is The Audience?

Challenge:
Who exactly is out there? What are their needs and expectations? How do you build truly effective systems to satisfy a diverse audience?

Recommendations:
Spend some quality time on defining who your user groups will be.

For example: is your intranet accessible only to organizational staff? Will you allow remote access for employees at home or at other offices? Will you open your intranet to vendors or customers? Answering these questions will go a long way toward defining the content and structure of your intranet.

Start with what you already know about your users.
If you limit access to employees, you can find your entire universe of users in the corporate phone directory. These are people you work with every day, and who have many things in common — not the least of which is a common place of employment.

Intranets that are open to customers and vendors are a different story. You many not know very much about the people in those organizations. Also, remember that as you open your network up to other organizations, it is exponentially more difficult to maintain any kind of security for your intranet information.

Intranet audiences, however, can be as complex as those found on the Web: different departments with different objectives and charters, different individuals with unique competencies and needs. Webmasters and content providers need to study their audiences to ensure appropriate and valuable content. Working with a finite number of potential users makes that task easier.

Involve your users in the intranet definition and creation process.
You might begin by conducting focus sessions with random employee groups to determine needs and expectations. This activity can also generate a list of potential online resources and evangelists as the intranet project gets under way. These groups should tell you about the basic computer competency levels of the employee population, their familiarity with

online services, their ideas about how the intranet could help them do their jobs better and other valuable information.

You might also conduct a user survey in other communication media like your employee newsletter. This pre-work will go a long way toward providing a valuable new employee tool right from the start.

Developing Content

Challenge:
Most organizations generate a large volume of internal communication. Add to that the enterprise-wide knowledge base and you can end up with a massive amount of information you could consider appropriate for your intranet.

How do you find out what's out there? How do you determine what's appropriate for intranet delivery? Who will spearhead the effort to repurposed existing content? Who will create new, original content for the intranet?

Recommendations:
Assemble an information providers committee to review content.
Don't try to gather and analyze potential content by yourself. Instead, identify information resources within the organization who may have an interest in posting their information on the intranet. This is usually more effective as a top-down activity initiated by you and supported by top management. One organization has found success in meeting with their information providers on a periodic basis to discuss content generation issues. As the group moves through the process they all learn much from each other about what content is important and valuable to share electronically.

Don't post everything.
Just as you would be selective about what you put into the employee newsletter or on the closed circuit television, be selective about intranet content. Make sure there is a good business purpose for the information. Then determine who should have access to what information. Establish clear posting guidelines during the process to avoid problems later on.

Start with the obvious.
Your organization probably has a wealth of information that would make appropriate content for your intranet. Some examples include:

- Employee and departmental newsletters
- Annual report
- Corporate mission and values
- Inventory
- Photo and graphic archives
- Product information

If you open up your intranet to your customers and suppliers, you may want to add some of the following:

- Online ordering and order tracking
- Customer support
- Customer service
- Catalogs
- Transaction records

Rule of thumb

Use this guideline to determine online content appropriateness: Can we add value to the content or to the organization by including this content on the intranet?

Structure

Challenge:

What if everyone wants a link from the home page to their content area? How will the site be structured at launch? How will it expand and change over time?

Recommendations:

Define structure first.

The architecture of your site needs to be designed properly right from the beginning.

Site architecture (document and file structure and naming) is very much a technical task. The content staff needs to be able to describe what the site will look like as it grows and expands. Planning for future expansion from the beginning will make site maintenance an easy task.

What are you main content areas?

In your initial content discussions you will need to decide on the major content areas — those with universal appeal to all of your users. These should be given priority attention on your home page.

Plan for additional information providers (IPs).

Take a snapshot of your organizational structure as it exists today. Determine who the likely content providers might be from within that structure. A good way to think about your structure is to have it mirror the organizational structure. Major groups or departments will probably want their own intranet content areas (mini-nets). You should probably choose to place all these in one area of the site with a single link from the home page.

Determine security needs.

Some department/groups will want their information accessible only to a select group of users. In these cases the content should be placed in a secure area of the site where it is password protected.

Measuring Results

Challenge:

Most management will want to be able to justify their investment in a project. Carefully planning objectives and managing expectations are important first steps. Providing timely and accurate feedback to management about the intranet requires good usage measurement techniques.

Recommendations:

Passively track usage

Almost every server-side software package on the market today includes a usage tracking capability. The most frequently reported categories of usage are number of hits and unique users. The number of home page accesses will give you a pretty good idea about how many times your intranet is being visited. Since many visitors go back to the home page several times during their visit to navigate around the site, the statistics can be misleading. A better measure of usage is the number of unique visitors. This is easily measured because each computer on your network is assigned a distinct address that is recorded by your server when accessed.

Actively solicit feedback.

The ability to obtain real-time feedback from users is one of the most powerful aspects of this new medium. Most successful intranets try to involve their users throughout the development and maintenance process. As site designer, your most important role is to make it easy for your users to give you direct feedback. For example, your intranet can include a "mailto" form as part of the standard footer throughout the site. This allows a user to provide feedback from any page anywhere on the site.

Conduct ongoing surveys.

Take advantage of interactivity by frequently asking your users to participate in surveys. Keep them short and focused on a single topic. Users tend to avoid surveys that take more than a minute or two to complete. Use lots of radio buttons and check boxes to speed the process, but always provide a text area for users to make specific comments. You'll find that some of your best features and enhancements come from user comments. Ask about the usefulness of an existing site area, attitudes toward a company issue or about specific improvement or expansion ideas for the site.

Give lots of feedback to users.

Use your intranet to build dialog. Post the results of surveys just as soon as possible. In fact, you might want to keep all your survey results in one area as a feedback archive for users. Your audience wants to know that you care about their input. If they see their comments or the results of the survey they took last week on the site, they will know that the feedback loop is complete. You may also want to use individual e-mails to begin one-on-one discussions with particularly involved users. These might turn out to be the people who help you expand and grow your intranet in the future.

Style Standards

Challenge:

Everyone in the organization has a good idea about how the site should look. Some of the designs you have seen may not be very efficient and interesting. How can you establish standards without inhibiting creativity?

Recommendations:

Publish a guide for information providers online.

Your information providers can make the difference between a good site and a great one. Your role includes providing them with the tools they need to do their jobs more effectively. You should produce a comprehensive information provider guide and publish it in both print and online forms. Your IP guide should include at least the following topics:

- Intranet basics
- Making content selections
- Planning your site
- Good site structure
- Good site navigation
- Encouraging feedback

Publish an online style guide.

Good design does not come easily. Corporations spend millions of dollars to establish and maintain a "corporate image" through the use of standardized design elements. Your intranet should be no different. You should develop a guide that covers at least the following topics:

- Backgrounds
- File names
- Footers
- Graphics
- Headers
- Live area
- Navigation area
- Page layouts
- Photos
- Site structure
- Style summary
- Tabling pages
- Writing guide
- Implementation of existing corporate style and graphics standards

Publish an online HTML guide.

Many of your information providers will want to construct their own pages. It will help all the way around if you publish a site-specific HTML guide that addresses the way you want your site to look. At a minimum, your HTML guide should contain the following topics:

- HTML basics
- Basic tagging
- Headlines
- Font sizes
- Text tags
- Lists
- Horizontal rules
- Image basics
- Image alt tags
- Image linking
- Hypertext links
- Paths
- Preformatted text
- Colors & Hexadecimal code
- Background images
- Basic tables
- Basic frames

Your company will have intranet and department-specific needs. Include these wherever they are applicable to the outline above.

Encouraging Interaction

Challenge:

Differentiate this new medium from the others by encouraging the user to do more. The real challenge when building an intranet is: Can you make the user experience more participatory and less passive?

Recommendations:

Concentrate on one user at a time.

Intranets are intensely personal systems. The network reaches one user at a time with an experience that is totally user-controlled. The best intranets find ways to reach out an include the user in the experience. Some obvious examples of user interaction are:

- On-line forms
- Surveys
- Questionnaires

Use new technology tools to increase interactivity.

The advent of Java as a programming language has opened the door to many more opportunities to encourage interaction. Custom programming can produce such online tools as retirement calculators and real-time inventory tracking systems. Placing these valuable tools on the site makes for a better user experience and gives your users more reason to come back frequently to the site.

Keeping the Site Fresh and Timely

Challenge:
Keep users energized and enthusiastic about visiting the site frequently.

Recommendations:
Look and feel issues.
Understanding the continuing need to keep the site fresh and new will help you develop a plan for ongoing maintenance. From the start, you should count on implementing a plan to frequently rotate key elements on your home page so users see a different look as they continue to access the intranet.

Placing the date and time on the home page is another way to give the appearance of fresh content. Many intranets offer a "breaking news" or "current weather" feature by making alliances with local newspapers or television stations to use their content on the intranet site as it is updated.

Content issues.
In any case, you should develop a plan to add new content throughout the year. This new content can correspond to organizational activities (United Way campaign, blood drive, Special Olympics, community events, etc.) or to the calendar (a new face for the seasons, holidays, etc.). Creating a set of organization-specific graphics for these special content sections goes a long way toward dressing up the site.

Organizational Issues

Resources
Challenge:
How much does an intranet cost? Can you justify the cost of the new project by showing savings in other traditional communication media?

Recommendations:
Capital
Many of the resources required to build and run an intranet already exist within the organization. If your organization currently operates an internal network, chances are the intranet can use that existing infrastructure with only minimal impact. You will need additional server hardware and software, but these costs are not prohibitively high.

People
Various organizations have assembled a wide range of personnel to build and operate intranets. A successful intranet project requires full-time positions with specialized skills

and training. Ideally, you should create a stand-alone team reporting to an online manager. If it is not possible to add all these new resources to the organization, you may want to consider bringing in outside resources to launch the project.

At a minimum, you will need two full-time positions on staff — Webmaster and Programmer. In some cases, these two positions can be covered by one very talented individual. Staff size can range from only two to many, but most staffs will look something like this:

> **Webmaster** — Overall responsibility for the site production andmaintenance
> **Content person** — creation of new content and re-purposing existing content
> **Graphics person** — creation of new art and interfaces and the re-purposing of existing graphics
> **Systems person** — design and maintenance of the intranet delivery system
> **Programmer** — writing HTML and other necessary code

Defining Roles and Responsibilities

Challenge:
Who will have overall intranet management responsibilities? Who will operate the intranet day-to-day? Do you add new staff or can you squeeze new responsibilities out of over-worked, existing staff?

Recommendations:
Modern organizations are need heavy and resource thin. They have been down-sized, right-sized and flattened to their limits. Internal resources are often stretched to the breaking point. And now you are going to ask them to take on another responsibility with the intranet.

You should treat the intranet as a totally new endeavor for the organization. This fresh thinking will help you resist the assumption that this new set of tasks can be stacked on top of other communication work already on the plate. It will also help you build internal support, which, in turn, may allow you to employ additional resources from outside your company.

Look within your existing IT/MIS department for your technical staff. Try to identify someone who spends lots of time on the Internet, or who runs a Web site out of their office at home. Chances are these people have the skills required to launch and maintain your intranet. Also they probablywill have the drive and enthusiasm necessary to create a successful intranet project.

On the content side, look within the traditional communication disciplines for some-one with video or multimedia background or interests. This person will ensure that the right content makes its way onto the intranet and follows established online publishing guidelines.

Involve top management in strategic oversight.

In most organizations an advisory committee or intranet board sets the strategic focus for the project. Normally this group is made up of executive-level members from the corporate staff. This group provides the vision and resources necessary to ensure a successful intranet project.

Place the staff where the energy is.

It really doesn't matter who "owns" the intranet. On-line publishing can find evangelists in virtually any function within the organization. Chances are, if you are reading this, you have an intense interest in online publishing. Unlike traditional media, online projects tend to begin as "guerrilla operations" on someone's desktop. Intranets are very much driven by online zealots within the organization.

Project Manager.   Typically, the intranet team is headed up by a mid-level manager who reports to the human side of the organization (human resources, corporate communication, training, etc.). This ensures that the project is content-driven and firmly focused on corporate goals.

Webmaster.   The Webmaster usually reports directly into the project manager and has overall tactical responsibility for the intranet. The Webmaster is typically a content-oriented person with some technical expertise online. In many cases, the Webmaster produces the actual HTML pages for the site. In other situations, the pages are built by a technical production staff.

Technical.   The technical elements of the intranet are usually provided by the IT/IS department personnel. Since the intranet usually operates over the existing computer network, IT professionals have a keen interest in the operation of the intranet. In some cases, the Webmaster may also serve double duty as the technical lead on the project, but that combination is unusual and can overwhelm a single employee.

Creative.   Many intranets have an online editor on staff to make all editorial decisions. This "wordsmith" creates new, original content for the site and re-purposes content from other sources (brochures, newsletters, product sheets, etc.).

Site "look and feel" is developed by a graphic designer with some knowledge of interface design. Designing for online is distinctly different from designing for the printed page. Network speed, file sizes and HTML restrictions play critical roles in determining design issues. Your designer needs to understand the mechanics of the online world to be effective in designing your intranet.

User Training

Challenge:

Assuming your employees will warm up to the new intranet may be dangerous. If you build it, they will come — but it may take longer than you had anticipated without some gentle nudging on your part.

Recommendations:

Construct an online tutorial.

One of the easiest ways to teach people about the site and its usage is through an online, on-site tutorial. Make it a prominent link from the home page. You may want to use streaming audio (if your system is audio-capable) to walk users through the basics of hypertext linking and the use of your site. If you can't use audio, create a series of text pages that perform the same function.

Create a User Guide.

A comprehensive, stand-alone, printed piece can be very valuable. Users can keep the guide at their fingertips during their maiden voyages on your site. Pattern your guide after traditional software manuals — except shorter and simpler. Use actual screen shots from your site to illustrate what content is available and where it can be found.

Conduct informal sessions.

Offer brown-bag lunch sessions for users. Keep them informal and interactive. Get people talking about their technophobias. You may want to construct an overview area on the actual site that you can use during the training — use the medium to sell the medium. Concentrate much of your session on the value to the user.

Conduct formal training.

If you have a computer training room with multiple workstations, use this facility to conduct formal intranet training sessions. The same rules apply here as above: Keep the training focused on user value. Let users express their technology fears. Use these sessions to collect information about future site improvements or refinements.

Promotion

Challenge:

There's no real budget to promote internal communication media. How can you beat the drum about this new medium without spending a lot of money?

Recommendations:

Use what you have.

Advertise your new medium by using your existing media. Use your employee newsletter to promote special content areas on the site. Use your closed-circuit TV system to make announcements about specific online content. In your United Way packets, include a mention of the special campaign area on the intranet. Paycheck stuffers can promote the use of benefits filing online. Use company bulletin boards to direct attention to public transportation routes and schedules online, or weather updates, traffic advisories, etc. This repetitious cross-promotion will go a long way toward building site traffic. Making an event out of the system's roll-out is also an excellent way to begin its usage in an enthusiastic, interesting way.

Intranet Best Practices

Place special content online.

Think of some special content that would attract your users' interest. Get people excited about judging an employee photo contest on the intranet. How about matching baby pictures with current executive photos? Online company trivia contests are fun and have the beneficial side effect of providing usefulcompany information.

Information Provider Issues

Controlling Access

Challenge:
Once the floodgates are open, how do you maintain some control over the site?

Recommendations:
Develop a comprehensive plan.

One of the most important tasks facing the intranet development team is clearly defining the policies and procedures that will govern the site. This document should put forth a set of governing policies as the framework under which the intranet will function as an official channel for corporate communication. It should delineate the governing structure (strategic and tactical); access and security strategy; copyright and other legal issues; (proper conduct and language online), and appeal processes.

The procedures guide should be a cookbook for how the site operates. This will be the Webmaster's bible. It should cover such topics as content approvals, update frequency, access privileges and backup plans.

Designate an online point person for each information provider (IP).

As departments and other groups step up to the table as information providers, they need to designate one person as their mini-Webmaster. This person will have total content responsibility for their area and will coordinate all online activities for the group. These people gradually become familiar with HTML and other online issues. In time, they can do more and more of their own production work. One warning, however: making something live — adding or modifying online HTML files on the active server — should be limited to the Webmaster or the site technical staff. It's easy to do a lot of damage to the site if someone without extensive knowledge and training tries to modify "live" HTML files.

Copyright and Legal Issues

Challenge:
Intranets are real-time networks with content from a number of sources. How can you maintain the integrity of your site and keep everyone out of court?

Recommendations:

Get your legal department involved.

Much of the law relating to online issues is being written today. At a minimum, you will want to include a member of your legal staff in your strategic oversight committee. That will keep potential legal issues from developing into major unforeseen problems.

Use existing conduct policies.

Almost every organization has a set of policies governing proper conduct in the workplace. Many also have rules governing the placement of content in traditional media — like employee newsletters. You should adopt these existing documents for use online. It shouldn't be necessary to prepare a new batch of regulations just because the medium is different.

Respect copyright.

Even though your intranet is only seen by employees within your organization, you still must respect all applicable copyright laws. Your organization probably has a policy on the use of copyrighted materials. Make sure you and all your IPs read it and heed it.

Glossary

Access Management The management of intranet applications.

ADN (Advanced Digital Network) Advanced Digital Network is a 56Kbps leased-line.

Address An address is the Domain Name on the internet.

Anonymous FTP (File Transfer Protocol) This gives other people outside of your company access to FTP but gives limitations on what they can transfer and where.

Application Netscape Navigator, Microsoft Internet Explorer, Microsoft Office and Adobe are all different types of applications. Applications can be used to for Web applications, word processing, graphic design, and spreadsheets.

Archie A robot that looks through FTP servers for certain information that a person requests. It is also a network-based utility program.

ARPANet (Advanced Research Projects Agency Network) The U.S. Department of Defense developed this area wide network in an experiement so it would work before, during, and after a nuclear war or attack. Developed in the 1960s era.

Bandwidth The amount of information being sent through a connection and is measured in bits-per-second. The faster your modem, the faster information can be sent.

Baud Sending and receiving bits per second.

BBS (Bulletin Board System) File downloading and uploading, announcements and discussions that can be accessed from other computers that are in different areas.

Beta group A number of people who test intranet/internet sites before they go live.

Binhex Converting files that are non-text into ASCII.

Bit The smallest unit of computerized data.

Bps (bits-per-second) The measurement of movement of data from one place to another.

Bridge A bridge moves packets between two or more connected networks.

Browser Software that lets a person read information on the Internet. The first well known browser was Mosaic; now the most popular is Netscape Navigator.

Buffering Storing data in memory before it is sent to the receiver.

Byte The amount of memory to store one unit.

cgi-bin cgi-bin refers to Common Gateway Interface, which are utility programs used on web pages only when something happens that you cannot see. For example, web pages with forms use cgi-bin, which processes the information that the user enters into it.

Chat group Communicating with other people through a network in real time. Text is the general format.

Circuit switching Connection to different sites through your telephone company network, which is done with a number called.

Client A client application of a software program, for example a web browser, always needs a server application to make it work. If the Web files are on a computer that has Web server software, your web browser can see these files, which can be anywhere in the world.

Contact Database An address book and electronic calendar that you can put onto your intranet for everyone to access.

CP/IP Protocal communication used by all computers on the Internet is called Control Protocol/Internet Protocol.

CU-SeeMe Live video-conferencing application.

Cyberspace All available information resources through computer networks

DCT (Direct Connection Telephone) A fixed IP address can receive direct calls through this internet telephone program.

DDF (Digital Document Format) Electronic storage of information.

DDS (Digital Data Service) Continuous circuit between two sites.

Digerati Knowledgeable people who are known for their involvement in the digital revolution.

DNR (Domain Name Resolver) Mac TCP element that allows a logical address(www.kinetoscope.com) to be resolved into a physical address (207.100.78.33).

DNS (Domain Name System) The server that distributes domain names used on the Internet.

Domain An example is "www.kinetoscope.com." A Domain is your site, which is made up of names or letters and dots that separate these names.

Glossary 215

Domain Name Each Web site has its own Domain name.

Download To unload. To copy files from one computer to another computer. This is sometimes done to work on a file without making change to the original.

Electronic files An electronic file is anything that can be read, stored or transferred from one computer to another. This can be sound, images, text or information.

E-mail (Electronic Mail) Each person who has electronic mail has their own address. Anyone who also has electronic mail and knows your address can send you information. Information that is normally text can also be sent to more than one person at a time.

Ethernet Ethernet networks computers in a LAN.

External Any Web page or site that is not inside a firewall. Anyone on Web can see these pages.

FAQ (Frequently Asked Questions) FAQs are questions that have been asked many, many times and are put into a web page or listed for all to see. FAQs show the question asked along with the answer.

Finger A tool to find information that is not personal, to locate people on internet sites and to see if someone has an account on a certain site.

Firewall A firewall is used for security to protect certain information. Only authorized people can read or use this information. To make the documents secure, the firewall separates a LAN into two parts.

Flat File Data that is stored in succession in text format.

Flat File Database One table database storage in text format.

FTP (File Transfer Protocol) The moving of files from one site to another on the Internet. FTP gives login capabilities for moving these files. Some sites are for public use while others are for internal use only.

Gateways A means of access from one network to another network. Information is first sent to a router. The router then sends the information to the computer asking for the information.

GIF (Graphics Interchange Format) A graphics format that can be viewed by all web browsers; it is most commonly used on Web pages.

Gopher A client and server program mainly used by colleges and universities to share information. It is not supportive of graphics and you cannot view web pages. Even though this is an older program it is still widely used today.

Grep Does search and replace operation on files.

Groupware Software that allows more than one person to work or access a project.

GUI (Graphic User Interface)   This can be used with almost any graphics program.

Home Page   This is the first Web page that you come to when you go to a site. Every site has a home page.

Host   Making available services to other computers through one computer on a network. This computer can provide one or more services.

Hot List   A Hot List, also known as a Bookmark, is a way to save addresses that you wish to return to at a later date. You can keep a list of them that your broswer maintains just by adding them to the list as you go to the sites. When you are ready to go back just click on the name of the site you want and it will automatically bring you to it.

HTML (HyperText Markup Language)   HTML is the programming or coding language used to make Web pages for the Internet. With this language you can link to different pages or sites, add graphics or images, text, and also set up the layout of your page. To see another site's HTML code, press the view menu and select source if you are in Netscape or Microsoft Internet Explorer.

HTTP (Hypertext Transfer Protocol)   To transfer Web pages over the internet HTTP the communication protocol, is needed. This is used for all web pages for example: "http://www.kinetoscope.com."

Hypertext   Hypertext can be a word, phrase or graphic that can be clicked on and will bring you to another document that can be viewed. This is also called a link.

Intelligent Agent   A program that will do tasks for you without your help, like search for a certain topic on the Web.

Interface   Showing information from one condition to another.

Internal   Any Web page or site that is inside a firewall. These cannot be accessed by anyone who does not have authorization. Internal pages generally contain company information used for employees of that company.

Internet   The internet is the sharing of TCP/IP communication protocols and a collection of inter-connected networks. The internet has grown tremendously in the past couple of years and no one person is in charge of.

Internet Explorer   Internet Explorer is the free Web browser from Microsoft.

Intranet   An intranet is a private site that is for internal orgainizational use only. It is placed behind a firewall and only authorized personnel can use it. It is mainly used for an organization's staff members and contains pertinent information regarding the company.

IP Address (Internet Protocol)   IP is an address separated by periods and always has a set of four numbers. These numbers can be from 1 ato 256. Every computer on the internet needs their own number or address. An example of an IP number is 207.100.78.33.

Glossary

ISDN (Integrated Services Digital Network) ISDN is a faster moving telephone service that can transfer data quickly and is basically used for people who want to see the internet from home.

ISO (International Standardization Organization) A world-wide federation that assists with aspects of manufacturing, trade, and communication internationally.

ISP (Internet Service Provider) A person or company who provides access to the internet. An ISP provider generally provides email and Web hosting along with the access.

Java A programming language that Sun Microsystems developed. Java can display animation and applets that you can download to your computer off of the Internet.

JavaScript Based on Java this scripting language allows browsers to run on a person's computer a program.

JPEG (Joint Photographic Experts Group) JPEG is a graphic format for vieweing images on Web browsers. It is generally used for photos.

Junction Sites A junction site is used for a company's intranet, which is usually made up of index pages organizing all of the information.

Kilobyte 1024 (2/10) bytes, which is a unit of computer memory.

LAN (Local Area Network) A LAN is a computer network usually used for one business, company, or university all located in one location. A LAN depending on the size can connect a few computers to hundreds of computers at one time.

Link Also known as a Hyperlink can be clicked on to move to another page of that site. The link is usually underlined a link and is usually a different color from the rest of the text so you can tell what is a link and what is not. Also graphics and images can be a link. For example, most sites have a back button that is a link. A link can also bring you to another site.

Listserv A listserv is the most common maillist on the Internet.

Login To receive access to a computer system you need an account name, which is called Login. This is different than a password because it is not private.

MBPS Megabits per second.

Message Board Discussion group where a user can post and reply to messages from other users.

MIME (Multi-purpose Internet Mail Extensions) The standard for multimedia mail contents in the Internet suite of protocols.

Modem An instrument that is hooked up to your computer and through a telephone system lets your computer talk to another computer. A moden also lets you hook up to the internet. It is the same as if you are on the telephone talking to another person.

Mosaic Mosaic was the first web browser that could be used with all computers. It was developed by students at the University of Illinois at the National Center Supercomputing Applications. This Web browser was free, so it led to the rapid growth of the World Wide Web.

MPEG Video compression.

NCSA (National Center for Supercomputing Applications) Location at the University of Illinois where Mosaic was developed.

Netscape Netscape is a Web browsercreated by Netscape. This Web browser is now considered the most popular to explore the internet.

Network Two or more connected computers sharing resource information.

Newsgroup Discussion groups.

NIC (Networked Information Center) A company like InterNIC that handles network information, like registering your domain name.

Node A computer connected to a network.

NOS (Network Operating Software) Software to control network operations. Some operations may be email, id information, security, etc.

NSF (National Science Foundation) Organization founded by the federal government.

Online To be online means you are connected to the Internet.

Open Standards Something that is public, like the Internet.

Packet Switching Packet switching is information being sent from one computer to another.

Password To get to the Internet you have to enter a password. Sometimes this can be done automatically so you won't have to do it each time. It is best to make your password something that no one would guess. If anyone obtains your password they can use it to get onto the Internet under your account.

PDF Formatted documents that can be electronically distributed and read.

Perl (Practical Extraction And Report Language) A programming language programs written with Perl are called scripts. This language is mainly used in cgi-bin scripts.

Plug-In An attachment to a larger program to add to its capabilities. An example is Shockwave.

PPP (Point-to-Point Protocol) Connection to the internet with a modem over a telephone line instead of dedicated cables. PPP is the software that makes this happen.

Provider Any company or person who provides access to the Internet.

Glossary

Protocol   A computer language that is used by computers to communicate with each other.

Publish   When Web pages are put onto a web server they are published. Only after they are published can another person see them.

Real Time Protocol   To transmit video or audio content over the Internet or an intranet.

Real Time Video   Transmittal of live video.

Replication   Data stored on two or more computers is called replication.

Root   The top of a file system in a directory.

Routers   Decision making sytem that decides which path traffic on the internet or data delivery will go to. It always choose the quickest path.

Script   A character-based interface utility program that is used with other programs, like Perl.

Search Engine   A network-based software tool to search for a topic or subject. After you pick a topic, the tool will bring back the addresses that have this information on the site. There are many different search engines today.

Serve   Any site that is not behind a firewall and can be seen by other computers is considered served.

Server   Any computer or software that services is considered a server. A computer can have more than one service on it.

SGML (Standard Generalized Markup Language)   This is a coding language that is like HTML, but makes content platform-independent.

Shareware   Downloadable software off of the Internet that is either a trial version or free.

SMTP (Simple Mail Transfer Protocol)   A general Internet electronic mail protocol.

SNMP (Simple Network Management Protocol)   The network management protocol for TCP/IP-based internets.

Surf   To browse or explore unknown sites on the World Wide Web without going to a certain destination.

Sysop (Systems Operator)   A person who performs the maintenance of a network or computer system.

T-1—An Internet connection for networks that is fast.

T-3—An Internet connection for networks that is fast enough to do full-screen and full-motion video.

TCP/IP (Transmission Control Protocol/Internet Protocol)   Most common communication protocol on the Internet today because of its reliability in the interconnection of different networks.

Telnet   Protocol that connects one host to another.

UDP (User Datagram Protocol)   UDP is the same as TCP. The only difference is it allows data exchange, but doesn't give a guaranteed delivery.

UNIX   A computer operating system that can be used by more than one person at a time. This system is common in universities and is becoming more and more popular in businesses.

URL (Uniform Resource Locator)   An example of a URL is the following: http://www.kinetoscope.com. A URL is how you identify a web page on the Internet.

Usenet   Discussion groups that can be on the Internet but doesn't have to be. These discussion groups are also called newsgroups and messages are passed on to each member of the newsgroup.

Video compression   Video compression is to make smaller the bits to transmit the digital video.

VRML (Virtual Reality Markup Language)   A launguage that lets a user explore third dimension.

WAIS (Wide Area Information Server)   This protocol can be used to create a database in full text.

WAN (Wide Area Network)   Companies that have more than one office and are located far from each other will use this network system to connect their LANs.

Web Page   Any document on the Internet is called a Web page. The Web page is written in HTML code and can be text, an image or animation, or movie with sound.

Web Server   Web servers are a type of software that give computers the ability to publish Web pages. This term is often used to refer to the computer running the Web server, but strictly speaking web servers are software, not hardware.

Web Site   A Web server containing any number of electronic Web pages in a directory is called a Web site.

World Wide Web (WWW)   The WWW is a global information network made up of web sites which have electronic pages. The electronic pages are viewed by a browser on either Microsoft Windows programs or an Apple Macintosh and you can access different information which includes text, images, and even sound. The World Wide Web was first created by scientists so they could share information.

WYSIWYG   WYSIWYG means what you see is what you get. A person can see what the document will look like while they are working on it or before the document is printed. Almost all word processors and web authoring programs now have this feature.

Intranet Battle Plan

(How to take the organization on-line and make them love it)

This Is War!

Scenario:

Sometime between today and tomorrow you will be involved in an intranet project. This will happen whether you are prepared or not. The on-line forces are massing all around your perimeter. You have no choice but to engage them.

Mission Statement:

Seize the opportunity that lies dead ahead. You and your team must be ready to face a challenge that will transform the way you communicate. In the end, it will change the way you do business. Your challenge is to understand this new phenomenon, learn its strengths and weaknesses, and execute a plan to use it to your advantage.

Tactics:

To engage this opportunity effectively you must consider and answer the following question:

| Closed — Autocratic | Open — Collaborative |

Where does your company or organization fit on this continuum? Does it feature an environment that is open and sharing? Does information flow freely, accurately and quickly in all directions?

You will find that the company's intranet project will closely reflect its communications style. More open and collaborative companies will produce richer, more interactive intranets. Closed and autocratic companies will produce intranets that are more like bulletin boards, carrying lots of topdown information. Your job as project leader will be much more rewarding if you begin your planning with a careful analysis of the culture in which your intranet will grow.

How much support (staff and resources) will you receive from management?

Typical intranets average an expenditure of about $25,000 in hardware, software, and other capital costs. You can get by on less. A typical staff consists of a Webmaster, a content person, a graphics person, and a systems administrator (can be Webmaster).

As you begin your planning, you should survey available resources within you organization — both physical and human. Can you find candidates for your intranet staff within the present organization? Will you be forced to look outside? Can you utilize some existing hardware to build your project instead of spending new capital?

Underfunding is one of the most devastating handicaps you will face in your role as project leader. Make sure you and your management are in agreement about how much money it will take to produce an intranet everyone will be happy with.

How will you maintain and expand your intranet?

Intranets, unlike other communications projects, are never finished. They must always be considered a "work in progress". The fastest way to kill a good intranet project is to launch the site and ignore it. Your on-line customers expect (no, demand) new and compelling content to appear regularly. You should begin planning your site growth and maintenance BEFORE you launch your initial site. Have a preset plan for changing graphical look and content on a regular basis. Determine who will handle the updates and expansion and make sure they understand the importance of their role in keeping the project fresh and useful.

What are the Communications objectives?

Sure intranets are cool. Sure they improve communication. But what will an intranet do for you and you particular situation? Make sure your plan includes some very well defined goals and objectives for your project before you begin. Make sure these are shared with management and your user community so everyone can stay focused on them as the site rolls out. These goals and objective should be clear and measurable so they serve as milestones for your progress. Also make sure that you keep everyone informed of your progress as the project moves along.

Who is the audience?

You probably will have several different audience segments — general, specific, and individual. You may even have people outside your organization as users. How much do you know about each of these audiences? How can you use that information to shape the intranet content and structure? It is extremely important to maintain a user focus during every phase of your project. Understanding the needs and desires of your audience — and giving it to them — will go a long way toward ensuring a successful project.

What is the content?

Intranets become the depositories for all manner of content. If you keep a customer focus you will be able to develop useful and timely content.

What is the structure?

All the useful and timely information in the world does little good if people cannot find it. Having a good, logical site structure is extremely important.

How will we encourage user interaction?

Intranets are interactive by their very nature. Your users will become active participants and energetic supporters of the intranet if they perceive they have a vital role in its success. You may want to encourage feedback through the use of email links on each page. Surveys and questionnaires are excellent ways to involve users in the intranet experience.

How will we respond to user feedback?

If you ask your users for their feedback and ideas, you need to be ready to respond to what they tell you. Failing to do that will choke off you communication with your users and stifle your project. Web surfers have come to expect an answer to their email within 24 hours. You should develop a plan that addresses the need for such quick response on your intranet.

How will we keep the site fresh and timely?

Your users want to see something new and interesting each time they visit your site. If they don't they will find other things to do with their time. Automating as much of the routine updating and maintenance will free up some time to create new content and change the look of the site. Simple CGI or PERL scripts (ask your technical person) enable content providers to update their own content right in their browser. The more you do to automate routine updates, the more time you will have to expand and innovate.

What are the roles and responsibilities? Content? Technical?

Putting together an effective project team requires skill and understanding of the task at hand. Where will you find your staff? Who will be responsible for content creation? Who maintains the server? What kind of outages can you tolerate? If you are supporting mission-critical applications or information on you intranet, your system maintenance plan will be much more rigid than if you don't. Will you recruit content providers from the various departments within your organization? Will they need training? Who will provide it?

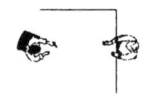

Will user training be necessary?

You may find a wide range of on-line skills and experience among your potential users. You can build a loyal user base by making sure everyone understands the basics of the on-line world. Who will handle this training? Can you provide it using traditional training methods? Who will pay for the training?

How will we promote use of the site?

Your intranet must be promoted — often and widely — to become an integral part of daily life in your organization. You should construct a comprehensive plan to promote your new intranet in all you other communications media. You might also want to use your intranet as the exclusive medium for some specific, valuable information. This will probably go a long way toward encouraging people to visit your site and visit it often.

Appendix: Intranet Battle Plan 225

Who controls access to the intranet?

You must make decisions about how open and accessible your intranet will be. On the one hand, if you allow free access to users, you may get inappropriate or offensive content. If you review and evaluate postings before they go "live", you run the risk of being labeled "censor." In any case you should publish some set of standards that regulate content on the site to prevent problems about the fact.

Who can post information on the intranet?

You must make decisions about who can post content on your intranet. Will you recruit content providers from other departments? Will you review their content before it goes "live"? Will you allow content providers access to the live server, or will you give them a "sandbox" server where they can build their content and where it can be stored until you or someone else make it live. Access to the live server is a touchy issue. Many intranets allow only one or two people into the live server. Others make it available to a wider group. Your decision should be based on the amount of control you want and the technical expertise of your support group.

What is the posting process?

You must determine the process by which content gets placed on you intranet. Hosting live Chat or having newsgroups (unhosted discussions) can prove to be a challenge. In some cases, all postings are reviewed before they are made live. In other cases, organizations take a "hands-off" approach to postings.

What about copyright? Other legal issues?

Just because your site is behind a firewall, you are not immune from prevailing laws. You should have a well publicized policy governing the use of copyrighted information on your intranet. Most copyrights prohibit their use even within organizations.

Index

A

Absolute information, 31
Adobe Acrobat, 16
Agent technology, 39
AltaVista, 38
Amazon Books, 37
America Online (AOL), 149, 172
Animation, 167, 168
AOL, *see* America Online
Approval process, 119
Archival information, 138
Audiences, determining, 71
Audio files, 168

B

Back-end resources, 91
Background images, 206
Battle plan, intranet, 221–225
BBS, *see* Bulletin board services
Benefits, of intranet, 9–30
  case studies, 18–23
  content providers, 25–30
    communications, 26–27
    customer and vendor relations/support, 29
    human resources, 25–26
    quality, 29
    sales automation, 28–29
    training and development, 29–30
  faster, cheaper, and easier, 13–18
    cheaper, 14–15
    easier, 15
    faster, 13–14
    instant, global distribution, 17–18
    makes everyone publisher, 15–16
  intranet prerequisites, 12–13
    budgetary buy-in, 13
    collaborative culture, 12
    LAN/WAN, 12
    technology and tools, 12
  intranet springboards, 9–12
    directives from chief, 10–12
    grass roots, 10
    guerrilla operations, 10
  online advantages, 13
  real-time interaction, 23–25
Benefits information, 20, 25, 72, 96
Best practices, for intranet, 199–212
  audience, 201–202
  communications objectives, 200–201
  developing content, 202–203
  encouraging interaction, 206
  information provider issues, 211–212
    controlling access, 211
    copyright and legal issues, 211–212
  keeping site fresh and timely, 207
  measuring results, 204
  organizational issues, 207–211
    defining roles and responsibilities, 208–209
    promotion, 210–211
    resources, 207–208
    user training, 209–210
  structure, 203
  style standards, 205–206
Beta testers, 162
Breaking news feature, 207
Brochures, 51

227

Browser, 58
　standards, 58
　window, expandable, 112
Bug Report, 89
Building intranet, 133–145
　building production team, 133–135
　　content manager, 134
　　designer, 135
　　editor, 135
　　illustrator, 135
　　intranet manager, 134
　　systems administrator, 135
　　technical manager, 134
　　Webmaster, 135
　　writer, 134
　content function, 137–138
　creative and technical people working together, 136–137
　effective online content, 138–139
　　archival information, 138–139
　　current information, 138
　　general information, 139
　　individual information, 139
　　special interest information, 139
　looking for staff, 135–136
　technical function, 142–145
　　programmer, 144–145
　　system administrator, 143–144
　typical development work flow, 141–142
　　converting, 141–142
　　mining, 141
　　posting, 142
　　surveying, 141
　　testing, 142
　　translating, 141
　where to find intranet content, 139–141
Bulletin board(s), 44
　announcements, 96
　services (BBS), 3, 10, 42
Buzzwords, 43

C

Capital costs, 47
Carpooling information, 72
Catch-22, 46
CBT, *see* Computer based training
CD-ROMs, 140, 150

Censorship, 172
cgi, *see* Common gateway interface
CGI, *see* Common gateway interface
Chat, 172
Claims forms, 72
Client browsers, 90
Code of online conduct, 81
Collaborative culture, 2
Collaborative technologies, 79
Command-and-control model, 78
Common gateway interface (cgi; CGI), 25, 55, 99, 157
Communication(s)
　Administrator, 9
　channel, two-way, 51
　climate, magnification of, 46
　floodgates, prying open of, 76
　gaps, closing, 189
　guidelines, 119
　inter-office, 191
　issues, organizational, 68
　knowledge, 194
　management, 4
　media, relationship of intranet project to, 82
　model, 32, 143
　objectives, 199, 200
　on-demand, 2
　organizational, 31
　politics, 33
　procedure, standardized, 53
　revolution, 31
　roles, 41
　theorist, 11
　theory, organizational, 7
Community
　activities, 27
　events calendar, 72
Company
　financial information, 72
　goals, 27
　organizational charts, 72
　sports news, 72
Competitive sites, 183
Computer
　based training (CBT), 29
　drawing program, 144
　literacy, 4, 148
　networks, 90
　policies, 20

Index

screen, designing for, 107
technical support, 83
users, low-end, 83
Concurrent engineering, 72
Conduct policies, 212
Connectionless environment, 54, 63
Consulting group, 179
Content
  appropriateness, 203
  decisions, 35
  experts, 163
  issues, 5
  manager, 134
  page, 166
  person, 208
  projects, updates on, 155
  providers
    advanced, 129
    intermediate-level, 129
    mature, 127
Converting, 141
Copyright, 81, 169, 212
Corporate identity guidelines, 68
Corporate logo, illegal usages of, 128
Corporate mission, 202
Corporate networks, 9
Corporate news bulletins, 20
Corporate policies, 20, 25
Creative group, 179
Creativity, process of, 137
Cross-platform publishing, 121–122
CRT screen, 140
Current information, 138
Customer
  programming, of secure areas, 39
  service, 1
Cute trap, 75

D

Daily status reports, 158
Database(s)
  automated reporting from, 188
  connectivity, 86
  development, SQL, 144
  generating customized pages from, 161
  Site Dynamics, 61
Decision-makers, 33

Default
  page, 93
  settings, 187
Departmental information, 27
Designer, 135
Designing intranet, 107–132
  approach to site style, 119–121
    advanced group, 121
    HTML beginners group, 120
    intermediate group, 120–121
  establishing online style guide, 130–132
  establishing unique look for intranet, 109–110
  intranet content providers, 128
    advanced, 128
    beginners, 128
    intermediate, 128
  limitations of hypertext markup language, 121–126
    content drives style, 126
    download time, 122–123
    graphics file sizes, 123
    networks, 122
    print vs. online, 122
    site attitude, 124–126
    style, 121–122
  look-and-feel issues, 108
  process, 110–119
    reviewing existing organizational style guidelines, 110–112
    reviewing other online style guides, 112–118
    talking to intranet committee, 118–119
  restrictive, 128–130
  writing for online delivery, 126–128
    information date stamping, 126–127
    one-voice edit, 128
    online linking, 127
    short and simple, 127
Development server, 154
Discussion
  areas, 22
  groups, 46
Document samples, 8
Domain name, 61
Domain Name Server, 54
Dots per inch (DPI), 92, 140

Downloading, 62, 63
   slow, 75
   time, 122, 166
Downsizing, radical, 76
DPI, *see* Dots per inch

E

EDA, *see* Electronic design automation
Editor, 135
Edutainment, 100
Electronic design automation (EDA), 28
Electronic files, 139
Electronic publishing terms, 8
Electronic revolution, 36
e-mail, 40, 42, 170
   form, 51, 156
   list, 158
Employee
   activities, 27
   benefits packages, 15
   handbooks, 20
   newsletter, 152
   phone listings, 96
   recognition, 26
Empowerment, electronic, 31–42
   creation of plan, 34–36
     filter, 35
     grapevine, 36
   everyone knowing everything, 39
   information power, 40
   new communications model, 40–41
     interactivity, 41
     nonlinear construction, 40
     real-time information, 40–41
   new communications roles, 41–42
     content provider, 42
     Webmaster, 41–42
   too much information, 38–39
   traditional comunications functions, 32–34
     gatekeeper, 32–33
     trap, 33–34
     way it was, 32
   winners and losers, 36–38
Encryption, 56
Enterprise systems, developer of, 66
Euphoria, 52
Evangelist, 10, 47
Excite, 38

Executives, 99, 147
Extranet, 29, 65

F

Feedback
   loop, 49
   encouraging, 48
   real time, 70
   responding to user, 161
   solicitation of, 204
File
   names, 120, 170
   structure, 203
   Transfer Protocol (FTP), 86
"Filling the shoebox", 141
Financial statements, 96
Firewalls, 39, 64, 86, 87
Floppy disks, 140
Focus groups, 88, 162
Font
   choices, 122
   initiative, new, 111
Footers, 170
Forum(s), 46, 98, 171
   hosted, 172
   management, 87
   topics, 99
   unhosted, 171
Front page, 93
FTP, *see* File Transfer Protocol

G

Gallows humor, 77
Gatekeeper, 7, 32, 35
General Manager, 9
General policies and procedures, 72
GIF, *see* Graphic Inline Format
Glossary, 213–220
Goals, unrealistic, 193
Grapevine, 7, 36
Graphical User Interfaces (GUIs), 3
Graphic Inline Format (GIF), 123, 140, 172
Graphics
   compelling, 130
   person, 208
   software, 136
   standard for, 173

Groupware solutions, 14
Guerrilla operations, 9, 209
Guest book, 23, 55
GUIs, see Graphical User Interfaces

H

Hackers, 150
Headers, 173
Health regulations, 25
Healthy company, 67
Hierarchy, preservation of, 33
History, organizational developments in, 5
Hit, 62
Home page, 69, 93, 165
    accesses, 204
    features, 180
Hosted forum, 172
HTML, see Hypertext Markup Language
HTTP, see Hypertext Transfer Protocol
Human resources department, 88
Hypertext link, 95, 206
Hypertext Markup Language (HTML), 10, 13, 54, 62, 149
    advantage of, 127
    authoring, 142, 162
    basics, 206
    beginners, 120
    creation of brochure using, 17
    document, 115, 116, 141
    files, modifying, 211
    guide, online, 205
    Guidelines, 183
    gurus, 121
    interface, 188
    pages, 184
    publishing, 15, 119
    tags, 11, 118, 174
    templates, 129
    text, 130
    waterfront, 121
Hypertext Transfer Protocol (HTTP), 13, 62, 142, 149

I

Illustrator, 135
Image mapping, 55
Improvement ideas, 155
Index page, 93
Information
    absolute, 31
    archival, 138
    availability of without overhauling, 198
    benefits, 96
    company financial, 72
    corporate, 74
    current, 138
    date stamping, 126
    gatekeepers, 67
    general, 21, 139
    individual, 139
    mission-critical, 154
    motivation about posting, 83
    official, 35
    overload, 196
    personal time, 73
    potentially troublesome, 40
    power, 40
    product, 96
    providers (IPs), 42, 77, 191, 203
    real-time exposure to, 2
    resources, identification of, 202
    right spin on, 35
    sharing, 1, 33, 79
    special interest, 139
    speed of access to, 201
    summary, 145
    Systems (IS), 1
    Systems Group, 91
    Technology Group, 91
    translating, 157
    treatment of as management asset, 80
    types of, 138
    unfiltered, 35
    vacation, 73
Inputs, monitoring of continuing, 119
Inspection records, 72
Interactivity, 69, 195
Interdepartmental competition, 77
Internal links, 95
Internal resources, 7
Internet
    phenomenon, 11
    protocol (IP), 53
    Service Provider (ISP), 86

surfing, 38
technologies developed for, 1
Intranet
  action plan, 48
  advantages, 7
  advocates, 44
  AT&T, 19
  attitude, 125
  audiences, 201
  battle plan, 221–225
  Blue Sky vision of, 70
  challenges and issues, 2
  Columbia Healthcare, 19
  committee, 18
  content people, successful, 137
  control of access to, 200
  corporate, 191
  cost of, 207
  definition, 201
  development, 17, 199
  Electronic Arts, 19
  elements, 167
  Eli Lilly, 20
  employee-only, 18
  expanding reach of, 163
  growth of, 198
  hardware, 85
  HBO, 20
  human side of, 6
  implementing, 200
  John Deere, 21
  launching, 147, 153, 200
  manager, 134
  misconception about, 80
  Mobil, 21
  moving toward empowerment, 2
  Olivetti, 22
  popularity of, 12
  prerequisites, 12
  project
    building successful, 189
    leader, 45
    major role in, 6
    manager, 66, 89
    strategic direction for, 154
  promise of technology, 2–3
  Sandia National Labs, 22
  session, typical, 64
  Site Dynamics, 179
  site
    day-to-day operation of, 142
    production of, 133
    remote access to, 87
    updating of, 143
  staff structure, 133
  structure, 93
  style, defining, 130
  technology, 7
  typical, 133
  ultimate goal of, 195
  user survey, sample, 100
Inventory
  levels, 28
  records, 96
IP, *see* Internet protocol
IPs, *see* Information providers
IS, *see* Information Systems
ISP, *see* Internet Service Provider

J

Java, 58, 206
Job postings, 26
Joint Photographic Experts Group (JPEG), 123, 140, 176
JPEG, *see* Joint Photographic Experts Group
Just-in-Time processes, 29

K

Knowledge
  base, organizational, 6
  worker, 78, 147

L

Labor markets, worldwide, 43
LAN, *see* Local Area Network
Layout design, 174
Lead Tracker, 188
Legal department, 212
Light through world, 108
Links
  kinds of, 95
  to other publications, 175
Local Area Network (LAN), 5, 10, 13, 57, 86, 91
Long-range improvements, 70

Index

M

Macro site navigation, 175
Mailto, 51, 98, 156, 170
Mainframe computer, 63
Maintaining intranet, 153–163
    automation, 156–160
        online templates for content providers, 158–159
        repurpose content from online sources, 160
    involving entire organization, 153–156
        ad hoc content committee, 155
        e-mail, 156
        management information services, 154
        online discussion, 156
        strategy committee, 154–155
        users, 156
    keeping fresh, 160–161
    recruiting and training content providers, 162
    recruiting and training online discussion hosts, 163
    responding to user feedback, 161–162
Maintenance automation, 156
Management
    challenge, 137
    forums, 87
    information systems (MIS), 154
    philosophies, 2
    presentations, 15
Managing intranet, 43–52
    clash with traditional systems, 45
    managing communication and change, 44–45
    managing effective intranet project, 47–52
        building initial support, 47
        developing action plan, 48
        encouraging interaction, 51
        keeping fresh face, 52
        keeping user focus, 49
        managing site growth, 51–52
        setting realistic expectations, 48–49
        sustaining momentum, 52
        understanding technology, 49–50
    taking organization's temperature, 45–47
Marketing intranet, 147–152
    educating and evangelizing, 148–151
        newbies, 148–149
        power users, 150–151
        surfers, 149–150
    not newsletter, 147–148
    promotion, 151–152
Mass transit schedules, 72
Mature organizations, 43
Microsoft site, 197
Mini-nets, 203
Mini-Webmaster, 211
Mining, 141
MIS, *see* Management information systems
Mistakes, common intranet, 191–198
    failing to build initial support, 191–192
    failing to encourage interaction, 195
    failing to keep fresh face, 198
    information overload, 196
    not focusing on users, 194
    not knowing technology, 194
    project leader not keeping up with technology, 197
    setting unrealistic goals, 193
    stalling, 196–197
    weak plan of action, 192–193
Model online site, 165–177
    structure, 165–167
        content page, 166–167
        home page, 165–166
        submenu page, 166
        top page, 166
    typical intranet elements, 167–177
        animation, 167–168
        audio, 168–169
        backgrounds, 169
        copyright, 169
        e-mail, 170
        file names, 170
        footers, 170–171
        forums, 171–172
        graphics, 172–173
        headers, 173
        layouts, 174
        navigation, 174–175
        photos, 176

site structure, 176–177
  text, 177
  video, 177
Momentum, sustaining, 52
Monthly quality reports, 158
Motivator, fear as, 9
Multimedia, 30

N

Navigation, 167, 174
  button, 127
  links, 95
  macro site, 175
  simple, 121
  text, 175
Netscape, 18, 34, 156, 197
Network(s)
  administrator, 168
  crippling of, 128
  crowded, 75
  Information Center (NIC), 53
Newbies, 148
Newsgroups, 41
Newsletters, 26, 51
Newspaper, major American daily, 37
NIC, *see* Network Information Center
Notification Agents, 69
Not Invented Here syndrome, 79

O

OCS, *see* Optical Character Scanners
Office phone extension list, 182
Official information, 35
One-voice edit, 128
Online
  backgrounds, 169
  content provider, 91
  delivery, 74, 107
  design, 112
  discussions, 171
  forms, 183
  games, 100
  HTML guide, 205
  humor, 125
  identity, 124
  knowledge levels, 148
  media, 23
  page, creation of, 116
  publishing, 6, 31, 34, 65
    features of, 109
    issues, workshops about, 120
  reference library, 97
  resources, 186
  sites, most successful, 98
  style guide, 110, 205
  technology, 74
  time sheets, 72
  world, 108, 165
Open door policy, 32
Optical Character Scanners (OCS), 140
Optical drives, 140
Organization
  charts, 25
  communication issues, 68
  healthy, 67
  hot topics, 99
  management style, 45
  master calendar for, 189
  mature, 43
  power base, 6
  software applications within, 97
Out of box thinking, 38
Overall appearance, 108
Overpromising, 193

P

Pages, building, 108
Pamphlets, 44
Password, 56
PCs, *see* Personal computers
PERL programming, 135
Personal computers (PCs), 12
Personal pages, within intranet, 92
Personal time information, 73
Personnel costs, 47
Phone directories, 20
Pilot program, 49
Plan of action, weak, 192
Planning intranet, 85–105
  allocation of resources, 85–87
    hardware, 85–86
    people, 86
    remote access, 87
    security issues, 86–87
  building in interactivity, 97–98

Index 235

defining responsibilities, 102–103
  content generation and maintenance, 102
  page construction and maintenance, 102
  technical support, 103
encouraging feedback, 98–100
  e-mail within site, 98
  forums, 98–99
  games, 100
  surveys, 99–100
enlisting management support, 101–102
  justifying resources, 101
  overcoming objections, 101–102
  steering committee, 101
  strategic planning group, 101
inside or outside, 85
obtaining user involvement, 87–89
  ad hoc committee, 88–89
  focus groups, 88
  soft launch, 89
  surveys, 87
protecting intranet from copyright and libel violations, 103–105
  copyright information websites, 105
  sidebar/boxed information, 104–105
selecting appropriate content, 95–97
  repurpose existing materials and information, 97
  surveying current enterprise for inclusion, 97
  what is appropriate for online use, 96–97
  what exists now, 96
surveying available resources, 90–95
  content resources, 91–92
  designing internal linking scheme, 95
  design and production resources, 92–93
  IT/IS resources, 90–91
  understanding nonlinear information, 93
Plant layouts, 96
Portable system, 149
Posting guidelines, 202

Power
  brokers, 36
  user, 150, 151, 180
  Web, 151, 152
Pre-press shops, 136
Press releases, 20, 27, 182
Pricing information, 28
Primary audience, 71
Primary user group, 150
Print
  designers, 92, 107
  production
    cycle, traditional, 16
    problems associated with, 17
Problems, unforeseen, 49
Product
  build plans, 72
  information, 96
  sheets, 15, 209
Production
  cycle, online, 16
  group, 179
  schedules, 28
Programmer, 144, 208
Programming languages, 150
Project
  budgets, 72
  damage to, 192, 193
  drivers, 192
  fulfillment, 52
  manager, 65
  schedules, 72
Promotion, 152, 210
Propeller-heads, 150
Publishing
  models, 24, 155
  online, 31, 34, 65
  process, 158
  terms, electronic, 8

Q

Quality documents, 72
Quarterly goals, 158

R

RAM, *see* Random Access Memory
Random Access Memory (RAM), 57

Resources, necessary, 199
Retirement information, 73
Retrieve button, 188
Return on investment, 47
Root
   domain, 61
   level, 176, 177
Rules, posting, 82
Rumors, 36, 67

S

Safety regulations, 15, 25
Sandbox server, 121
Savings plan, 73
Secure Sockets Layer (SSL), 55, 56
Secure storage, 40
Security strategy, 211
Self-sufficiency, 79
Server
   hardware, 136
   Side Includes (SSI), 55
   software, 90
   systems, existing, 142
Shopping cart, creation of, 64
Site
   attitude, 124
   maintenance, 52, 157
   navigation, 165, 205
   sections, naming, 126
   structure, 176
Site Dynamics intranet, 179–189
   "eat your own dogfood", 179
   home page features, 180–185
      advantages, 181
      major content areas, 181–185
   links, 186
   need, 179–180
   process, 180
   resources, 186
   tasks, 186–187
   tools, 187–189
      bottom line, 189
      calendar, 189
      Lead Tracker, 188
      Time Tracker, 187–188
Sneaker net, 57
Soft launch, 89

Software applications
   non-standard, 97
   off-the-shelf, 197
   prepress, 93
Spreadsheets, 14, 96
SQL database development, 144
SSI, see Server Side Includes
SSL, see Secure Sockets Layer
Staff addresses, 182
Stalling, 196, 197
Start-up costs, 47
Storage media, 140
Strategies, of intranet, 65–83
   determining audiences, 71–76
      primary users, 71–73
      secondary users, 73
      what is wanted, 73–76
   establishing realistic goals, 65–66
   politics, 67
   project parameters, 82–83
   reworking strategic communications policies and practices, 81–82
   site growth, 69
   site rollout plan, 69–71
   surveying communications resources, 76–77
   "unnatural acts", 78–80
      harnessing teams, 79
      keeping it alive, 79–80
      sharing information, 78–79
      using information seomone else invented, 79
   what intranet adds to what exists, 67–69
   what is at stake, 77–78
   who stands to lose, 80
Streaming audio, 169
Stringers, 162
Style
   challenges, 128
   guides, 184
      to facilitate page production, 114
      online, 205
Submenu page, 166
Supervisory meetings, 87
Support, problem with, 192
Surveys, 46, 87, 141, 204
System administrator, 135, 143, 208

Index

T

TCP/IP, *see* Technology, of intranet, transmission control protocol/Internet protocol
Technical decisions, 136
Technical group, 179
Technical literacy, 194
Technical manager, 134
Techno-geeks, 150
Technology
  bandwagon, 11
  companies, 160
  gap, 4
  hype surrounding new, 48
  innovator, 45
  negatives, 75
  -related problems, 194
Technology, of intranet, 53–64
  connectionless environment, 63–64
  domains and URLs, 53–54
  firewall issues, 64
  how intranet works, 60–62
    hypertext markup language, 62
    hypertext transfer protocol, 62
    uniform resource locator, 60–62
  intranet overview, 54–59
    browser standards, 58–59
    cgi, 55
    image mapping, 55
    LAN/WAN, 57–58
    page security, 56
    remote management and monitoring, 56
    server guidelines, 57
    SSI, 55
  putting together, 64
  standards and concepts, 54
  transmission control protocol/Internet protocol (TCP/IP), 53
Technophobia, 147
Templates, online, 158
Text
  breaking up, 127
  navigation, 174
  on-screen, 177
  size, 122
Thumbnails, 173, 184
Timesheets, 96
Time Tracker, 187

Top page, 93, 166, 184
Training
  components, 30
  formal, 210
  programs, 44
  traditional classroom, 29
Translating, 141

U

Unfiltered information, 35
Unhosted forum, 171
Uniform Resource Locator (URL), 60, 98
Universal Resource Locator, 54
UNIX platforms, 13
Update screen, 188
URL, *see* Uniform Resource Locator
User
  group, primary, 150
  guide, 149, 210
  input, 41
  interaction, encouragement of, 199
  survey, 202

V

Vacation information, 73
Value-added dimension, 78
VGA monitor, 111
Video(s), 51
  conferencing, 41
  files, 177
  network, closed-circuit, 152
  records, 88
  teleconferencing, 69
  training, 96
Voice mail, 40

W

WAN, *see* Wide Area Network
Web
  checking weather on, 160
  criticisms, 160
  development technology, 14
  devices, portable, 3
  page, 14
  server, 14, 54, 60

site(s)
　keeping fresh, 161
　people operating existing, 136
　real-time reporting on, 37
　U.S. Corporate, 24
　technology, 3
Webmaster, 114, 153, 208
Weekly progress reports, 158
Wide Area Network (WAN), 12, 13, 57, 91, 135
Wordsmith, 209
Work in progress, 52

World Wide Web (WWW), 54, 82, 123
Writer, 99, 134
WWW, *see* World Wide Web
WYSIWYG, 16

Y

Yahoo, 38

Z

Zip drives, 140